The Poetics of Cruising

The Poetics of Cruising

Queer Visual Culture from Whitman to Grindr

Jack Parlett

University of Minnesota Press

Minneapolis

London

Published by the University of Minnesota Press
111 Third Avenue South, Suite 290
Minneapolis, MN 55401-2520
http://www.upress.umn.edu

ISBN 978-1-5179-1103-4 (hc)
ISBN 978-1-5179-1104-1 (pb)

A Cataloging-in-Publication record for this book is available from the Library of Congress.

Printed in the United States of America on acid-free paper

The University of Minnesota is an equal-opportunity educator and employer.

UMP BmB 2022

Contents

Introduction

A Look

> *Pleasures are like photographs: in the presence of the person we love, we take only negatives, which we develop later, at home, when we have at our disposal once more our inner darkroom, the door of which it is strictly forbidden to open while others are present.*
>
> —Marcel Proust, *In the Shadow of Young Girls in Flower* (trans. James Grieve)

> *When a man recognizes another man's desire, he is also learning something about the other's identity, not exactly what kind of person he is, but what kind of group he belongs to.*
>
> —Leo Bersani, *Homos*

Three Photographers (1975–1979)

In 1976, twenty-two-year-old photographer Sunil Gupta moved to New York City from Montreal, where his family had relocated from India some years earlier. Although Gupta was already involved in both photography and gay politics, interests he had developed during his time as an undergraduate in Montreal in the years following gay liberation, he had ostensibly come to the city to study for an MBA. Living in the London Terrace building on West Twenty-Third Street in Chelsea, Gupta found himself at the heart of "a gay public space such as hadn't really been seen before."[1] At the encouragement of the esteemed street photographer Lisette Model, Gupta gave up the business degree and enrolled in her photography course at The New School. In his recollections of this period, Gupta describes the artistic and erotic climate of New York in adjacent terms—"I just got drawn into the whole moment of early '70s documentary stuff that was happening here, in terms of photography and also the gay scene, both of which suddenly exploded in front of me here"—and foregrounds the street itself as a space of exploration and experimentation.[2] "It was the first time I was living in a city that seemed full of photography," he remembers, both in terms of the number of commercial galleries and museums exhibiting photography and the experiential plenitude of the city; the sense that "the real life of the street was our theatre." Before long, the erotic and aesthetic site of the street, and one street in particular, became Gupta's primary subject.

Christopher Street, which Gupta describes as his "natural habitat" during this period, spans the western section of Greenwich Village, extending all the way from Sixth Avenue to the Hudson River. By the mid-seventies, it was a well-known cruising area for gay men. It played host to a multitude of bars, clubs, shops, and social spots including, most famously, the Stonewall Inn at its easternmost end, and the Oscar Wilde Bookshop, the city's first gay bookstore, which opened in 1967 and moved to Christopher Street in 1973. Armed with his Leica camera, Gupta spent weekends walking up and down Christopher Street and photographing the men he saw. Although the resulting collection of images, simply titled *Christopher Street 1976*, possesses a documentary function, for Gupta the photographic act was not just a way of documenting cruising. It was like cruising itself, and the level of interaction it involved was familiar to him, as he "was used to going up to people anyways." Some of the men in the photos look away, seemingly—or perhaps studiedly—unaware of the camera. Others look directly at it. Gupta's photographic subjects were, in this sense, doubly solicited, both by the lens of the camera and by the man "looking through the viewfinder."

Cruising, as I will go on to argue in the chapters ahead, is a profoundly optical phenomenon, a perceptual arena where acts of looking are intensified and eroticized. The presence of Gupta's camera thus augments the latent theatricality of these encounters; the sense that his subjects, at the moment of transient and passing interaction, are playing not only to the real spectator before them but to the imagined spectators suggested by the medial figure of the camera. Gupta's images light upon the cruise at its moment of initiation, not the hookup that will hopefully, if not invariably, follow. In this regard what they capture is an eroticism at its most incipient, yet on the other hand these images also mark an endpoint. Because Gupta's subjects are mostly captured in passing, their disappearance is signaled just beyond the frame of the photograph that freezes them in time. A person walking down the street in any given city will likely experience this phenomenon numerous times a day—a moment of optical interaction with a stranger, however brief, that is swiftly subsumed into the city's incessant flow of time and people. But Gupta's images capture something more particular: a look that is charged and directed; a look that is the very currency of an entire sexual culture most commonly—and often nostalgically—associated with New York in the 1970s. Thus, while the photographs signal an abundance of potential sexual encounters, they in turn locate a quiet melancholy in such abundance. The sense, as Gupta put it recently in a talk, that there were "so many men" and "so little time."[3]

This comment about promiscuity is no doubt shot through with a retrospective awareness of the HIV/AIDS epidemic that followed, less than a decade after these photographs were taken, but it also speaks more whimsically to the sense of new endless possibility that attended cruising culture in this period. If cruising, as Leo Bersani has it, is a form of "sexual sociability," its intrinsic danger is not "that it reduces relations to promiscuous sex, but rather that the promiscuity may stop."[4] The efficacy of cruising in the street, in this regard, could far exceed what Gupta described in this talk as cruising's more capitalistic iteration in bars and clubs, which involves the financial bargain of buying drinks, for example, and often proscribes a focus on solitary pleasure. Choosing one partner from an available pool of many could easily resemble a form of erotic individualism whereby the "promiscuity may stop." On the street, however, encounters are largely freed from the choreography of the bar and exist instead as a series of intensified looks, looks which may come and go but nonetheless leave an impression. Faced with the seemingly endless erotic potential of Christopher Street, Gupta's project locates photography as a site of possibility; an erotic alternative to consummation itself. Shooting on the hoof was a "cheap way of having them all," of creating a "catalogue of all the guys I wished I'd slept with," like a visual "wishlist" (a phrase that nonetheless has its own capitalistic associations).[5]

This visual "wishlist" of erotic prospects speaks to the vital role played by fantasy, because in the face of the risk that the "promiscuity may stop," it is through imagined acts of consummation and connection with passing strangers that the cruising subject may find a way of "having them all." Back in the much "smaller town" of Montreal, Gupta and a "literature-oriented buddy who liked cinema" made up "fictional narratives about still frames" they had taken and "tried to make up stories about people like us who were young, single, gay men."[6] After "going to the same bars every weekend for a few months, you've kind of seen everyone," so "we invented fictional names and backgrounds for people." These acts of invention were, for Gupta and his friend, a response to the over-familiarity of Montreal's gay scene, and yet this same fictional impulse is present in *Christopher Street* for quite the opposite reason—New York's overabundance of possible lovers. The street portraits of *Christopher Street* zoom in upon (presumably) gay male subjects and present them for imaginative projections by the viewer. From the raw details of their self-presentations—what these men are wearing, how tall or broad or slim they are, how they wear their hair—arise any number of questions. Who is this person? What is his story? What would it be like to go to bed with him? Gupta's photographs invite viewers to inhabit the peripatetic vantage of street cruising and in turn to participate in a conjectural exchange about their subjects. In dramatizing this optical scenario they suggest, ultimately, that the "look" of cruising is itself photographic; that the desirous look shared between strangers is itself an imaginative act of capture.

Just a year later, in the similarly vibrant gay hub of San Francisco, Hal Fischer was interrogating the codes and customs of erotic fantasy in gay cruising culture. If Gupta's peripatetic images of men walking in the "habitat" of Christopher Street provide a vivid portrait of a time and place—marked by the prevalence of particular fashions—Fischer's numerous photographic projects in the late 1970s offer an inventory of the cultural meanings of such fashions. Fischer's photographs of gay men attest, as he writes in the foreword to *Gay Semiotics,* to how "gay people have developed a semiotics intended both for identification and/or visibility within the larger culture, as well as communication among themselves."[7] These photographs demonstrate an intricate repertoire of signals and accessories, earrings and handkerchiefs placed deliberately in this or that ear, this or that pocket, all of which indicate not only sexual availability but your expressed "role" as either "active" or "passive." He continues:

> Gay culture has established a set of public, sexual prototypes. In
> gay magazines men are pictured in situations which were initially
> inspired by established male fantasies. Within the gay community
> certain characteristics of the fantasy have been adopted as fashion,
> thereby creating a "gay look," i.e. Gay Prototype, the cowboy;
> Contemporary adaptation, flannel shirts, jeans, short hair.[8]

The adaptation of such "looks" has an intriguing chronology; they are
born of "established male fantasies," photographed as "situations" in
magazines and then adopted into everyday life, thus becoming another
kind of cruising code, one that refers back to sexuality via the fantasy
narrative it is attributed to.

In his 1979 series *Boy-Friends,* which is composed of anonymous portraits of men accompanied by a short text describing or imagining an
encounter with them, Fischer further teases at the relation between the
semiotic and the narrative. The types represented in his photographs
here give way to miniature character-led cruising stories, like "A Hip-
pie," which begins, "Shoulder length hair and black leather jacket; he's
a Haight-Ashbury hybrid. Eye contact, he gestures me over." Each man
is also given a number, like "B75SF-46," a reminder of the proximity between the delineation of types and more official and even sinister forms
of cataloging by industrial or sociolegal bodies.[9] The proximity between
image and text in *Boy-Friends* serves to emphasize the semiotic nature
of erotic fantasy and a reliance upon preexisting or familiar cultural
matter. Dreaming up an erotic encounter with a "cowboy" involves not
the invention of a new figure but the queering of a masculinity that is
ubiquitous in the American imaginary from Western films, for example.
As with the other archetypal media images that Fischer cites and recon-
structs in *Gay Semiotics*—the classical, the natural, the urbane, and the
leather—the adoption of the "look" by gay men walking the streets is
the result of an intricate appropriation. This adaptation of preexisting
images from gay and straight sources comprises a mode of performance
through which to enact or elicit fantasies. The "adapted items are essentially neutral in the culture at large," Fischer writes, "but form a style
within the gay culture," one that is only legible to certain eyes.[10] In the
chapters that follow, style will emerge as one of cruising's communica-
tive faculties, a way of inflecting the erotic "look" through an attention
to the way one looks, sartorially speaking or otherwise.

There is a prevalence of certain stylistic features in Gupta and Fischer's images, then, like mustaches and denims, that are rooted in the semiotic conventions of a particular time and place. Back in New York, at the westernmost end of Christopher Street and beyond, the photographer Alvin Baltrop was documenting another kind of cruising culture, where desire was less entangled, to some extent at least, with the prevailing gay archetypes of the day. The largely abandoned Hudson River piers on the west side of Manhattan were frequented by men for sex throughout the 1970s and '80s, and are equally as iconic as Christopher Street in the queer imaginary of the city's past. Where Christopher Street was an artery of the gay Village, the derelict piers comprised a quasi-pastoral and even wild space of alterity, synonymous with a shadowy past of organized crime and reappropriated as a home for any number of the city's social outcasts. Men of different stripes—working-class truck drivers and middle-class denizens of the Village bars, for example—visited the piers in search of sex, away from the public glare of the streets. Although, as Jonathan Weinberg writes in his art history of the piers, there is the danger of imagining that participants "shed all their inhibitions and conventional behavior when they stepped onto the docks," finding "sexual partners along the waterfront" was in fact still "prone to be highly competitive and often frustrating," but they nonetheless provided an alternative to the more stratified spaces of the Village.[11]

Baltrop's photographs, which were mostly taken between the years 1975 and 1986, attest to the ambivalent world of the piers in wide-ranging ways. They demonstrate, as Fiona Anderson writes, that "while many of the men who cruised the piers wandered there from the adjacent bars, others were those intentionally excluded from such spaces," and many "were homeless, overweight, disabled, older, poor [...] African-American or Latinx."[12] As an African American artist himself, Baltrop was a relative outsider both to the dominant gay culture and the exclusionary New York art world. He worked as a postman and as a club bouncer during the same period in which he produced his most enduring works, and ensconced himself in the life of the piers by moving into his van, poised with his camera to capture whatever was going on. Baltrop would often go to extreme lengths—scaling the heights of the piers' structures in order to photograph them from particular angles—and he used the police radio he had acquired from his days as a cab driver to keep abreast of criminal activities. Among the more haunting examples of his work is a photograph of a dead body being fished out of the river, surrounded by police officers. The piers were as much a place of danger as they were of refuge, and Baltrop captured, Douglas Crimp writes, the "harsh realities of the place," from the "sad fates of teenagers who lived there," to the "terror of psychopaths preying on vulnerable men," and "even the risk of falling through a rotten floorboard or stepping on a rusty nail."[13]

Like Christopher Street for Gupta, the piers for Baltrop were an erotic and artistic site, a place where he both cruised and created. Among the range of scenes he captured is an attendant fixation upon the erotic look of the cruiser. Antonio Sergio Bessa suggests that the "object of desire for Baltrop is often seen from afar, enmeshed in a pile of debris that at once frames the subject while making it inaccessible," and the photographer's signature vantage point, capturing figures and sex acts from the distance of a neighboring pier, speaks to the importance of inscrutability to queer desire, often forced below—or behind—the surface of public visibility.[14] But recurring throughout Baltrop's work are also portraits of men—like Gupta's passing subjects—"who were happy to become exhibitionists for the camera at close range."[15] Among Baltrop's various and uncatalogued images—he did not attribute dates or titles, such that any arrangement of them is somewhat arbitrary—we find arresting faces punctuating any sequence with a direct intensity. One in particular, of a man sitting with his back against the wall, inhabits the optical scenario of cruising. It invites us to measure him up, just as he appears to be measuring us up with a look at once antagonistic and flirtatious. He sits against the wall with one leg stretched out, his hand grabbing his crotch and an open tin of Miller Lite beer between his legs. He wears an open shirt that shows his chest, sleeves rolled up to reveal his lower arm muscles quietly exerting themselves in his crotch-grab, along with denim jeans and workman boots with roller skates attached. Under the aspect of Fischer's gay semiotic model, we might attribute the man's style to the Western archetype, say, though we are left wondering, in the imaginative space forged by Baltrop's close-range composition, about the other aspects of his story.

Taken together, the works of these three photographers offer vivid portraits of gay male urban culture during a period widely regarded as the halcyon days of cruising, the post-Stonewall and pre-AIDS years when sex and possibility were palpable on the streets and in the piers.

Indeed, Gupta, Fischer, and Baltrop's works are vital parts of cruising's archive, an archive that is itself large and unwieldy. As Fiona Anderson notes in *Cruising the Dead River,* her study of David Wojnarowicz and the piers, there is a compelling friction between cruising's evanescence and its archival ubiquity. "Cruising," she writes, "even as it exploits urban anonymity and is structurally dependent on movement and ephemerality, has a queer historical orientation that is both imaginative and material."[16] At the same time, the process of archiving and remembering cruising's material traces is not always a smooth one. Although Baltrop exhibited his work during his lifetime at The Glines, the bar space of a gay theater organization, and even at the bar where he worked as a bouncer, he was still a relatively unknown artist when he died of cancer in 2004 at the age of fifty-five. It wasn't until the publication of Douglas Crimp's 2008 essay on Baltrop in *Artforum* that the art world began to take heed of the artist's significant archive of photographs, which are now held by the Bronx Museum. The museum's 2019 exhibition on Baltrop demonstrates the renewed and rising interest in his work. But this resurgence, as Mia Kang argues, is multipronged and bittersweet: if the "rise of ethnic, gender and sexuality studies in the academy" has "led to an increase in scholarship and exhibitions addressing artists previously excluded from canon formation," an artist "like Baltrop," who did not follow a familiar trajectory according to the art world's vectors of success, "could only gain entry belatedly—and more importantly, too late for the man himself to receive its benefits."[17]

Published in the catalog of the Bronx exhibition, Kang's observations are valuable for drawing attention to the way that the reclamation of Baltrop in numerous circles can lead to a flattening of the work along certain axes. His "life and work present the discipline of art history with a challenge," in that his photographs "tend to be written about in either formal *or* documentary terms, and those terms interact variously with an opposition between a utopian *or* abject view of queer social life."[18] Baltrop's recent inclusion in various art historical narratives is thus not only born of inclusion per se, but occurs against a larger backdrop of interests. His status as a documenter of cruising, along with more established photographers like Fischer and Gupta, has come to fruition in the context of a larger cultural interest in gay cruising, and in particular in the ways it was captured and constituted in New York and San Francisco in the 1970s. In the years 2018 and 2019, each of these photographers had a solo exhibition of their cruising photography in New York or London, and accompanying catalogs of those photographs have recently been published. The simple question "why now?" has no simple answer, but rather speaks to several intersecting concerns about the contemporary moment's relationship to a queer past.

In blurbs, interviews, and catalog essays, Gupta and Fischer have framed their seventies work in the retrospective terms of a pre-AIDS atmosphere, and these recollections speak to the vitality and exhibitionist charisma of their photographs from this period. But as well as remaining mindful of the less than enlightened elements of the halcyon days of seventies gay sexual culture, we must also resist, Anderson argues, "the sense of viral momentum that often accompanies popular, or at least heteronormative, narratives of gay life in the 1970s," exemplified by the "moralistic suggestion of a causal relation between the diverse cruising cultures of the late 1970s and the advent of HIV/AIDS in the early 1980s."[19] If the revival of interest in gay seventies photography speaks, indirectly, to contemporary attitudes toward HIV/AIDS in an age where the advent of preventive medication (PrEP) for those who can afford it all too easily invites talk of being "post-AIDS," the interest is no doubt also related to the contemporary status of cruising culture. The "gay public space" Gupta identifies in his images has today largely moved online, regulated by geosocial dating apps like Grindr and Scruff. In his book on the piers, Weinberg writes that we "love to complain that the virtual world of the internet, computers, and cell phones has destroyed our humanity," such that many "of our accounts of sex and romantic relationships today are built around a longing for a past when people supposedly had more authentic connections with one another."[20] Weinberg resists conventional thinking here, as Bersani famously does in his classic 1987 essay "Is the Rectum a Grave?"[21] by suggesting that the "anonymous sex" of the past was hardly an enlightened phenomenon. Indeed, Weinberg writes, it is comparable to the "supposed alienation of the early twenty-first century."

Contemporary app culture has altered the nature of cruising in any number of profound ways, from the virtualization of space as a digital grid to the more sinister and discriminatory ways in which "premium," fee-paying Grindr users could, until 2020, filter the type of men they are exposed to on that grid.[22] It is thus easy to see why the relative unsophistication of "analog" cruising becomes its own kind of nostalgic fetish in the face of the digital, and only makes the work of Gupta, Fischer, and Baltrop more compelling as a document of historical practice. Where cruising in "real" time and space operates according to the contingencies of encounter, apps serve to regulate the space of cruising and determine users' chosen pathways through it. The incipient and contingent now of a cruising encounter is reified on Grindr as "Right Now," the unit of time that delineates a given user's desire for casual sex. The interpersonal immediacy of the street is replaced on Grindr by the vexed evidentiary function of the image, where "pics"—of faces, torsos, and other body parts—are a primary currency. To look at Gupta, Fischer, and Baltrop's work under the aspect of contemporary online sex culture is thus to observe both deviation and a sense of continuity. While these photographs may provoke a longing for a past that reveals, in the face of Grindr's more banal and instrumental interface, how far we have fallen, they nonetheless also reveal that cruising has long been a visual culture where image and self-image play a constitutive role.

Just as the seventies cruising culture captured by these then-young gay photographers developed in dialogue with the increasing accessibility of photography as a form, where students and novices could more easily get hold of a portable Leica camera and document the world around them, so the imagistic culture of Grindr has flourished through, and alongside, the development of smart phones. In fact, this intermingling of cruising and images has a longer history still than this brief survey of cruising photographers would suggest. Gupta, Fischer, and Baltrop are significant figures in the canon of the art of cruising, which is to say art that not only documents cruising but also speaks to its status as an imaginative capacity and an aesthetic phenomenon. Their identification of cruising's photographic essence at a particular historical moment can steer us through the magnitude of gay New York's archive. But it is in an altogether different creative form, this book will argue, that we find the relation between cruising (as an optical interaction between queer subjects in time and space) and visuality (as a perceived aesthetic heightening) most clearly articulated.

Gay New York

Rehearsing the history of three queer photographers from the 1970s might be an unusual way to begin a study primarily concerned with poetry and literary texts. To establish these increasingly ubiquitous images of mustachioed men in shorts and leather as the backdrop for the book's picture of cruising risks perpetuating the decade's insatiable hold upon contemporary imaginings of the city's queer past. As Doug Ireland wrote in a piece for *New York* Magazine back in 1978, there "have always been parts of our city that have served as gay cruising areas," such as "Washington Square Park in the 1940s" and "Third Avenue near the Queensboro Bridge in the 1950s," among others.[23] The post-Stonewall moment does not possess a monopoly on what constitutes a gay tradition; as Walter Holland writes, there is a "mythic view of Stonewall as the moment when a deep wall of silence and invisibility was magically lifted and gay identity and culture were instantly constituted," and this view has been "deconstructed by the work of George Chauncey," whose 1994 study *Gay New York* "shows the existence of a rich and diverse 'gay' past even at the start of the [twentieth] century."[24] One of the major interventions of Chauncey's now-classic history is precisely its identification of vibrant social and sexual cultures in the late nineteenth and early twentieth centuries, long before the advent of an "out" public culture for gay men, as well as the observation that the look has long been an important tactic in such cultures.

Because of the "cultural injunction" in the early twentieth century "against men looking at other men in the sexually assertive way they gazed at women," Chauncey writes, "a 'normal' man almost automatically averted his eyes if they happened to lock with a stranger, whereas a gay man interested in the man gazing at him returned his look."[25] The phenomenon that art historian Rebecca Zurier terms "urban visuality," the "social and cultural habit of looking as a social and cultural practice in cities," where "city dwellers become knowing interpreters of a potentially bewildering overload of visual information and learn to assess strangers optically," can be traced in the life of New York City at least as far back as the turn of the twentieth century.[26] Thus, in their directness and immediacy, Gupta, Fischer, and Baltrop's images from the seventies crystallize a mode of erotic looking that can be identified throughout the history of gay life in the city and, I will argue, across a number of literary texts. These photographs actualize a "look"—a term I am using to denote both a gaze and a form of sartorial or even archetypal self-image—that is in fact a frequent and striking trope among several New York poets.

The Poetics of Cruising explores this relationship between cruising, photography, and the visual in the work of a number of writers, from Walt Whitman in the nineteenth century to Eileen Myles in the twenty-first, and also locates its initial crystallization in nineteenth-century Paris, in the work of Charles Baudelaire and Walter Benjamin's account of it. In establishing this formulation, the book does not seek to enshrine, transhistorically, a delimited "gay" or "queer" canon of New York writing—such a task is ever thwarted by historical particularities. Laying a claim to Walt Whitman or to Langston Hughes as gay or queer writers, for example, is no simple matter; although there is evidence these writers had sexual relationships between men, scholars still debate the pertinence and appropriateness of using terms which precede, or else do not adequately describe, their erotic lives. Whitman was writing before and during the period when desire between men began to be framed linguistically in a manner familiar to us today, and as John Boswell writes, the "word 'homosexual,' despite its air of antiquity, was actually coined in the late nineteenth century by German psychologists, introduced into English only at the beginning of the present [twentieth] century."[27] Similarly, inasmuch as the examples of Frank O'Hara and David Wojnarowicz comprise a historical continuity in regard to gay life in New York before and after Stonewall, it would be reductive to try and fit Eileen Myles neatly in this category, not least because there has been a relative erasure of lesbian cruising, and of female and nonbinary writers, from the history of cruising. And, as we shall see throughout this book, this history is not just one of community but of exclusion, where certain gendered and racialized bodies are marked and policed.

In other words, a "gay" sensibility does not map out consistently in this history, and in the course of attending to these three writers chronologically I am not suggesting a linear equivalence that leads from, say, 1855 to 2018, but rather seek to consider correspondences across these divergent historical moments. As its complex historical fate has shown, the term "gay" feels insufficient and even exclusionary. "While conceived as an act of resistance to homophobic oppression," writes Bersani, "the project of elaborating a gay identity could itself be discredited" for "delineating what is easily recognizable as a white, middle-class, liberal gay identity," as if the act of "looking for a gay identity predetermined the field in which it would be found."[28] Thus it is in a structural sense, in the first instance, that the word "queer" proves particularly useful.

"Queer approaches to understanding the past and present," Mark W. Turner writes in *Backward Glances,* his study of cruising in London and New York, can eschew the "levelling out of history" and the "grand narratives" of continuity, and can get "beyond binary thinking ('gay' and 'straight'), of the sort that has defined so much of the way urban modernity is understood."[29] Queer, in its elasticity, is amenable to the transhistorical by rejecting binary or deterministic labels, and moves past the methodological etiquette of appropriateness versus anachronism, as recent entries in the Whitman debate that argue for his queerness have suggested.[30]

This book keeps both terms, "gay" and "queer," in play, and contends that the urban space figured by these texts can still be fruitfully named as that of "gay New York," to return to the title of Chauncey's book, which spans the years 1890 (just two years before Whitman's death) to 1940. Gay was one among a number of terms used to describe homosexuality in this period, Chauncey argues, many of which were "not synonymous with *homosexual* or *heterosexual*" but still represented "a different conceptual mapping of male sexual practices," each with their own "specific connotation[s]." Still, it is perhaps the most commonly accepted member of a family of words that mostly, in spite of their differences, refer back to sex between men.[31] The word "queer" is also included along with "faggot," "fairy," and "trade," but in this lexical assemblage it meant something different to its more recent redefinition as a critical term, a term that could "be taken," Bersani writes, "as delineating political rather than erotic tendencies."[32] The "gay New York" that forms this book's field of enquiry thus refers to the city as both an imaginary and a localizable site, one that provides an umbrella term for the divergent portraits of queer life in the city that these texts provide. The ground covered ranges from Whitman's Brooklyn Heights in the 1850s to Myles's East Village in the 2010s, and the question of what constitutes these queer spaces is, of course, radically different in each of these periods. While Gupta's vision of Christopher Street in the mid-seventies, as a "gay public space such as hadn't really been seen before," seems like the consummate landscape of gay cruising, I am not seeking to impose a postliberation vantage upon Whitman's New York, for example, nor O'Hara's, even if the culture of the West Village in the sixties was continuous with the more open and tangible form that cruising took in the years following Stonewall. What I am suggesting in bringing these writers together in this study is that

they each, in their focus upon the look as an instrument of erotic perception, queer the respective urban spaces they inhabited. Out of this
assemblage something like a "gay New York" emerges, and although its
constituent iterations may not be directly reproducible across time, they
are parallel examples, nonetheless, of a queer relation to urban space.

What this assemblage also offers, then, is a vivid glimpse into the
ways that cruising has been conceptualized in relation to the visual
culture of given historical moments. Although Whitman's cruising in
Brooklyn or among the crowds of Broadway is well documented, there
is much in his work to suggest that his devotion to the love between
men and, more particularly, the love between strangers, is intimately
linked with his interest in daguerreotypes and burgeoning forms of
portrait photography. Similarly, Langston Hughes's poems of looking
and cruising are mediated by traditions of street photography and montage, a connection that is taken up explicitly—and to explicitly queer
ends—by Isaac Julien's 1989 film *Looking for Langston*. Frank O'Hara's
little-known film texts from the 1960s help to illuminate his cruising
poems, revealing a queer erotic fixation with film stars that is replayed
on the streets of Manhattan, just as David Wojnarowicz's unpublished
poetry from the 1970s allows us to reinterpret his better-known photographic and prose works.

What does "gay New York" look like today, fifty years on from the
Stonewall riots? Most apparently, the ongoing gentrification of the city
and, as Sarah Schulman suggests, of the mind, continues to endanger the
radical potential of what the city has to offer queer and subcultural communities.[33] The Hudson River piers, which, as Christopher Castiglia
and Christopher Reed point out, themselves "became a locus of memory, marked by casual graffiti—much of it, as the AIDS crisis developed,
explicitly memorial," have now all but "disappeared," former memorial
sites lost to the process of regeneration.[34] Where David Wojnarowicz's
visual art could once be found, like the graffiti Castiglia and Reed describe, on the crumbling walls of the piers, it is nowadays viewed in museums like the Whitney, home of the 2018 Wojnarowicz retrospective,
whose new Renzo Piano–designed building sits on Gansevoort Street,
a block away from Piers 51 and 53, both of which have now been turned
into parks. But perhaps the most significant change wrought upon queer
urban space in recent years is the virtualization of the space of cruising
by apps like Scruff and Grindr.

Created in 2009 as a means for gay men to communicate, date, and meet for sex, Grindr approximates the arena of cruising using a virtual grid comprising user profiles that are displayed in the order of their proximity to you at a given moment. These profiles are shown in the grid as images; what is shown in users' profile images is at their own discretion, though full-frontal nudity is not permitted, and some users choose not to display an image at all for anonymity's sake. Within a profile, which is accessed by tapping on this image, a user can choose to display such information as Height, Ethnicity, Body Type, Relationship Status, Sexual Position, and HIV Status. A user can also choose the "Tribe" that best describes them, from a list that includes the following types: Bear, Clean-Cut, Daddy, Discreet, Geek, Jock, Leather, Otter, Poz, Rugged, Trans, and Twink. (Grindr's grid of course often reproduces discriminatory attitudes, of a piece with the fetishistic and even violent economy of preference that can govern actual encounters on the street.) Finally, there is the option for a user to display why they are using the app through the "Looking For" function, stating that they are looking for Chat, Friends, Dates, Networking, or Right Now. To be looking for right now is to turn the act of virtual perusal into the act of cruising at one remove, mediated by the technology that governs what is available to explore. Provided with this information, to differing degrees, users can pick and choose who to communicate with from the available network of men, determining who they are to share their "right now" with.

Grindr may have altered or adapted the "now" of cruising to its own ends, and in the book's coda I will explore both how cruising culture has changed in its wake, and how contemporary poets like Danez Smith have carved out the distinctive textual space of the "Grindr poem" to reflect on this. But in the chapters ahead I will be considering how these historically particular texts from Whitman onwards can speak to the "now" of the present moment as icons of a queer cultural past. By staging acts of looking, I will argue, these cruising texts invite their readers to participate in the optical erotics they establish. This occurs most often through triangulation. A Whitman lyric, for example, makes available (at least) two kinds of address simultaneously, such that we imagine the "you" of a given poem as being both an imagined addressee particular to the poem's compositional situation—the cruisee—and us ourselves, who thus occupy a third position within the poem's interlocution. And it is no accident that some of Whitman's most explicit extensions to future readers are figured analogously as encounters occurring in the urban environment, like his invocation of the "others who look back on me because I look'd forward to them" from the urban vantage of "Crossing Brooklyn Ferry."[35] This line describes both the immediate optical situation of looks between strangers in the street—the backward glance of cruising—and the parallel interplay of backward and forward that attends the poet's relation to his readers, who "look back" upon him as he looks "forward" to them from a historically distant time and place.

Indeed, like the often brief and random back-and-forth of cruising, the hermeneutic "look" of a text's reception can also be contingent or fragile, and similarly prone to missed signals and misreadings. As Jonathan D. Katz puts it in introducing a collection of portraits representing same-sex desire, the "social universe of sexual desire, in painting, as in life, is so often of necessity communicated through the most subtle gestures, glances, and codes."[36] Whitman's poetics of presence is correspondingly animated by an anxiety to be seen and understood, to be affirmed by the look of the other, and it is bolstered by the hope that textuality itself can maintain and revivify the possibility of communion between poet and reader. However, while the erotics of this second-person address is not quite unique to Whitman, the directness of his invocation of the reader as a historically distant "you" is a central idiosyncrasy of his particular textual project, and one not exactly reproduced in the work of his successors. What is the place, then, of the reader in cruising texts that implore their onlookers less directly, which is to say texts that instead narrate an encounter between a self and an object who is not "you," but a third-person "he"? If O'Hara and Wojnarowicz's texts seem more inclined toward apprehending strangers who are rendered in the third-person, this is not to say that the reader does not still come to occupy something akin to the triangulated third positionality I described above. As in cruising, a text need not be looking squarely at its reader to retain its uncanny capacity to look back. It is here that the visuality courted by these texts comes to bear, for insofar as they frame cruising encounters as photographic or cinematic, these texts themselves might then be thought of as ekphrastic; as texts that render and describe their desired strangers as visual objects that share, in some sense, the properties of artworks. Though the ekphrastic text, in its tendency toward description over apostrophe, may seem to sideline its reader as an onlooker who is situated at a further remove from the object of attention, is the writer's act of reading not, in another sense, an implicit extension to their own reader?

In the introduction to his instructive book on queer ekphrasis, Brian Glavey writes of the "situatedness of ekphrasis that hinges on the forms of sociability involved in responding to artworks for readers, a scenario with at least three rather than two players" and which "is not simply about seeing" but "also about showing and sharing."[37] The reader of a quasi-ekphrastic cruising text, then, such as Wojnarowicz's apprehension of a man "handsome like some face in old boxer photographs, a cross between an aging boxer and Mayakovsky," is not only witness to an act of looking, but is instantiated by the text into a way of looking.[38] If ekphrasis "is, in this sense, pedagogical," Glavey continues, then this "sociability" might encourage a reader not only to inhabit the vantage of the "I" as if they are inside the time and space of the text's situation—a testament to immediacy, vividness, and the stirring of empathy—but also to turn this way of looking back upon the speaker and the text itself. In other words, a text that performs an act of close reading, in homing in upon a desired stranger, correspondingly invites a kindred effort from its own reader.[39] Such a mode of reading in turn invites an interrogation of the text's "I," the reader's own desired object, who is constituted at once by the particulars of form and the biographical matter of authorship. The reader thus becomes suspended, similar to the "Lucky Pierre" of O'Hara's "Personism,"[40] in a triangulated cruising scenario, compelled to visualize both the passing stranger of the text's situation and the no-less-strange speaker who mediates this encounter; a speaker who is himself suspended between an abstract "I" and "David Wojnarowicz," for example.

This capacity of texts to enact the look back that they describe touches upon recent methodological debates around what Rita Felski describes, in her critique of "context," as the "transtemporal movement and affective resonance of particular texts."[41] Such movement indeed recalls the sense of agency and posterity that Whitman seeks for his text, and in turn himself, in "Crossing Brooklyn Ferry." Using Bruno Latour's notion of "nonhuman actors," Felski asks "what would it mean for literary and cultural studies to acknowledge poems and paintings, fictional characters and narrative devices, as actors?" The "bogeyman in the closet" of this conversation is the "fear that acknowledging the agency of texts will

tip us into the abyss of a retrograde religion of art" or else insipid proc-
lamations about universality and timelessness, so "context" is presumed
to safeguard against these by invoking that which is outside, or to one
side of, the text (583). And yet, as Felski writes, there "is no zero-sum
game in which one side must be conclusively crushed so that the other
can triumph" (584). Rather, the cruising works I am concerned with
solicit a kind of reading that flouts any such fixed line between text and
context. Their erotics depend on a closeness to form that is simultaneous
with attending to the particulars of their production, and to the circumstances of their author's lived experiences as cruisers of the city. The
call of Whitman's "you," after all, draws its potency from its historicity.

That poems can look back or attain "transtemporal movement and
affective resonance" in a variety of ways is, on the surface, no more particular than the nature of reception writ large. And yet, I am suggesting,
this capacity is queer, or has particularly queer potential, and finds rich
analogical expression in the optical mechanism of cruising. The notion
that a poem of cruising might in turn cruise us suggests that the status
of texts as actors needn't remain at the level of the nonhuman. Walter
Benjamin once wrote, on a scrap of paper that will prove significant in
the next chapter, "Words themselves have an aura; [Karl] Kraus described this in particularly exact terms: 'The closer one looks at a word,
the greater the distance from which it returns the gaze.'"[42] Words are
rendered here not merely as actors or extensions of action; they resemble persons themselves, glancing back, perhaps taking on the countenance of the "loved one" or the "lover" Benjamin elliptically describes
in the next, incomplete paragraph of this note. This account of reading
recalls the feared, "retrograde" religion of art that Felski refers to, and resembles Alfred Gell's anthropological theory of art where "we approach
art objects" as "indexes," as if they had "physiognomies like people," for
when "we see a picture of a smiling person, we attribute an attitude of
friendliness to the 'person in the picture'" [. . .] just as a real person's
smile would trigger the same inference."[43] If the "inference" of animate
or interpersonal presence is the condition of the "index" in the realm of
visual art, a perception of "agency" that these textual accounts of cruising narrate in their absorption in the look as a live and visual encounter,
then they share in that same "abduction of agency" *as* texts themselves,
their "index" the linguistic phenomenon through which a reader detects
a physiognomic presence.

The stakes of this model of reading for a queer poetics lie, then, in the seeming perversity or naivety, or indeed perverse naivety, of an investment in the animate. As Glavey writes, "whether obtuse or otiose, old-fashioned or utopian, modes of thought tied up with an attention to form are queer in the sense that they care about things too much or in all the wrong ways."[44] Indeed queer theory abounds with these constitutive tendencies toward excess or wrongness that are sustained in relation to the supposed efficacies of texts and artworks, objects of study that are brought to life, correspondingly, through the queer art of reading. "Close reading," Kevin Ohi writes, "offers a way to access the potentiality of the literary work—not to settle it, once and for all, in a meaning that masters it, but to rewrite it, perpetually," and in this schema "potentiality" refers to that "recurrent topos in queer writing, where it is a mode of sexual and political critique and where imaginings of utopian sexual possibilities take shape in readings and rewritings of precursor texts."[45] Elizabeth Freeman similarly identifies in queer studies a formalism that seeks to carve out a space of solace, "a longing for form that turns us backward to prior moments, forward to embarrassing utopias, sideways to forms of being and belonging that seem, on the face of it, completely banal."[46] The utopian act of reading that anchors José Esteban Muñoz's 2009 study *Cruising Utopia: The Then and There of Queer Futurity* is, in the first instance, exemplary for my own purposes. Muñoz frames his formulation of the utopic around a poem that is itself a reading of a photograph, James Schuyler's "A photograph," a text that "harnesses multiple temporalities" and suggests that a relation to the visual—exemplified by the speaker's ekphrastic relation to a photograph of a happier time—is itself a negotiation of proleptic retrospection.[47] In the act of recollection, Schuyler's speaker illustrates "a type of affective excess that presents the enabling force of a forward-dawning futurity that is queerness" (23).

The placement of this poem, as a text illustrative of "moments of queer relational bliss," suggests that the utopian or ecstatic temporality Muñoz theorizes is something that can be learned or taught, or pedagogical, as Glavey has it. It is a way of looking at something—a poem, a photograph, a person—and this important ekphrastic dimension of Muñoz's argument is often neglected in accounts of *Cruising Utopia*. More obviously, there is also the suggestiveness of Muñoz's title, which he explains thus: "The mode of 'cruising' for which this book calls is not

only or even primarily 'cruising for sex.' I do see an unlimited potentiality in actual queer sex, but books of criticism that simply glamorize the
ontology of gay male cruising are more often than not simply boring"
(18). I hope to follow Muñoz's word in offering an account of gay male
cruising that is neither decorous nor boring; which neither glamorizes
cruising as an ahistorical paradise nor repeats the same old tropes. Like
Muñoz, who puns on the "look" or glance of cruising as both an exca-
vatory and erotic gesture when he writes that the book's "critical methodology can be best described as a backward glance that enacts a future
vision" (4), I too am interested not only in cruising for sex per se but in
the incipient and intricate temporalities the act brings to light.

In as much as the optical encounter of cruising is an immersion
in the present, it is also, as Paul K. Saint-Amour writes, after Muñoz,
a present that is "the only temporality that could harbor the utopian
touch of past and future."[48] Saint-Amour's article illuminates and builds
upon Muñoz's diagnosis of the present as an oppressive here-and-now
in order to identify what he coins the "literary present," a given of literary studies, the widely shared "practice of writing predominantly in
the present tense when writing about literary works," as if the text and
its author were live, or alive.[49] Saint-Amour explores and complicates
the assumptions of the literary present in fascinating ways, particularly
its relation to futurity, and I find myself needing to state at the outset of
this book—as he does at the end of his article—a renewed though self-
conscious faith in this wiliest of tenses. It is, after all, with recourse to
the literary present that the cruising texts I am concerned with are seen
to be looking at us, right now. Perhaps this mode of temporal intercon-
nection is what Freeman means by that longing that looks forward to
"embarrassing utopias," or, as Muñoz has it, the "longing that propels us
onward, beyond romances of the negative."[50]

Tyler Bradway has recently connected this sense of longing to the
notion of "bad reading," a mode of affective relation to texts where "we
suspend the institutionally sanctioned critic as the originator of the affective relations of reading" and attend instead "to the aesthetic object's
affective agency—its capacity to foster new relational models for reading."[51] Such models would look beyond the "dialectic of suspicion and
empathy" inherited from Sedgwick toward affects that include "stupe-
faction, anxiety, masturbatory pleasure, exuberance, shameless immod-
esty" and so on; they would weather the potentially "embarrassing" or

"retrograde" implications of finding and seeking queer kinship, even solidarity, in texts from across great historical distances.[52] And, indeed, of taking Whitman at his word when he writes in "Crossing Brooklyn Ferry" that it "is not upon you alone the dark patches fall" (*LG*, 138). That our encounters with queer texts, like our hook-ups and the looks that initiate them, can feel embarrassing, pleasurable, shameful, wounding, and utopic, as if, to quote Frank O'Hara's 1954 poem "Homosexuality," "we'd been pierced by a glance!" (*CP*, 181–82), is the main argument of this book.

In chapter 1, I extend a backward glance to nineteenth-century Paris in order to illustrate this imbrication of cruising, looking, poetics, and photography. Baudelaire's poem "À une passante" ("To a passing woman"), as well as Walter Benjamin's account of it in relation to the interpersonal-aesthetic phenomenon of the aura, are both frequently recruited to tell the origin story of urban modernity. In this chapter I carve a new path through this material to identify its resonance for queer looking, particularly with regards to the erotic and photographic capacity of poetry itself, and compare Baudelaire's poem to Whitman's "To a Stranger." This comparison also brings to light the ambivalence of cruising's look, the fact that it can be utopic and illuminating, but also wounding, violent, and scopophilic, which I pursue at greater length in Whitman's work in chapter 2. Whitman's celebrations of cruising in Manhattan, an environment he names the "City of Orgies" in the title of one poem, are connected, I suggest, to his fixation upon portraits and daguerreotypes. Although this connection seems most apparent in Whitman's cruising poems, a similar erotics of looking is also palpable in poems of wounding and war. Whitman's definition of a textual and erotic magnetism gathers together these various strands in his poetic thinking, and provides a gloss upon his own cruisy solicitations of his readers.

In chapter 3, I identify Langston Hughes's relation to Whitman as loaded with queer meaning, and locate the presence of Whitman's legacy as a poet of cruising in Hughes's 1925 poem "Subway Face." Using that poem's fixation upon looking, desire, and interchange, I turn to Isaac Julien's 1989 film *Looking for Langston* as an optic for Hughes's own furtive representations of queer love and interracial desire, and trace his use of textual cruising as a mode of resisting the white gaze in his photographic and quasi-photographic works from the 1950s. In chapter 4, I begin by identifying how race, desire, and cinema intersect in Frank

O'Hara's work, and argue that his well-documented love of the movies is intimately linked to his interests in cruising. Through a close reading of *Act and Portrait,* a rarely discussed film collaboration with the artist Alfred Leslie, I identify how O'Hara's poetic eulogies to cinema and to the erotic strangers of the streets, whom he apprehends as if they were movie stars, are both steeped in the semiotics of cruising, which in turn provides a way of thinking about his own flirtatious poetic style.

In chapter 5, I study David Wojnarowicz's unpublished poetry alongside his photographic project *Arthur Rimbaud in New York* and suggest that, for Wojnarowicz, the shared glance of cruising is a distinctively photographic phenomenon that is also closely linked to the temporality of masturbation. Following these strands in his work, I argue that the simultaneously wounding and erotic dimensions of looking are thrown into relief by the specter of HIV/AIDS that haunts his writing. In the book's coda, I address the question of who is traditionally excluded from the practice and history of cruising, and explore how the poetry of Eileen Myles, from the 1990s through to their more contemporary output, critiques, both directly and obliquely, the gendered inequities in the queer community. This analysis of Myles's work, in particular their poem "Hot Night," precipitates a turn to the contemporary moment, and a reflection upon the changing nature of cruising and looking "right now," in the age of Grindr.

1

Passing Strangers

Love at Last Sight

Wondering as to the nature of "aura," Walter Benjamin once scribbled the following observation on an Acqua S. Pellegrino notepad:

> The one who is seen or believes himself to be seen [glances up] answers with a glance. To experience the aura of an appearance or a being means becoming aware of its ability [to pitch] to respond to a glance. This ability is full of poetry.[1]

From a distant perspective this object has its own aura; although it is mechanically reproduced in a published collection of materials from Benjamin's archive, this passage appears closer in this form to its so-called authentic origin, shedding the layers of mediation which characterize its more familiar disseminations in the complete, published essays where it reappears.[2] It is all the more evocative for the tangible sense of place it suggests. The S. Pellegrino tagline at the bottom of the paper—"La Migliore Da Tavola" (The best table water)—recalls the kind of notepaper you might expect to find on a hotel bar or café table in the inside-outside of a Paris arcade, say, a place where you are "one who is seen," where you might answer the looks of passing strangers "with a glance" and afterwards jot down the experience. It is possible to glean from this fragment, then, the very milieu of cruising—a scene of looking, watching, and subsequently, of writing. The aura is one of the most ubiquitous of Benjamin's concepts, referred to frequently both in his own work and in Benjamin scholarship, but its usage in this note is distinctive. Here, the aura is inflected, implicitly and first-personally, with the imagined experiences of its author, lent an urban and interpersonal resonance that refers back to the analogy around which this coinage functions.

As Benjamin writes in "On Some Motifs in Baudelaire," the "experience of aura thus arises from the fact that a response characteristic of human relationships is transposed to relationships between humans and inanimate or natural objects."[3] Analogies provide optics, and this transposition lights upon the way that aura is, in Miriam Bratu Hansen's words, "not an inherent property of persons or objects but pertains to the *medium* of perception, naming a particular structure of vision" that "enables the manifestation of the gaze, inevitably refracted and disjunctive, and shapes its potential meanings."[4] Reciprocated glances in "human relationships" act, for Benjamin, as a particular "structure of vision" vis-à-vis singular artworks, a means of conceptualizing aura (which is predominantly used for describing a feature of aesthetics) in terms of an interpersonal animism that is endangered by reproduction. Yet this note, in its suggestion of a scene of writing that might also be a scene of watching, highlights the term's applicability not only to an object/ beholder relation, but the reciprocated human glance per se. To consider this juncture in Benjamin's analogy, across which the "aura" might travel from describing an artwork back to describing a person, is thus also to consider its possible other variants—artworks which contain persons, or the contexts in which persons might themselves resemble artworks, torn between the static and the animate.

The three-line fragment at the top of the note—"Eyes staring at one's back / Meeting of glances / Glance up, answering a glance"—narrates an exchange of looks and is lineated like verse, bringing to mind an accompanying inversion: if the "ability" of aura is full of poetry, might "poetry" also be "full of" this ability? In the Baudelaire essay, Benjamin posits the eponymous subject as the consummate lyric poet of the city, a writer alive to the contingencies of the crowd and the phantasmagoria of urban experience, which can both intensify and threaten this capacity to respond to a glance. Baudelaire's sonnet "À une passante" renders the auratic exchange as a scene of heartbreak, one where modern love meets the shock of the urban glance at the threshold between the singular and the repetitious:

La rue assourdissante autour de moi hurlait.
Longue, mince, en grand deuil, douleur majestueuse,
Une femme passa, d'une main fastueuse
Soulevant, balançant le feston et l'ourlet;

Agile et noble, avec sa jambe de statue.
Moi, je buvais, crispé comme un extravagant,
Dans son œil, ciel livide où germe l'ouragan,
La douceur qui fascine et le plaisir qui tue.

Un éclair... puis la nuit! —Fugitive beauté
Dont le regard m'a fait soudainement renaître,
Ne te verrai-je plus que dans l'éternité?

Ailleurs, bien loin d'ici! trop tard! *jamais* peut-être!
Car j'ignore où tu fuis, tu ne sais où je vais,
ô toi que j'eusse aimé, ô toi qui le savais!

[All around me the deafening street was wailing.
Tall, slim, in the garbs of mourning—a sorrow majestic—
A woman passed, with refulgent hand
Lifting, swinging her flounce and hem.

Agile and noble, her limbs of a statue.
Me—I drank, tensed up like a madman,
From her eyes, the pallid sky that gives rise to tempests,
The softness that grips, the pleasure that kills.

A flash... then night! —O brief beauty
Whose glance suddenly rebirthed me,
Shall I only see you again in eternity?

Away, far away from here! Too late! Perhaps never?
For I don't know where you flee to, you don't know where I go,
O you who I might have loved, O you who knew it!][5]

This poem stages the apprehension of another person's aura, which is to say the woman's disturbing ability to glance back, her agency, signaled by the fact, as Mark W. Turner writes, that "she, too, reads the street visually."[6] This ability in turn marks her out; Janet Wolff writes "we may also ask whether a "respectable" woman in 1850s would have met the gaze of a strange man."[7] Whether a widow, as her attire suggests, or a prostitute, as her look back could imply, the *passante*'s "regard" (glance) is significant for the poet. A glance is optical, meaning to "cast a momentary look," but it can also mean to "strike obliquely," perhaps not unlike the "plaisir qui tue" (pleasure that kills), as though the meeting of glances is an exchange of some violence. The "éclair" (flash) of the third stanza corroborates this—one is, after all, said to be "struck" by lightning or an assailant—and also gestures to another possible meaning. In translating Benjamin into English, Howard Eiland and Kevin McLaughlin have elsewhere opted for "glance" as a translation of the German word *Blick,* which, they explain, "in earlier usage meant 'a flashing,' 'a lighting up,' 'a shining.'"[8] *Blick* is also the term Benjamin uses to describe the aura in the German text of his Baudelaire essay.[9] For both Baudelaire and Benjamin, this flash can signal aura's undoing. Eduardo Cadava notes that "Benjamin's vocabulary of lightning helps register what comes to pass in the opening and closing of vision," often the "irruption of events or images, and even the passage into night" (as in Baudelaire's sonnet, "Un éclair . . . puis la nuit!") Frequently too it is posited as necessary for creation, being "the movement of writing and inscription," but also destructive: "What is illumined or lighted by the punctual intensity of this or that strike of lightning, however—the emergence of an image, for example—can at the same time be burned, incinerated, consumed in flames."[10]

Baudelaire's poem gives voice to this burning out in its mournful "O"s, for no sooner has the poet seen this passing woman than she vanishes in this flash, a lighting up that eschews the epiphanic or celestial associations of light. A proximate analogy is the flash of the camera, which registers the fleeting urban encounter as though it were as transient as a snapshot. Timothy Raser describes this poem as displaying the "urge to capture the passing moment, for fear of losing it forever," in a manner that is "inextricably bound into modernity and photography."[11] Baudelaire's on-the-record conception of photography in "The Salon of 1859," in which he lambasts the camera for the threat it poses to the imaginary capacities of art, indeed emphasizes its "true duty" to preserve "precious things whose form is dissolving and which demand a place in the archives of our memory." But Baudelaire had in mind "tumbling ruins" and fragile "manuscripts," not passing women whose forms dissolve in crowds.[12] "À une passante" may court the photographic in several ways, but not without presenting a certain experiential tension between the live, passing nature of momentary urban encounters on the one hand, and the more fixed, reflective forms of attention denoted by photographic "archives" of memories on the other. Benjamin navigates this by reconceptualizing the live-ness of the metropolis and the reproductive capacities of photography as mutually informing and ambivalent symbols of progress in the midst of modernity. For Benjamin the camera acts as a mechanism of mass reproduction threatening the auratic phenomenon of the singular glance, for that which "withers in the age of mechanical reproduction is the aura of the work of art," divorced from an originating "tradition" or "unique existence"; thus instead taking dispersed form in a "plurality of copies."[13] In other words, in a construction which exemplifies the way this essay seems peculiarly double-minded about its own position: "from a photographic negative [. . .] one can make any number of prints; to ask for the "authentic" print makes no sense."[14]

In this regard Benjamin synthesizes strands of Baudelaire's thoughts intended as resolutions of one another, and suggests the ability to reproduce is photography's greatest threat to the realm of art, where Baudelaire sees that ability as grounds for its relegation from that realm. In his essay on the poet, Benjamin conceives of this diminishment as homologous with the impact of the metropolis upon the consciousness whereby *Erfahrung*—the terrain of a preconscious, personal, Proustian form of memory—is usurped by *Erlebnis,* an exterior world of sensation whose relentlessness precludes access to such memory.[15] Dianne Chisholm expands upon Benjamin's identifications in the Baudelaire essay of the "sexual shock that can beset a lonely man" and the "love which only a city dweller experiences," suggesting that for Benjamin "love in the big city is inextricably bound to commodity traffic," and that encounters with strangers culminate only in "but fleeting consummation" before they pass on, "destined for mass circulation and repeated exchange."[16] This flash of apprehension in "À une passante" thus resembles the alienating multiplications of both the urban crowd and the camera, swallowing the image of the passing woman not into a void of disappearance but the chaos of "mass circulation."

In translating the poem, another kind of reproduction, Clive Scott makes literal work of this loss by transforming it from a sonnet to a villanelle. This transformation "made necessary" the "projection of the encounter, not, as in the sonnet, as a unique and once-and-for-all event, but as something repeated, habitual, as a kind of Muybridgean cinematic sequence, a series of frames slightly differentiated from each other, where the repetition itself takes the woman away, confirms her in an otherness."[17] This otherness is not to be confused, however, with singularity:

however unique your encounter with this woman may seem, it is likely being repeated somewhere else, around the corner, only moments later, which the mind's eye can replicate as if part of a Muybridgean projection. Reading Benjamin's "aura" into Baudelaire's sonnet exposes the way in which the "wellspring of poetry" is, for Baudelaire, thwarted by the city. Benjamin's text has become a crucial companion to this poem, a poem whose "importance," Scott writes, is "owed substantially to its appearance in Benjamin," and he seeks to "incorporate this cultural fact" in his translation.[18] He does this by paraphrasing in the final line Benjamin's oft-cited observation, which first appeared in a 1938 essay on Baudelaire and later in "On Some Motifs," that this is a poem of "love" not at "first sight," but "last sight."[19]

The "rue assourdissante" (deafening street) emerges from Benjamin's analysis as a compositional setting that is not apprehended per se, but as a perceptual field already mediated and mediatized, like the "Muybridgean cinematic sequence" that Scott draws out in his translation work. Philip Auslander locates, in Benjamin's statement about photographic negatives and their copies, an "ontology" that the category of liveness paradoxically shares, for the live can contain its own capacities for repetition just as "photographic media" can partake of the "ontology of disappearance" and "provide an experience of evanescence."[20] In this light, the gaze's mediation through the camera is thus already immanent in the urban environment, as a "structure of vision" and way of being in the city that ever awaits passing objects for perceptual consumption. Susan Sontag writes that photography "first comes into its own as an extension of the eye of the middle-class *flâneur,* whose sensibility was so accurately charted by Baudelaire" and of whom the photographer is an "armed version [. . .] reconnoitering, stalking, cruising the urban inferno, the voyeuristic stroller who discovers the city as a landscape of voluptuous extremes."[21]

As neat as this description is, of a direct parallel between the photographer and the walker, and of cruising and composition, the connection it suggests is predicated upon a shared sense of voyeuristic detachment that is sweepingly attributed to both urban walking and photography, as though the peripatetic *flâneur* might in turn also prove to be an analog for the scopophilic "male gaze" famously identified by Laura Mulvey in narrative cinema.[22] While the nature of the gaze in urban walking can seem forensic and nonparticipatory, insofar as it might often be structured, as in photographic media, around "gazing at other people's realities" (as Sontag puts it), this doesn't quite tell the whole story.[23] The "voluptuous extremes" of the "rue assourdissante" in Baudelaire's sonnet are not experienced by the poet with "detachment" or "professionalism," nor is the passing woman apprehended by him in the way that "a detective apprehends a criminal."[24] The power relation suggested by those descriptions, conferring the photographer-walker with a perceptual sovereignty, is upended by the starkly emotive texture of Baudelaire's poem, its affect based upon what *cannot* be possessed or even fully seen in this "urban inferno."

That Baudelaire's poem seems unable to take pleasure in its own voyeurism, which is to say unable to mobilize a nonparticipatory "look" whereby the gazing subject is immune from shock or injury, in turn poses questions as to what it might mean for looking to constitute a form of ethical practice. How might looking, in other words, as an optical relation between subject and object, be recuperated as an exchange in which the former does not subsume the latter? The work of Kaja Silverman is instructive in this regard. Her study *The Threshold of the Visible World* theorizes the potentiality of a responsible mode of looking. In such a mode, the "subject's frame of reference" would not "triumph [...] over that of the external image, whether it derive from an artistic representation or a human being"; such a mode of looking would succeed in neither appropriating nor diminishing the object-as-other at the moment of apprehension.[25] Silverman identifies in Benjamin's numerous accounts of the "aura" a dual process of "investiture" (*Belehnung*). On the one hand, to "invest the other with the ability to return our look is seemingly to accept the other as an other, or [...] to concede that he or she is also a subject"; on the other, it is a process of exaltation that entails the "radical *idealization* of the other," and "his or her elevation to the status not only of the beloved, but of the very *cause* of desire" (95). As an essentially intersubjective operation, auratic desire involves a negotiation of the distance-within-closeness that Benjamin identifies as a condition of aura's legibility, one that constructs "an identificatory relation between the viewer and the auratic object" and requires "the object's insertion into a representational network sufficiently complex to 'light' it up in new ways, and so to solicit the spectators' imaginary relation to what would otherwise remain merely alien" (99). If "À une passante" does not, for reasons that will become clear, quite realize the project of ethical or productive looking that Silverman espouses, this reading of Benjamin nonetheless brings a new valence to the way in which the poem "light[s]" up its object. This illumination is an act of reciprocity between subject and other. It is not only a conferral upon the other, but is rather akin to "the brilliant luminescence with which certain insects adorn themselves to attract those of the same species," an analogy of light that Proust's narrator uses to describe the "solitary" gay cruiser on a train platform, searching for the reciprocated gaze of one who also "speak[s] the unusual tongue."[26]

Baudelaire's "flash" can thus be considered not merely as an estranging instrument of the urban, nor as the mechanical intervention of the voyeuristic photographer, but rather as a different kind of light-source, akin to the light in whose glare the poet negotiates his complex relation to the "alien" apparition who passes him, and which illuminates the instant of her "insertion into a representational network." A more fertile analogy, then, would read the photographic resonance of the poem's earlier section less as an invitation to collapse the figures of "photographer" and "stroller" into one, as though the perceptions of each are acts of detached or voyeuristically empowered authorship, than to consider its mediatized field of vision as itself being in some sense photographic, this encounter *as of* a photograph.[27] The flash does not preserve the passing woman but causes her to disappear and thus returns to the semantic plenitude of the "glance," which illuminates and wounds with a "punctual intensity." She may already be an image circulating in a chain of reproductions, her gestures merely adjuncts of commodity traffic's pageantry, but the passing woman also somehow retains an aura under threat, and retains that ability to send a glance back and wound her beholder with the "plaisir qui tue," a phrase cognizant of its own fatalistic impossibility. Roland Barthes's oft-cited coinage of the photographic *punctum* offers one way of accounting for the pain inflicted by the passing woman. The *punctum* is a conceptual sibling to the aura—for James Elkins, both of these concepts allow their authors to bring "something ineffable, private, or even sublime" into the orbit of their critical arguments—but it foregrounds wounding over exaltation.[28] What is wounding, in fact, is precisely this sense of the ineffable:

> I decided then to take as a guide for my new analysis the attraction I felt for certain photographs. For of this attraction, at least,

I was certain. What to call it? Fascination? [...] What it produces in me is the very opposite of hebetude; something more
like an internal agitation, an excitement, a certain labor too, the
pressure of the unspeakable which wants to be spoken.[29]

Baudelaire's poem buckles under a similar pressure of beholding, a knife-
edge between excitement and bafflement that agitates between exact
sensations—the "douceur qui fascine" (the softness that grips)—and the
frustrations of not knowing—"j'ignore où tu fuis" (I don't know where
you flee to). What fascinates, for Barthes and for Baudelaire, is not only
the expressive reticence which demands of the beholder a "certain labor"
of absorption, but the very contingency of its arrival. This attraction is
reserved only for "certain" photographs or women in the street, who may
appear as if from nowhere and seem, as with the aura, to be close and distant simultaneously. Baudelaire's "rue assourdissante" is Barthes's "glum
desert," the field of perception in which "suddenly a specific photograph
reaches me; it animates me, and I animate it. So that is how I must name
the attraction which makes it exist: an *animation*" (20).

The speaker of Baudelaire's poem is more like the beholder of a
photograph than its creator. He does not author this passing woman
into being but feels singular in his relation to her, and thus takes on the
imaginative work that would make her more tangibly "exist" through an
"animation." She passes, apprehended already in motion, and yet still
seems curiously still, with "sa jambe de statue" (her limbs of a statue).
The frustration which here fuels desire gravitates around observing a
form of life somehow frozen. She is confined by a frame, or the intran-
sigence of statuary, and is conceived of as an abstraction, animate only
in the sense that she moves. Barthes famously develops his theory of
attraction with recourse to the "two elements" of photography "whose
co-presence" establish that attraction (25), the *studium* along with the
punctum. The former describes the visual textures that viewers of photography are accustomed to look for as subjects of a shared culture and
a given field of information. The latter is not so volitional, and "it is not I
who seek it out [...] it is this element which rises from the scene, shoots
out of it like an arrow, and pierces me" (26), an "accident that pricks
me" (27) which is not necessarily tempered or restrained by this intertexture. The *punctum* cannot be intended by the creator of the appearance from which it arises but must be an "accident," seeming to strike

by chance, like the sudden emergence of a singular glance from within a crowd. To imagine the vantage of "À une passante" as photographic is to observe in the transition from its first to second line a transition from the *studium,* the thematic of the city for which the deafening street stands, to the *punctum* effect of the passing woman's emergence, a *tableau parisien* made woundingly intimate. In the poem's affective universe this urban encounter is both uniquely irrevocable and infinitely repeatable, neither first nor last in a "plurality of copies." Barthes's *punctum* lights upon the way the aura might survive reproduction; how a person, like a photograph, a form which "mechanically repeats what could never be repeated existentially" (4), might continue to glance back, and puncture in the process.

What are the implications of these "wounds" in relation to Silverman's call for a look that does not "effect" the "destruction" of its object?[30] On the surface, at least, it appears to be the looking subject who incurs such destruction at the hands of the *punctum.* Yet, as Silverman writes in a later chapter, while "*Camera Lucida* dramatizes the possibility of apprehending the image-repertoire from an unexpected vantage point," it ultimately neglects to perform any "realignment of self and other," such that "Barthes's own sovereignty vis-à-vis the object remains unquestioned" (184–85). Because the *punctum* derives from the viewing subject's own "memories" it can all too easily fall into solipsism; "something inaccessible to any other viewer" that ultimately "attests to the unquestioned primacy of the *moi*" (184). (Recent critiques of *Camera Lucida* have further illuminated the vexed politics of this "primacy of the *moi,*" including its racial implications, and I will address these issues later in this chapter.) And even though Baudelaire's poem exalts its object and registers the shock of the "prick" at the moment when the relationship between self and other threatens to be rearranged, "À une passante" ultimately gives voice only to a solipsistic crisis of looking, not its possibilities, and it cannot help but fetishize the more vulnerable figure of the passing woman in the process. I read Silverman's notion of "productive looking"—the "constant conscious reworking of the terms under which we unconsciously look at the objects that people our visual landscape" (184)—as a formulation at once utopic and urgent. To conceive of these reformulated acts of looking as utopic does not mean that they are always experienced joyfully, nor that they do not disturb, but it does suggest that they are felt as generative in the ways that Baudelaire's encounter does not. If the "aura" and the *punctum* offer suggestive ways of reading "À une passante," they nonetheless resonate with regards to this poem as melancholic structures of vision, voiced by a speaker absorbed in an everyday lyric tragedy, licking his wounds.

Indeed, facing "À une passante" itself can induce a sense of déjà vu not dissimilar to the one at its heart, where over-familiarity and strangeness are caught in a bind between the *passé* and *unheimlich*. Albert Thibaudet, writing in 1924, even suggests that for the Parisian city dweller, who may experience "ces regards" (these looks) as many as "dix fois" (ten times) on a given day, "le grand alexandrine" (the great alexandrine) of Baudelaire's poem would rise palliatively in the memory to "remplir" (fill) the void that gapes between urban strangers.[31] This notion, of a city poem folded into the life of that city and the minds of its inhabitants, where the intertexture of its rhythmic qualities provides a soundtrack and salve to the kind of ubiquitous experience it describes, might also find a contemporary equivalent in the pop song, heard through headphones and seeming to address the stranger one passes while listening: hello, is it me you're looking for? Like such songs, Baudelaire's sonnet has acquired the air of cliché, a literary earworm whose cultural catchiness is unshakable but which risks being worn out itself. It foregrounds iconic characters of urban experience—the *flâneur* watching, the mysterious stranger passing—and gives voice to the exhaustion of their failure to be reconciled. Further multiplications abound: not only does the figure of the "passante" seem to recur numerous times in *Les Fleurs du Mal*, as Susan Blood observes, but Benjamin's account of this poem, by now a canonical "cultural fact," has been much enfolded and anthologized.[32] Nonetheless, "À une passante" retains a particular power to pierce the surface of time and reception not only because of the mnemonics of its alexandrines (as Thibaudet describes) but because it endures as a wellspring, a consummate example of poetry's "ability" to witness a glance, and to register the relation of desire to urban modernity.

In beginning with this poem alongside Benjamin, Barthes, and Silverman, I have sought to reintroduce it in relation to this book's central concern, which is to say the way that poems of the city, poems whose contingent and momentary desires gravitate around interpersonal encounters, are informed by the lives and deaths of images. Both aura and *punctum* are ways of seeing that are neither wholly active nor passive, describing effects done unto a beholder by works which nonetheless depend upon that beholder's "attraction" for their vitality. In this vein, it is the realm of the aesthetic—and in reflective encounters with artworks—where the renegotiation of self and other can be pondered and performed, and where the limit-points of the *punctum* and the aura illuminate the stakes of looking. How "realizable," Silverman writes, is "such a renegotiation in everyday life?"[33] The problematic associations that mediate our encounters with others, which Silverman describes in terms of Jacques Lacan's notion of the "screen," are often products of the unconscious, but draw upon culturally recognized or shareable data. As such, these associations are often immediate or automatic, and thus hard to unpick "through a simple act of will," for no "look can extricate itself in any absolute way from the snares of the self" (173), although the space given to such extrication is no doubt different in the halls of a museum than in the more hectic space of the streets. This imperative to "entertain an ethical relation with a particular other" thus has less "to do with our immediate, largely involuntary reactions to him or her than with how we subsequently reinscribe those reactions at the level of consciousness" (173). Such reinscription can here refer not only to an act of consciousness but of composition, and so it is within a poetry of the everyday that the tensions between the immediate and the composed, or the spontaneous and the written, might come into fruitful play and offer potential remappings of desire. All of which is to suggest that to find such a remapping, we must look toward a radically different figuration from that of Baudelaire's poem.

A New York Minute

It is by way of a seemingly random cameo appearance in another Walter Benjamin essay, named fortuitously after New York's "Central Park," that the cruising literature I am concerned with comes into view. Baudelaire's sonnet may offer a canonical instance of the "love which only a city dweller experiences," but it is also suggestive as a text that throws counterexamples into relief:

> That Baudelaire was hostile to progress was the indispensable condition for his ability to master Paris in his verse. Compared to his poetry of the big city, later work of this type is marked by

weakness, not least where it sees the city as the throne of progress. But: Walt Whitman??[34]

Baudelaire and Whitman are strange bedfellows, as is suggested by Benjamin's double question mark. Among a number of available ways for approaching a comparison between them, which could include Whitman's popularity in France, having been translated into French by poets like Jules Laforgue, Benjamin frames it here in terms of respective notions of the city as a "throne of progress."[35] Benjamin's account of Baudelaire's hostility is a contestable one, but I understand "À une passante" as one instance of it (rather than a representative example of Baudelaire's thoughts about "the city"), providing as it does a reference point and a critique of the kind of fleeting urban intimacy that Whitman frames altogether differently. This is the kind of intimacy that might seem unthinkable without the formulation of modern urban space as Whitman recognized and experienced it, insofar as the metropolis spatializes and reinterprets intimacy by enforcing proximity between strangers. Urban spatial relations, Anthony Vidler writes, after Georg Simmel, offer "important indications of social processes, of the interaction between human beings conceived of and experienced as *space-filling*."[36] It is the space between Baudelaire and the passing woman that offers a conceptualization of the poet's estrangement, an exemplary condition of modern city-dwelling, so what distinguishes Whitman's sense of the urban from that expressed in Baudelaire's poem, then, can be framed in terms of his differing reconciliation of this proximity.

Whitman's poem "To a Stranger" (*LG*, 109), whose title alone recalls that of "À une passante," is an example of such reconciliation. Mark W. Turner makes an explicit comparison between these poems in his study of cruising and describes "To a Stranger" as "the poem" from "Whitman's oeuvre" that "we ought to compare with Baudelaire," both as a companion piece and a counterexample.[37] One immediate difference between them is the object of Whitman's address, for in being directed toward "a Stranger" it leaves room for the sense of that term not merely as the immediate figure before the poet but the stranger as a figure more broadly, one who in Simmel's words contains "the nearness and remoteness of every human relation," for "strangeness means that he who also is far is actually near."[38] The poem reads:

Passing stranger! you do not know how longingly I
      look upon you,
You must be he I was seeking, or she I was seeking,
      (it comes to me, as of a dream,)
I have somewhere surely lived a life of joy with you,
All is recall'd as we flit by each other, fluid, affection-
      ate, chaste, matured,
You grew up with me, were a boy with me, or a girl
      with me,
I ate with you, and slept with you—your body has
      become not yours only, nor left my body mine
      only,
You give me the pleasure of your eyes, face, flesh, as
      we pass—you take of my beard, breast, hands,
      in return,
I am not to speak to you—I am to think of you when
      I sit alone, or wake at night alone,
I am to wait—I do not doubt I am to meet you again,
I am to see to it that I do not lose you.

While "To a Stranger" is a short poem, it unfolds like many of its longer counterparts over the course of just one sentence, and thus enacts a tense relation between line and syntax wherein the caesuras and typeset breaks that divide Whitman's long lines are merged into the poem's presentation as one coherent temporal unit. The relation between line and sentence in Whitman's poem illustrates a continuous now, a time that comes into being incipiently. This incipience is made up of a number of temporal constructions, like the present participles "passing," "seeking," and the odd combination of the present tense with an infinitive, "I am to wait" and "I am to see," as if the being of "I am" is bound up with futurity. This containment is distinct from the fragmentary finesse of Baudelaire's *rimes riches,* which involve a phonetic back and forth between both whole lines and hemistiches, akin to the poet's distressed look here and there for the vanished passing woman.

    These sonic differences embody these poems' divergent senses of time. Where Baudelaire ends his encounter in the impossible past subjunctive mood, Whitman apprehends his stranger in relation to an idyllic past, this moment part of a fluid temporality: "I have somewhere surely lived a life of joy with you." The word "surely" at once destabilizes this line and also provides the poet with a foothold felt as a kink in the language, a self-reassurance, and a way of expressing a chronological impossibility (this person has only just been encountered) that nevertheless feels intimately possible in this moment. This sense of an almost-congruity between past and present resembles Benjamin's suggestion that "it is not that what is past casts its light on what is present, or what is present its light on what is past; rather, image is that wherein what has been comes together in a flash with the now to form a constellation."[39] The moment of Whitman's poem is not merely a now, but a present tense experienced alongside a sensation of false memory which is felt "as of a dream," at once like something dreamt seemingly out of nowhere and something that "comes to me" in the way a dream might upon waking. Benjamin's suggestion that an auratic object's "glance is dreaming, draws us after its dream" as a kind of distance,[40] appears here as an erotic closeness, neither body belonging to "yours" or "mine" only, and this "sexual shock" will be harnessed, will become a moment preserved through recollections to come: "I am to think of you when I sit alone." William White's collection of Whitman's *Daybooks and Notebooks* corroborates the importance of such solitary moments of recollection for the poet, filled with entries like "driver [...] big, young, blonde," and "little black-eyed Post boy at ferry," entries which read like they could be rehearsals for poems of preservation.[41] The now of "To a Stranger," framed around the impulse to record and recollect, is thus legible as a now in relation to a past and a future, such that this encounter emerges as a temporally multiple form of love at neither "first" nor "last" sight. The end of Baudelaire's poem, on the other hand, looks ahead only to a future of repetitious mourning, rounded out by its grieving "O"s. Whitman's coda, on the other hand, suggests a beginning, and strikes a note so definite as to sound almost threatening; "I am to see to it that I do not lose you," a sentiment that would not sound out of place if uttered by such urban figures as the detective or the stalker.

Thus if Baudelaire's enmity toward progress is "the condition" of his "ability to master Paris in his verse," as Benjamin writes, Whitman's view to the contrary might then be thought of as the condition for his own negotiation of urban and poetic time, his way of animating a passing tableau and making it "exist," through his attraction, beyond its transient parameters. The *punctum* as a summit of feeling depends in Barthes's writing upon the nonintentional; Whitman's stranger, too, must "not know how longingly I look upon you," a phrase locked in a semantic bind of cause and effect, for it is precisely this not-knowing that creates longing, that pricks. Whitman's ability to shape the meanings of his encounter is thus a particular "structure of vision," where such meanings are legible when situated within a temporal mélange that exceeds the empirical unfolding of the now and thus obscures its ending. The oddness of the poem's final line narrates this purposiveness acoustically, and registers sonically the poet's clasp of control over this encounter, giving it a "seeing to," and thus also reminds us how this dreamt "life of joy" is too a form of seeing, a poetic sequence that tangibly courts the visual. At the moment of apprehension the poem performs a juncture between the static and the moving, as if the opening apostrophe to the "Passing stranger!" is also a kind of verbal halting, freezing the object of perception in time such that the poet can "look upon" it and, as above, introduce other time zones into the momentary.

As Anne Dufourmantelle writes, regarding the temporality of risk, cameras "produce suspense in the form of still images. Their function: the pause."[42] To be in suspense is to assess the risk of engaging with a stranger whose character is unknown; to conceive of this process as photographic is to witness its actualization. Mary Ann Doane describes the "conceptualization of the instantaneous photograph as point" as a site of possibility; it "allows for thinking the image as a critical specification of time" and "entails a halting of time; the image is perpetually 'on the verge' of completion."[43] This poem's slowing-down suggests a reaching toward a sense of "completion," in which "You give me the pleasure of your eyes, face, flesh as / we pass—you take of my beard, breast, hands, / in return," that is felt as a tension between word and image. This sequence of body parts, which again plays out monosyllabically, seeks to approximate the trajectory of this gaze with recourse to order, traveling downwards from "eyes" to "flesh" (which here perhaps reads not as synecdoche for the body itself but as a description of the muscular regions of arm and chest), and from "beard" down to "hands," as though inscribing in textual form the act of looking someone "up and down." (And this is a look which does not only scrutinize or take "pleasure of" but might also in the process offer out an erotic or flirtatious signal.) Yet, like the earlier "surely," the clarification that this glance occurs "as we pass" places a kink in the sequence. It introduces a caveat in which the directionality of the poet's list of body parts rubs against the simultaneity suggested in "as," which is to say that we look at the same time as we pass. When passing a person "in the flesh," after all, we are not granted the same attentive time in which we look "upon" a still subject or a portrait.

This moment seems thus curiously torn between the ekphrastic and the immediate, both conferring a chronology to the erotic gaze while at the same time scrambling it. It conveys in miniature the way the static might still involve forms of movement, the way that the tableau of a body which the poet seeks to arrest involves the passing of eyes across its surface and the perception of details in a manner akin to montage, just as that body itself passes by toward the threshold of the next, yet-to-be-seen frame. To preserve the pleasure of a passing gaze, then, involves that same temporal intervention by which the ostensible present tense is made unstable, both frozen and flowing, giving way to a porosity with past feelings and future perceptions. This catalog of passing body parts comports itself as occurring in the external and reciprocal realm of optical perception between persons. But what, as far as it can be made separable, about the more interior lyric echo chamber in which images "come to me as of a dream"? The dream-like succession of Whitman bears evident parallels to cinema, and while his relation to photography and portraiture is well documented, the sense of his work as proto-cinematic is less frequently touched upon. Robert Richardson makes the bold claim that "Walt Whitman's remarkable achievement, for example, has had at least as great an impact on film form as it has had on modern poetic practice," while Barry K. Grant observes such an impact in the work of a particular early filmmaker, Sergei Eisenstein, who referred to "Walt Whitman's huge montage conception" in his own writing.[44] Richardson writes of Whitman's emphasis of "something other than order" as being akin to the way "montage was later to work in film [...] a technique of simply aligning images in such a way as to create a logic of images themselves," and Whitman filled his "poetry with long catalogues of particular things, people, and places, in much the manner in which any good documentary film builds itself up from details," and this act is the remit "simply [of] one who bears witness to things."[45]

This account of poetic montage speaks to the well-known, expansive catalogs found throughout *Leaves of Grass,* lists that assume the gaze of a speaker looking upon the exterior world of streets and landscapes and corroborate Whitman's own analogy that "in these *Leaves* every-thing is literally photographed. Nothing is poetized, no divergence, not a step."[46] And yet conceiving of this documentarian impulse as a form of bearing witness seems more closely related to the "evidentiary or in-dexical relation to what we take to be the 'real'" that Benjamin assigns to photography, whereas "cinematic pleasure is intimately tied," Silverman writes, "to its capacity to posit a world apart from and discontinuous with the one we inhabit, but capable of preempting the latter within the domain of the present."[47] While Whitman, historically speaking, can only anticipate the auratic setting of the movie theater, a setting that Silverman cites as key to "cinematic pleasure," it is worth noting that the cinematic quality of his work cannot be accounted for merely as an extension of photomontage's "indexical" function. Indeed, Whitman's proto-cinematic representations of looking and passing are intimately linked with the mysterious pleasures of the "world apart" that moving images offer.

This "world apart" also operates not only according to the spatial distances that separate viewer and screen, but the temporal distance between apprehension and recollection. The perception of a desired stranger as existing in a "world apart" thus anticipates their transfor-mation into memory while also accounting for the otherworldly frame through which they are perceived. It is in this vein that the perceptual "world apart" which comes to light in Whitman's episode of urban de-sire has parallels with pornography, the actualization of sexual fantasy. In turn, it is then no surprise that the particular form of glancing per-formed in this moment is not only, to return to Benjamin's words, full of poetry, but a quasi-masturbatory mode of recollection in tranquility. The speaker of "To a Stranger" vows "to think of you when I sit alone or / wake at night alone." Invoked as a means of not losing the desired addressee, this recollection is cast here not only as an act of writing, a recollection made possible by the composition of a poem that "bears wit-ness" to the original encounter, but also as an act of private imagining at bedtime. This moment thus also suggests, in its temporal variety, that the activity of creation has already taken place, and it is in the midst of such an act that the passing stranger is activated as a renewable source of plea-sure. In other words, the stranger enters, at the moment of passing, into the erotic archive of the observer's mind; more colloquially, his "spank bank." The act of erotic creation, of reconstructing through images the "life of joy" that takes place "somewhere" other than the scene of passing, is also temporally coexistent with that scene, as if preempting recollection. The poem's parallels, in this regard, with the technique of montage have less to do with documentary than with daydreaming, and the poem takes the external world of the street not as its object of representation but as the occasion for writing into being another world, an alternate sequence infused with desire and reiterability. This other world constitutes a response both to the potential loneliness of urban life and to a more essential solitude taken as a condition of desire itself. Self-pleasure thus arrives to fill in the gap between the known and the ineffable. It provides, as it were, a mode of company. And yet the urban erotic scheme that "To a Stranger" sketches is not merely a product of the solipsistic "love which only a city dweller experiences" as broadly conceived by Benjamin. What Whitman lights upon in this poem is a way of harnessing pleasurable looking that has a queer history all its own.

Queer Eyes

"To a Stranger" provides one optic upon Benjamin's elusive distinction between Whitman and Baudelaire. Though its urban setting is implicit, and is not framed directly as a "throne of progress," Whitman's poem recuperates pleasure from the "love which only a city dweller experiences"; glimpses, even, at a utopic horizon. Another, quite obvious distinction between the poems is the question of gender—although "To a Stranger" again only implies a furtive same-sex desire, Baudelaire's poetic-photographic composite frames a resolutely heterosexual encounter that cannot help but recall the dangers posed to women in urban spaces and, concurrently, the scopophilic wielding of the "male gaze" against women's bodies within visual culture. It is no accident that "À une passante" is a common locus for a number of feminist critics, such as Janet Wolff and Deborah L. Parsons, for whom it throws into relief the historical status of women walking the streets.[48] (The differing stakes for women cruising are something I address in the book's coda.) If it is therefore self-evident that questions of danger and pleasure apply differently to gay male cruising, Leo Bersani suggests that there are still greater distinctions to be drawn between heterosexual and homosexual desire which, I argue, also map on to the differences between Baudelaire and Whitman's texts. He writes:

And it is in defining erotic desire as epistemological catastrophe that Proust himself becomes a novelist of heterosexual—or, at least, heteroized—love. [...] In its somber glamorizing of a desire grounded in the irreducible opposition between an empty subject and objects of desire that might but won't reveal and return the subject to himself, Proust masochistically celebrates difference as the very condition of desire, thus renouncing the privilege his homosexuality might have afforded him of recognizing, and loving, himself in an hospitably familiar otherness.[49]

Although these descriptions of an "epistemological catastrophe" and an "irreducible opposition" are particular to Proust, they might also describe the founding pathos of "À une passante," a poem whose speaker is unable to find himself in another. Whitman's poem, on the other hand, exemplifies a love born of sameness, one that allows the poet to love "himself in a hospitably familiar otherness."

In this same essay on cruising and sociability, Bersani finds in Freud a surprising formulation: "at the very origin of psychoanalysis" can be found "the outline of a conceptualizing of queer desire as somehow exempt from the destructive sociality of straight desire" (50). Because the so-called perversion of homosexuality eschews the Oedipal conflicts upon which heterosexual desire is predicated, the "psychoanalytically defined homosexual [...] wanders in the world—cruises in the world, we might almost say—in search of objects that will give him back to himself as a loved and cared for subject," and "homosexual desire for others is, in this account, motivated by the wish to treat oneself lovingly," to encounter new love objects "without introjecting them" (55). In "Friendship as a Way of Life," Foucault on the other hand remains more suspicious of the notion that the cruising is what distinguishes homosexual and heterosexual desire:

One of the concessions one makes to others is not to present homosexuality as anything but a kind of immediate pleasure, of two young men meeting in the street, seducing each other with a look, grabbing each other's asses and getting each other off in a quarter of an hour. There you have a kind of neat image of homosexuality without any possibility of generating unease, and for two reasons: it responds to a reassuring canon of beauty, and it cancels everything that can be troubling in affection, tenderness, friendship, fidelity, camaraderie.[...][50]

We might wonder who the "others" Foucault refers to are, and whether he is gesturing here to a "neat" image of cruising that plays to the straight outsider's gaze and "glamorizes," to return to Muñoz's phrase, its ontology. Tom Roach names this model of queer, Foucauldian friendship "shared estrangement," the practice of a radically "impersonal relationality," and although Bersani differs from Foucault in arguing that "there is indeed something unique to queer desire and sexual behavior that lends itself" to this relationality, where Foucault moves away, as here, from the scene of desire, the "two thinkers share the belief that queer practices and communities are privileged sites for instantiating a post-identitarian politics."[51]

Bersani and Foucault's accounts of cruising suggest that it is a cultural and theoretical battleground, a queer search for the self, on the one hand, or for relation, on the other, that incorporates nostalgia, "concessions," "canon[s] of beauty" and the vexed question of a possible camaraderie. The cruising texts I examine in this book attest to the simultaneity of these things; Whitman's poem, for example, in its avowed and fulfilled quest for the "he I was seeking," frames the act of "seducing each other with a look" as an act with the potential for "affection, tenderness, friendship" and so on. For a less sincere portrait of the look's potentiality, we can look to Frank O'Hara, whose ethos concerning the actual process of cruising was often parodic. He once wrote facetiously to friend John Ashbery about a December 1963 feature in the *New York Times* which covered the State Liquor Authority's closure of two gay drinking establishments, and gravely addressed an increase in overt homosexuality in the city. He was particularly struck by journalist Robert C. Doty's observation in the piece that some "homosexuals claim infallibility in identifying others of their kind 'by the eyes—there's a look that lingers a fraction of a second too long.'"[52] This pseudo-anthropological interest in the private and furtive culture of an increasingly visible minority anticipated the controversial 1970 book *Tearoom Trade,* in which sociologist Laud Humphreys went undercover in cruising spaces. His resulting study offers an inventory of cruising and behavioral norms in public bathrooms, a space where the "eyes [...] come into play."[53] Diagnostic and voyeuristic as both Doty's exposé and

Humphreys's study are, they nonetheless attest accurately to the crucial role played by eyes in cruising's language, not only as the medium of observation, but as the instrument of a particular kind of glance.

This glance of cruising is itself a site of identification, and not only of "identify[ing]" other "homosexuals." In his similarly acerbic early poem "Homosexuality," O'Hara identifies the "act of taking off our masks" as if "we'd been pierced by a glance!" (*CP*, 181–82). O'Hara treats the notion of the piercing glance incredulously and makes light of the hackneyed Freudian association between the eye and the penis, which Otto Fenichel describes as a scopophilic "matter of course" where the "eye fixed in a stare stands for the penis in erection"; a prick.[54] But the poem nonetheless sustains the reading that this multiply penetrating glance might be interpellative; that it might prompt both veracity and silence, as if theatrically revealing the gay men behind the masks while compelling them to keep their "mouths shut." It is somewhat typical of O'Hara's poetry to invoke the political only to sidestep it, and this poem neither beams with gay pride nor enshrines public sex as a celebratory act of openness. As Turner writes, this poem "is in part a jab at queeny homosexuals, but it is also the work of a keen cruiser who knows the various scenes well."[55] And it still pursues, if glancingly, the connection between cruising and selfhood, the candid act of self-reflection while "tallying up the merits" of the city's latrines, from "14th Street" to "53rd" (*CP*, 182).

While the poem warns us against taking it too seriously, yoking wonder with the dirty public restrooms where the consummation of cruising encounters often takes place, this moment reflects suggestively on the way such encounters allow one to be seen (without a mask) and thus to see oneself as if from without (in a bathroom mirror, perhaps). This is an identity observed multiply through public bathrooms that have the characteristics of persons, sometimes "drunk" (14th Street) and other times "at rest" (53rd). These latrine self-portraits suggest a picture of cruising as a process of moving between sites without a clear endpoint that enables cruisers to observe their own absorption in the act. The homosexual subject identified by Bersani, on the other hand, arrogates the desired objects he encounters not quite as mirror-images, as in O'Hara's latrine tableaux, but as a series of "always, however minutely, inaccurate replications" that render "the search for the self *out there* [. . .] beneficently fruitless."[56] This admission of the unrealizable coexists with the "danger" that cruising may nonetheless lead to an approximation of that original desire to refind the self, and poses the "danger" that "promiscuity may stop" and "our connection" to others may end up "degenerating" into a relationship. Worse, cruising is at risk of recuperation by accepted ethical categories of relation; if it "make[s] us feel as, perhaps even more, worthy than a comfortably monogamous straight couple" it becomes "even less interesting than marriage."[57] We must then be compelled, Bersani argues, to "specify the ways" in which "outrageous practices [...] may or may not require us to elaborate new ethical vocabularies."

Bersani's account of cruising as a "training in impersonal intimacy" draws upon Simmel's notion of "sociability" to reconstruct a "new" kind of orientation vis-à-vis "otherness."[58] In this regard, as a forum of objects and others, this articulation of cruising intersects with the phenomenological, and calls to mind Sara Ahmed's suggestion that queerness might be thought of as "a matter of how one approaches the object that slips away—as a way of inhabiting the world at the point in which things fleet."[59] The fleeting traffic of cruising bodies becomes, for Bersani, an "exceptional experience of the infinite distance that separates us from all otherness," because

> in cruising—at least in ideal cruising—we leave our selves behind. The gay bathhouse is especially favorable to ideal cruising because, in addition to the opportunity anonymous sex offers its practitioners of shedding much of the personality that individuates them psychologically, the common bathhouse uniform—a towel—communicates very little (although there are of course ways of wearing a towel ...) about our social personality (economic privilege, class status, taste).[60]

It is curious to encounter Bersani's description here of the bathhouse as a site of "ideal cruising," or as a place where selves might be left behind, given that he famously de-idealized that same space in his classic 1987 essay "Is the Rectum a Grave?" Here, in "Sociability and Cruising," the ideal form of the bathhouse offers an "intimacy between bodies no longer embellished or impoverished, protected or exposed."[61] Is this the same space as that "ruthlessly ranked, hierarchized and competitive" space identified in the earlier essay, where "looks, muscles, hair distribution, size of cock, and shape of ass determined exactly how happy you were going to be"?[62] Although Bersani is discussing a historical, pre-HIV/AIDS iteration of the bathhouse in "Is the Rectum a Grave?," he is also putting paid to the wider notion that sex between men is somehow latently democratic or utopic, a fallacy which relies upon the figure of collective nudity in the bathhouse to venture such a claim. Bersani's work on cruising and sociability is compelling and theoretically rich, but this reevaluation of nudity as a social "shedding"—rather than as one among many forms of erotic performance—both jars with his earlier text and draws attention to the ways in which his more recent work is curiously mute about the parameters of non-"ideal" cruising, which is not only a psychic or libidinal exchange. Cruising, in other words, with clothes on.

While Bersani's insights are instructive, his more recent essay seems wedded to a theoretical endeavor that renders the space of consummation—i.e., the bathhouse—as cruising's ground zero, such that the nature of the interaction between object and other is forced to the background. In the chapters ahead, I favor the street as the consummate, if not "ideal," site of gay cruising, precisely because, unlike the latrine or the darkroom, it does not necessarily denote consummation, orgasm, or even hooking up, though I do also look at other important cruising locales such as the bar, subway, and piers. The "intimacy with an unknown body" that reveals an infinite "distance at the very moment we appear to be crossing an uncrossable interval" need not only refer to touching flesh, but to the field of cruising on the street, too, where potentially infinite looks are exchanged, perhaps precariously, in the glare of the public.[63] I seek to build upon Turner's observation that "we need not get trapped in the assumption that the visual encounters of urban modernity are necessarily alienating, that the act of the looking is always already inscribed by the script of the city," for the "cruiser's intention is to find in the passing glances in the streets that person whose gaze returns and validates his own."[64] The optical intimacy of looking offers its own ways of idealizing or reimagining desire, and negotiates states of closeness and distance through the act of reading another person. In some of the texts I discuss, in particular those by Wojnarowicz, the look precipitates a narrative drive toward sexual consummation, in public or private. In others, the moment of optical contact between strangers is the event itself. What is being offered in the following chapters is primarily an account of looking, and of the relation between its theory and practice, but this look in all of its complexity—its seeming ability to freeze time, to forge momentary kinships—cannot be abstracted from the activity in which it may comprise the first step. I will thus use "looking" and "cruising" as distinct but mutually informing terms—a look can easily become a cruise, and a cruise just a look.

Looking, I argue, is a way of wresting intimacy from the transient, a process that operates at an optical and, in turn, a visual level. By optical I mean the relations of sight between strangers; by visual, I mean the image that is created out of such an encounter, an aestheticization through writing that is tethered to the referential field of visual culture. There is an experiential friction here, between the analogous capacity of visual technologies to frame and capture and the liveness of street encounters, but I am suggesting that it is precisely this invocation of the visual that breathes life and longevity into optical exchanges that might otherwise be merely passing or transient. The transport of these encounters into the realm of memory is neither straightforwardly chronological nor performed merely in the act of writing, but through their very conceptualization as images within that writing. This form of photographic attention may indeed offer a solution to Bersani's anxiety that the "promiscuity may stop." As Michael Snediker writes, while "cruising, for some, is teleologically inextricable from the hook-up that follows, for many, cruising's pleasures are the pleasures of the cruising scene itself."[65] Conceived of apart from the constraints of consummation, which is to say the constraint that the cruise must always have a happy ending (as it were), cruising's look can perform the imaginative work of projecting multiple endings with multiple partners, can invest each optical encounter with an eventfulness.

As the photographs by Gupta, Fischer, and Baltrop have illustrated, this imaginative projection of a stranger's story, the imagined past that is made legible in the immediate present and determines a possible future, takes place at the level of the *studium*. In this regard, the look of cruising, as Fischer reminds us, has a semiotic dimension; as Wayne Koestenbaum writes, the travel between "*studium* and *punctum*" has "an underground affinity with cruising," which is not only "a sexual readiness" but akin to a "readerly readiness—a willingness to pick up codes."[66] Whitman, for example, was writing in a period long before the everyday semiotics of sex between men were as codified as they became in the early twentieth century, and long before the camera was anything like a handheld or peripatetic technology. Yet he often frames his accounts of desire between men, as well as his poetic project writ large, in terms of the "roughs," including the sailors and stevedores he would pick up on the Brooklyn waterfront.

As Hugh Ryan writes in his recent history of queer Brooklyn, "the puls-
ing heart of this new American city was the Fulton Ferry landing," which
"provided an endless chance to marvel at the greatness of young men."[67]
Whitman's work, Ryan continues, offers "tantalizing codes" as to "the existence of a subculture of working-class white men who loved other men.
Many of these were laborers that he (Whitman) met while walking along
the docks, or taking the ferry, or going for a bracing swim in the ocean."[68]
Indeed, as I will explore in the next chapter, Whitman himself sought to
approximate the demeanor of the "roughs" in the frontispiece portrait of
the first edition of *Leaves of Grass* in 1855.

Frank O'Hara was similarly interested in rough trade. His love of
Hollywood extended not only to the camp appropriation of female star-
lets, but to the eroticization of figures like Marlon Brando, whose cultural presence was a reproducible and prototypical iteration of the kind
of rough and rebellious masculinity that held currency in gay cruising,
and O'Hara writes about encountering Brando-types on the streets of
New York. David Wojnarowicz's erotic fantasies of working-class masculinity are also structured around real figures, and passing men are recast
through the bohemian renegade theater of French cultural forebears.
His writing frequently frames strangers who look like Jean Genet or are
"handsome like some face in old boxer photographs, a cross between
an aging boxer and Mayakovsky" (*CK*, 13–14), and his photographic series *Arthur Rimbaud in New York* features his friends as models roaming
the erotic wastelands of the city's derelict piers and wearing a mask of
the French poet's face. These examples, which will be developed in the
subsequent chapters on these authors, point on the one hand to a deft
mining of culture on the part of gay men, and on the other to a fetish for
a certain kind of masculinity that is coded as white and working class.
It is through the *studium* of encounters, then, the studied stylishness
performed by the subjects of Gupta and Fischer's cruising portraits, that
potentially transient encounters are recuperated, reinterpreted, and preserved as images. Indeed, the frisson of encounters inscribed in these
cruising texts seems to derive from the rendering of the field of cruising
as an array of semiotic surfaces and types; of objects that nonetheless
retain some agency in their exchange with the cruising subject.

Yet the fact that the semiotic seems inextricably linked with the perceptual economy of cruising does not mean it is unproblematic, and the
rendering of walking bodies as so many erotic objects also has troubling
implications. There is firstly the matter of what is at play, ideologically,

in the prevalence or predominance of certain types. Bersani, for one, in his critique of the exclusionary spaces of gay cruising in "Is the Rectum a Grave?," expresses suspicions about the supposed efficacy of the "gay-macho style," and suggests that it is less a "subversive" parody of masculinity, as it is intended to be, than something that may in fact express "complicities with a brutal and misogynous ideal of masculinity."[69] Even leaving this criticism of a particular gay sartorial "look" aside, there are larger implications of the cruiser's tendency to make a fetish of type. If, to return to Silverman, no "look can extricate itself in any absolute way from the snares of the self," then what are the "projections" that occur "over and over again, in an almost mechanical manner, when we look at certain racially, sexually, and economically marked bodies?"[70] In chapter 3, I argue that Langston Hughes's work, as well as its excavation by Julien's *Looking for Langston,* speaks precisely to the fetishistic optical violence that is routinely done unto the Black male body.

Even the metaphors of violence that are often applied to acts of looking, like Baudelaire's wounding glance or Barthes's *punctum,* bear troubling histories when wielded irresponsibly. Recent work by Jonathan Beller has argued that Barthes's formulation of the *studium* and *punctum* as "programs of apprehension" cannot be disentangled from questions of race, in that images of slaves and racial others are "the rhetorical figures, the discursive, and arguably material media for the derivation of the supposedly ontological character of a visual *technology*" throughout *Camera Lucida.*[71] Barthes deploys images of slavery as exemplary of the "prick of the Real" while disavowing their semiotic content, thus making slavery supplementary to the photograph, and in this regard Beller's critique recalls Silverman's claim that "figures depicted in the photograph serve only to activate" the author's "own memories, and so are stripped of all historical specificity."[72] But it is also, Beller argues, that Barthes's own description of the pain of photography "precisely echoes—albeit in apparent ignorance—Frantz Fanon's description" of "coming under the white gaze."[73]

To think of the wounding nature of photography, then, is also to recognize that "the mortification of the flesh before the lens and the mortification of the flesh under a white gaze [...] are not merely analogous but are mutually constituting."[74] Although, as Beller concludes, the recognition "that contemporary visuality is bound up with racism and slavery [...] does not amount to reparations," it places vital pressure on the metaphors of wounding that Barthes uses in *Camera Lucida,* and serves to expose its author's blind spots.[75] Indeed "visuality" as we know it, writes Nicholas Mirzoeff, referring to the "totality" of visualizations as comprising "information, images and ideas," had its first domain in "the slave plantation, monitored by the surveillance of the overseer."[76] There are parallels here with Silverman's reading of Franz Fanon in relation to the Lacanian screen, and the image of the plantation recalls Fanon's discovery of "my blackness, my ethnic characteristics" as mediated by "slave-ships."[77] Mirzoeff, in a manner akin to Silverman's discussion of relations with others, posits the "right to look" as an ethical response to the oppressive field of visuality. The right to look begins "at a personal level with the look into someone else's eyes to express friendship, solidarity, or love," and it "must be mutual, each person inventing the other, or it fails." This look "claims autonomy, not individualism or voyeurism"; it "is common, it may be the common, even communist," for "there is an exchange, but no creation of a surplus."[78]

To what extent might this "right to look" be exercised within the optical mechanism of cruising? The "look" of cruising not only entertains a "surplus" of meaning; it positively eroticizes the "second longer" stare and draws upon a resolutely semiotic vocabulary. Cruising's look does not efface the Lacanian screen as much as use it as an arras to hide behind, at the expense of those for whom looking is experienced as a violence on a daily basis. Analogies of wounding thus figure, ambivalently, in the optical capacities for voyeurism, objectification, and violence at play in cruising encounters. Indeed, the resonance of what I term a wounding intimacy is present throughout the cruising texts I discuss in the chapters ahead, less in opposition to the utopic dimension of looking than as part of a tense simultaneity with it. Part of the frisson of gay male cruising is the risk of danger, but the language of piercing and wounding found in the work of these writers—from O'Hara's more whimsical "as if we'd been pierced by a glance!" to Wojnarowicz's recurring reference to the "wounding nature of a neck [...] seen among the crowds"—suggests the latent presence of a more profound sense of violence, a violence which poses an even greater threat to gendered and racialized bodies.[79] It is in Whitman, however, as I will explore in the next chapter, that we can see most clearly cruising's multiple dimensions—the utopic and the wounding—which is to say that "To a Stranger" tells only part of the story.

2

Walt Whitman, Looking at You

Suspended Pictures

In an early poem called "Pictures," which can be found in a notebook from "about 1850" and which evidently predates *Leaves of Grass,* Whitman describes an inventory of images collected in the mind's eye.[1] Although the poem is framed around memory and the process of memorialization, it also casts an intriguing light forward upon Whitman's life's work, gesturing toward conceits and concerns that would remain central to his textual project in the decades that followed. Its scope is capacious and in an earlier note Whitman writes that each verse will present "a picture of some characteristic scene, event, group or personage—old or new, other countries or our own country."[2] To find a variation upon the poet cruising—an act, as I have begun to suggest, that is vital to Whitman's poetics—we need look no further than the following tableau, set in ancient Athens (*LG,* 560):

> Here and there, couples or trios, young and old, clear-faced,
>   and of perfect physique, walk with twined arms, in divine
>   friendship, happy,
>
> Till beyond, the master appears advancing—his form shows
>   above the crowd, a head taller than they,

The scene is demonstrably not New York—or at least not the New York suggested by "To a Stranger," where the "divine friendship" of love between men is concealed and passing—but it reads as a homosocial idyll that might be conceived as possible even within the glare of the urban everyday, an excavation of a cultural past that projects a possible future. Emory Holloway, in his introduction to the stand-alone published edition of the poem, characterizes "Pictures" as a work that contains the "germ of a number of later poems," and glosses this scene of walking in ancient Greece as a clear precursor to the "Calamus" section of *Leaves of Grass*:

> There can be little doubt that one of the sources of "Calamus" was Whitman's early knowledge of Greek friendship, though he may have been unaware when he wrote "Calamus" that Greek friendship also had a sad decadence.[3]

Holloway neglects to elaborate on the nature of this "sad decadence," which here sounds euphemistic, like the kind of phrase one might use to describe an F. Scott Fitzgerald novel. But this phrase also recalls what Eve Kosofsky Sedgwick describes as that "peculiarly close, though never precisely defined, affinity between same-sex desire and some historical condition of moribundity, called 'decadence,' to which not individuals or minorities but whole civilizations are subject."[4] Save for the "master" who is "advancing" somewhat ominously, this moment in "Pictures" does indeed seem "unaware" of any "sad"-ness outside the frame. It is a scene of "divine friendship, happy" which does not trouble over even such matters as gender identification, or specifications as to the nature of these "couples or trios." In this regard it anticipates Whitman's later conceptualization of adhesiveness, a term for love between men that he borrowed from contemporary phrenological discourses, and which was legitimated with a pseudoscientific air without any explicit invocation to suggest that adhesive contact goes beyond anything less wholesome than "walk[ing] with twined arms."

This proto-cruising scene looks back to an imagined construction of antiquity, a cultural precursor to the gay male sexual practices that were becoming legible in New York during Whitman's lifetime, and as well to the liminal cruising spaces of the Brooklyn waterfront and Pfaff's, a beerhall on Broadway and Bleecker Street frequented by Whitman that was a known meeting spot for men seeking men. But the symbols of antiquity also look forward in anticipation of unrealized democratic futures. This chapter will be concerned, then, with the importance of looking at Whitman's work as both a temporal and an erotic phenomenon. Most obviously, I am referring to the optical look between strangers, that crucial instrument of perception in what Whitman terms, in the title of one of the Calamus poems, the "City of Orgies"; a place, indeed, where relations between eyes bear an orgiastic quality. But these acts of looking, for Whitman, are also intimately connected with the visual, and just as this Athenian scene is imagined in a poem called "Pictures," many of the cruising encounters found in Whitman's work are rendered in relation to his interests in photography and daguerreotypes. Indeed, this scene from "Pictures" bespeaks a particular mode of aesthetic attention that points to the poet's fixation with forms of still and moving images. It suggests a temporality that exceeds stillness, a duration ("till") that unfolds as a succession of motions, "walk[ing] with twined arms" and "advancing."

If, in "Pictures," the occupation of a memory palace is a form of conquest, a kind of mental excellence capable of bringing images drawn from sources both cultural and personal into the orbit of a single mind, the poem suggests that this possession also pulls off the feat of suspending these images between the fixity of their representation and the flux of their original iteration. In Whitman's picture gallery, pictures are hung "suspended" between the process of reification that makes their arrangement on a wall possible and the sensuous immediacy of the lives they contain, scenes of dynamic gesture and movement; a video of the heart, to borrow Christopher Ricks's phrase, that flashes by.[5] Whitman was contemporary with developments in animated photography that would make such a gallery possible, like Muybridge's work on locomotion in 1877–78, one of the period's most notable discoveries. This poem predates such developments, and if it is overreaching to claim that it predicts the advent of the moving image as a classifiable object, it nonetheless attests to a capacity to figure motion through movement between lines, rather than frames. Lineation has been a key focus in critical attempts to consider Whitman's work as protocinematic, where the trademark catalogs of *Leaves of Grass* suggest parallels with montage. A short 1966 essay by Alice Ahlers is one of the earliest attempts to suggest this relation; she writes that Whitman approximates cinematic "fast motion" by listing "words, images, and ideas one after the other," and "slow motion" through "repetitious description," but takes as given that lines and frames easily map onto one another.[6] This chapter will instead consider images in Whitman's writing as tense objects, distributed across the spectrum of the still and the moving, the whole and the part, the dead and the animate. These pairs are not so much polarities as conditions in determinate relation with one another, each recalling or gesturing to their other.

The pictures in Whitman's imagined gallery attest to the multiplicity of this visual imagination, but they also recall the poet's actual visit to a picture gallery, where what was striking was a certain visual stillness. In 1846, while he was working as a journalist and editor at the *Brooklyn Daily Eagle*, Whitman went to Plumbe's Daguerreotype Gallery at Broadway and Murray Street in New York City. You will see more *life* there," he wrote in an article about his visit, "more variety, more human nature" than in "any spot we know of."[7] As in "Pictures," Whitman evokes this space in writing through deictic narration, a surrogate for the "peering gaze" surveying the gallery's pictures, signaling that "here is one now" and then "another, nearby." The cumulative effect of this "great legion of human faces, of human eyes gazing silently but fixedly upon you" as you pass from one to the next creates the impression of a "peopled world" experienced as an "immense Phantom concourse." This journalistic account bears tangible linguistic echoes to the register of poems published much later in the numerous editions of *Leaves of Grass*, as though his body of work might be conceived of as an extended practice of certain ideas whose respective iterations play out in different lights, or are apprehended through numerous apertures. This notion of the "phantom concourse" in particular anticipates the poetic assemblies that became notable set-pieces in his writing, lists which often—in keeping with the form's epic roots—unfold as processions, like the "shadowy processions of the portraits of the past users" of machines in "Song of the Broad-Axe" (*LG*, 158). This relation between processions and portraits, yielding a pageant made up by images, is corroborated by an earlier note outlining the idea for "Pictures":

> Poem of Pictures. Each verse presenting a picture of some characteristic scene, event, group or personage—old or new, other countries or our own country.[8]

The movement from picture to picture both in the poet's mental gallery and in Plumbe's, the former a kind of memory itself and the latter a memory of a place rendered in journalistic prose, puts the persons seeing—both the poet and his reader—in a position of liminal perception, where "old" and "new" collide, and "other countries" emerge. The procession on the "phantom concourse" stages this spatiotemporal blur by leaving the sense of movement ambiguous; do we walk by these pictures, on a guided tour of the poet's memory palace, or are we fixed stationary as an audience transported to another plane, with the pageant of the living and dead possessing our line of vision? In epic form the catalog typically introduces a pause where the action proper is suspended and the list takes over; it marks an aspect shift within the same narrative world. In "Pictures" this succession of scenes is the main event, without the firm ground of an external reality, which remains present only as the material of memory. Even those images that are culturally or historically corroborable, like "Shakespeare" or "Adam in Paradise" (*LG,* 561–62), arise within the act of lyric remembering: the things that I have seen, that I have read.

This intersection between the transitory and lasting speaks to the images in "Pictures," themselves a jumble of the "old" and "new" which hang "suspended" between the past of their occurrence and the indefinite futurity of their preservation, as portraits "on the walls hanging" and "carefully kept." Like a daguerreotype gallery, where the portraits are "mute as the grave" but can nonetheless deceive us into identifying "the semblance with the reality" (*BDE*), these pictures are given new life by being archived in a poem, and some seem more alive still by their seeming capacity to move, described through details that suggest something beyond the still frame. Moving portraits such as these, I argue, are consonant with the experiential and indeed erotic uniqueness of urban modernity, the "City of Orgies" that is home to "shifting tableaus" (*LG,* 107). Thomas E. Yingling writes, glossing Michael Moon's work, that "sexuality in Whitman"—as in this orgiastic city—"is intertextual with (and thus not simply a screen for)" other "discursive concerns," including "democratic and mystical cosmic unions," as well as unions with images.[9]

The moving Athenian scene anticipates, as Holloway somewhat cagily notes, those scenes of adhesiveness in "Calamus," but those scenes themselves wear different faces. In this section of *Leaves of Grass,* in which the poems whose situations most resemble acts of cruising are to be found, happiness is interlaced with shame, and the familiarity of "divine friendship" is invoked alongside the uncanniness of anonymous encounters, as in "To a Stranger." The sequence thus makes for an ambivalent whole, in which homosexual desire is at once utopic and estranging. The visual quality of "Calamus" is thus not merely an extension of the image-as-memory mode that a poem like "Pictures" establishes but a statement of intent for the poet in his life's project. The pictures of encounter that emerge in "Calamus" are a means of recuperating such encounters from the transient temporality of the urban environment and the threats posed by social attitudes which force adhesiveness beneath respectable visibility. This poetics of cruising is thus multiply adhesive, both gravitating around connections between men and in turn yielding its own connectivity between temporalities and "suspended" images. The urban encounter is then invested with futurity through anticipated remembrance and the amorous weight of a submerged and shared past, which makes the strange familiar.

Calamus in the Streets

The Calamus section indeed begins away from "other people." Its first poem, "In Paths Untrodden," frames the love between men in relation to a solitary pastoral scene, the "growth by margins of pond-waters"; a "secluded spot" where the poet "can respond as I would not dare elsewhere" and "celebrate the need of comrades" (*LG*, 97). Since its inclusion in the 1860 edition of *Leaves of Grass*, "Calamus" has always begun with this poem, which thus establishes metonymically the rural compositional situation from which the sequence arises, itself named after the phallic-like calamus plant growing by these untrodden paths. "Calamus" moves between several locales, from pond-waters to Louisiana ("I Saw in Louisiana a Live Oak Growing," *LG*, 108), the "capitol" ("When I Heard at the Close of Day," 105) and "Manhattan" ("City of Orgies," 107), the latter of which will be the main concern of this chapter. These settings are cast in a relation whereby the pastoral is coded as a scene of reflection, an escape from the "life that exhibits itself" in other settings, and thus also acts as a taking stock of that life. To be "away from the clank of the world" allows the poet to develop the negatives of the images he has made out of the urban everyday, the pleasures

he has been "offering to feed my soul," rooted in "songs" of "manly attachment" that he "project[s]" along "that substantial life." This poem
exemplifies Michael Snediker's observation that many of Whitman's
"cruisy" or "proto-cruising" poems figure a "speaker alone," in scenes of
solitude that "rehearse, reiterate, or prepare for earlier and future erotic
encounters," and speak to the act of composition as a reworking of raw
material in the roughness of pastoral seclusion.[10] It turns snatches of
remembered glances into the sensible material of art, which pertains not
just to aesthetic form but to its execution as song and celebration, and
apostrophizes the democratic potential of "manly attachment."

The relation between memory, composition, and the rough is metaphorically elastic, and can be conceptualized in terms of written
iterations—as in notes or drafts—and the photographic stuff of negatives and images in development. Whitman's journal of encounters with
young men, resembling something like a cruising diary, demonstrates
the former. These "pleasures" are in initial and miniature form, made
up of situational or physiognomic details that aid remembrance: "Sat-
urday night Mike Ellis—wandering at the corner of Lexington av. &
32nd st. —took him home to 150 37th street, —4th story back room—
bitter cold night," or "James Sloan (night of Sept 18 '62) 23rd year of
age—plain homely, American."[11] Graham Robb writes of these "com-
pressed jottings" as the "dry ingredients that could later be used to produce delicious memories and fill the future society of comrades with
bodies and faces," as if the act of erotic looking is a form of harvesting,
giving shape and definition to an idealized future.[12] While these "notes
of encounter" attest to the role of writing or jotting in the cultivation
of "delicious pleasures," the actual urban "songs" that the poet projects
in paths untrodden emphasize the visual dimensions at play amid the
"clank of the world." The poems frame these encounters as scenes or
tableaux and emphasize the look or the glimpse as an instrument of realization. Whitman's rough jottings about the "roughs" he loved, being
made up predominantly of young working-class men, preserve specific
instances of a mode of vision that the poems celebrate more generally,
without names or details, and through their own acoustic iterations.

This mixed metaphorical "clank" is never louder than in "City of Orgies" (*LG*, 107), the sequence's most explicit invocation of Manhattan as
a site of erotic looking:

City of orgies, walks and joys,
City whom that I have lived and sung in your midst will one
    day make you illustrious,
Not the pageants of you, not your shifting tableaus, your
    spectacles, repay me,
Not the interminable rows of your houses, nor the ships at the
    wharves,
Nor the processions in the streets, nor the bright windows with
    goods in them,
Nor to converse with learn'd persons, nor the bright windows with
    soiree or feast;
Not those, but as I pass O Manhattan, your frequent and swift
    flash of eyes offering me love,
Offering response to my own—these repay me,
Lovers, continual lovers, only repay me.

In its very *mise-en-page* the poem embodies a distinction Whitman makes in "In Paths Untrodden" between "the life that exhibits itself" and "the life that does not exhibit itself, yet contains all the rest." To read this poem aloud is to make vocal a bathos of enumeration; the succession of negative particles lends the feeling of a poet stalling or delaying his main observation with counterexamples. The action of loafing here takes a strangely epic turn. The continual negative apostrophes dwell in the bombast of the pageants they claim to reject, which says something of the dominance of the "life that exhibits itself." These relentless "spectacles" exhibit modes of belonging to the city and offer a conception of the city as a work of art itself, "an anarchic and unstoppable proliferation of images" in which these "shifting tableaus" resemble *tableaux vivants,* a "series of living and moving images" where the "crowds do not provide a mere backdrop or audience" but are "at the center of the stage."[13]

If, as Laure Katsaros writes, the New York of *Leaves of Grass* "becomes like a living American Museum" akin to the spectacles of the contemporary entertainer P. T. Barnum, this is apprehended less as a maximal blur than as a sight in which desire resides in the shapes the cruiser makes out from within the spectacle.[14] It is after all the covert and less exhibiting "flash of eyes" that contains "all the rest"; the only things that can "repay" the walking poet are the successive but singular intimacies carved out within this proliferation. If Whitman claims to make "illustrious" the Manhattan in which he has "lived and sung," he is remunerated for singing its praises by the fleeting and feelingful encounters with strangers that it allows him. David S. Reynolds writes that Whitman was "appalled in the 1850s when holiday celebrations began to be mass-oriented spectacles by professionals," and suggests that such illustrious lines elsewhere in his work as "I celebrate myself" ("Song of Myself," *LG*, 26) are an attempt to "restore the idea of celebration" back to the "personal."[15] Whitman's preoccupation with spectacles frames the poem itself as an alternative and personal act of celebration.

And this is not just any celebration, but an orgy. The poem's first line convenes a site-specific, phonetic "orgy" by merging the sounds found in "walks," "joys," and "city." The word's association with revelry suggests that the poem's very cause for celebration also relates to the celebratory, as though looks between strangers are akin to an orgiastic ceremony. In supposing these strangers to be "lovers," Whitman gets at the erotic resonance of "orgy" and its meaning as sex between multiple people. Consistent to both definitions is a loss of self, subsumed by Bacchanalian ecstasy or a corporeal erotic mass. Read thus, these looks have an imagined physical efficacy in conjoining the anonymous, something that also occurs in "To a Stranger": "your body has become not yours only, nor left my body mine only." Whitman's notion of "adhesiveness" also imagines this potentiality as corporeal, defined as that which "fuses, ties, and aggregates, making the races comrades, and fraternizing all" (although it is important to note that Whitman's racial politics in his later years markedly veer from this utopic formulation).[16] In an 1876 preface Whitman inflects this imagined political adhesiveness with its homosexual resonance, which is described in relation to the "special meaning" of "Calamus"; the "beautiful and sane affection of man for man, latent in all the young fellows" is needed for the "United States" to be "effectually welded together" (*LG*, 657). This orgiastic "flash of eyes" thus semantically echoes "adhesiveness" and embodies the latter term's particular relation to love between strangers. "Here is adhesiveness," Whitman signals in "Song of the Open Road" (*LG*, 130), and do "you know what it is as you pass to be loved by strangers? / Do you know the talk of those turning eyeballs?"

This phrase seems to describe both the verbal talk of those whose eyeballs are turning (the gazing strangers) and, more strangely, the verbal expressiveness of the eyeballs themselves, as though glancing—that paralinguistic feature of encountering strangers—nevertheless possesses a secret ocular language. Like the "surely" of "To a Stranger," the "balls" harnessed to the "eye" here place a kink in the verse, resulting in a markedly more visceral moment wherein we imagine eyes not as features of a face but instead as isolated from a body, and this potential violence of disembodiment will be a concern later in this chapter. Simmel identifies the "eye-to-eye look" as a predominant feature of the metropolitan experience, an interaction which developments such as public transportation have enforced between strangers. It is something that "intertwines human beings" (as per an orgy) but leaves no "objective trace," unlike "the word spoken and heard." The "talk" of eyeballs is thus not literally audible, nor is it "transmissible," being "dissolved directly in the event."[17] This untraceable quality accounts for the address of Whitman's question, "Do *you* know," and the sense that this talk is rendered in a language understandable to some and not others. The difficulty in hearing it is no doubt compounded by the "swift flash," and knowing the "talk" thus amounts to wresting meaning from ephemeral and irruptive moments of apprehension.

This precarity is an important diversion for the cruiser, and the predominance of looking and passing by in the city can also be wielded as a means of assimilation, as in another Calamus poem entitled "A Glimpse" (*LG*, 112):

> A glimpse through an interstice caught,
> Of a crowd of workmen and drivers in a bar-room around the
>   stove late of a winter night, and I unremark'd seated in a
>   corner,
> Of a youth who loves me and whom I love, silently
>   approaching and seating himself near, that he may hold
>   me by the hand,
> A long while amid the noises of coming and going, of drinking
>   and oath and smutty jest,
> There we two, content, happy in being together, speaking little,
>   perhaps not a word.

The poem's first line positions it ekphrastically; a voice explains a tableau glimpsed only through an "interstice," "caught" like a snapshot through an aperture focused, with "glimpse" also bearing the archaic meaning of a "momentary shining, a flash." The vantage point laid out in the first line at once suggests the impossibility of Whitman peeping at himself through this interstice, as though this poem were a desirous fantasy, and also dictates the reader's position in relation to this image. The partiality of this viewpoint is figured in the poem's play between lines and the overarching single sentence, as though the crack in the wall through which this poem is visible similarly delineates its grammatical parameters. Yet this singularity can contain multitudes; Michael Moon identifies "interstitiality" as a framing device through which Whitman can represent "fulfilled homoerotic desire," which can be concealed from the public glare by this word's sense of the "only intermittently or fleetingly perceptible."[18] This form of duplicity, the sense that the poem's tableau can mean multiple things according to the knowledge of the spectator, in turn dictates the extent to which its homoeroticism goes "unremark'd." Like the spectacles of "City of Orgies," the surrounding theater of acceptable masculinities—"drinking and oath and smutty jest"—provide a camouflage or distraction from the poem's main event, and call to mind a proto–gay bar like the aforementioned Pfaff's, where Whitman would drink and meet men in the 1860s. This interstitiality is also analogous to the "swift flash" of peripatetic apprehension outside of the bar and in the public glare of the city, which is also silent ("speaking little") and passing, as in "To a Stranger." That very silence allows queer interaction to be double-tongued; on the one hand it is merely a look between strangers; on the other, the first step in a cruising encounter. This gets at the dual meaning of "passing" in that such partiality allows interactions to "pass" as a palatable form of kinship to the uninitiated. As an image captured interstitially, "A Glimpse" suggests that even within a quasi-photographic capture of a scene there is always more than meets the eye.

The textual activity of a poem thus enacts the sense in which the "talk" of "turning eyeballs" is a site whose multiplicity of meanings is helped along by its leaving no "objective trace." Unlike the "word spoken and heard," this talk finds furtive home in the poem itself. This negotiation of "talk" also provides a way of understanding the "objective" speech of Whitman's cruising poems, in particular his play with pronominal lyric conventions, as being similarly double-tongued, cruising the reader who is in the know. In an essay on "Calamus" and lyric, John Hicks writes that "the persona adopted by the poetic *I* seems to follow from the *you* Whitman seeks to address rather than the other way around," and that frequently in poems in which the addressee is unspecified, "the default referent" of this indeterminate *you* becomes "*you* yourself—the reader."[19] This play with apostrophe is present in "To a Stranger," whose address to the "Passing stranger" describes both someone its speaker passes in the street and the strange reader passing through this text. But this expanded apostrophe is more particularized than that of a "default referent." In other words, Whitman is not just cruising *any* reader here. The poem "Among the Multitude" (*LG*, 115), both in its published form and in a suggestive manuscript, tantalizes its "you" by gesturing to a certain readerly knowledge:

> Among the men and women the multitude,
> I perceive one picking me out by secret and divine signs,
> Acknowledging none else, not parent, wife, husband, brother,
>   child, any nearer than I am,
> Some are baffled, but that one is not—that one knows me.
>
> Ah lover and perfect equal,
> I meant that you should discover me so by faint indirections,
> And I when I meet you mean to discover you by the like in
>   you.

Berlant and Warner write that "making a queer world has required the development of kinds of intimacy that bear no necessary relation to domestic space, to kinship, to the couple form."[20] Like "City of Orgies" and "A Glimpse," this poem situates itself in the midst of traditional categories of kinship, that of "parent, wife, husband, brother," as a way of demarcating a "divine" subjective difference. It thus amounts to another instance of Whitman's poetics of deferral. This difference is again legible in terms of knowledge, and the sense in which it follows that if "that one knows me" then he must also be versed in the "talk" of "turning eyeballs," without which others are "baffled." Turning eyeballs can also suggest a portrait of reading, eyes scanning across lines of text, and the focus upon a secret talk hermeneutically flirts with the reader, and extends the challenge of taking up the position of the special "one" who can fill in the poem's gaps. Its omissions of gender, or of an explicit erotics, invite us to follow the poet's "faint indirections."

This is made clear in an earlier, more directly addressed manuscript version dated 1857–59, and titled "To ~~Those~~ One Who Will Understand":

Among the men and women
of all times, [I perceive that] you pick me
out by secret and divine
signs, ~~[You know me—you draw close]~~

You acknowledge none else—not
parent wife husband, friend,
any [nearer or dearer to you] than I am. -
Some are baffled—but you are not baffled—you
know me. —

~~O young man! O woman!~~ O
my lover and equal! I
meant that you should discover me [so] by my faint
indirections,

And I, when I meet you, mean
to discover you by the
same in you. —²¹

The "O . . . !" apostrophes of this version are tempered into an "Ah" in the published version, whose longer lines render the poem now as a fluid and incipient coming into being where the heavily punctuated manuscript and its short lines suggest a more fragmented visual experience, of eyeballs turning more sharply. The "one" of "Among the Multitude" becomes "you," the reader, an addressee who by entering into the solitary act of reading this poem is supposed different from the other "men and women of all times" who may come to encounter it. By introducing the direct address from the start, as opposed to holding off until the second and final stanza in the published version, Whitman renders the space of the poem more explicitly as both that of the urban multitude but also the space of reading, and it yields an encounter between text and reader in which the phenomenological proximity to one another surmounts even those relations that are notionally "nearer and dearer." But this draft is again a contested interpretive surface, and cruises us insofar as it only yields its meanings to us if we apply a secret knowledge and follow its "indirections." Whitman's crossed out "O young man! O woman!" is one such red herring. To state that the use of an indeterminate gender of address is merely a way of hiding the underlying and solely male "comradeship" would simplify such use, and ignore its queerer elasticity. Michael Davidson observes that the "eternal debate" over Whitman's sexuality has been "framed within an identitarian (and heterosexist) logic," the notion that if he is "interested in stevedores and boat captains" he is "therefore not interested in women."[22] This kind of masculinist framing misses the larger democratic implications of Whitman's self-declared poetic project and his avowal of writing "poems of women entirely as much as men" ("A Backward Glance O'er Travel'd Roads," *LG*, 482). Davidson instead turns his attention to Whitman's "cross-dressing" as a nuanced feature of his poetic language, with specific reference to the twenty-ninth bather section of "Song of Myself," where the poet adopts a "feminine position in order to participate erotically with other males" and in so doing puts forth a more complex version of "new emerging sexual categories" in a manner that invites queering.[23]

Like "Among the Multitude," "To a Stranger" also remains available to a more conventional heterosexual reading, but bears its queer resonance in the openness to be read alternately. Its blurring of gender ("he I was seeking, or she I was seeking") is cognizant of what "you," its reader, does or does not know. Written into these poems is a demand that we do more than glimpse them, or conversely that we are able to "know" them with only a glimpse. In response, they claim to know us through our own act of looking. The city poems stand out in "Calamus" not only because they represent specifically the "comradeship" between strangers, but because the experiential model offered by looking at strangers in cities lends these poems a reflexivity, and the sense that they are themselves thinking about how to represent homoerotic desire in a poem and the importance of the reader in such representations. These poems discover a way of glancing back at their reader through celebrating and harnessing fleetingness. Read together as a sequence in isolation, these poems begin to proffer a coherent poetic strategy of confession through indirection that blends the mystery of flirtation with the solidarity of intimacy. Their sense of gay pride is not that of pageants or parades but of the city's more private processions; the flashes of eyes that sustain the sexually curious walker with the suggestion of abundance and possibility, along with snatches of togetherness, however transient, to be recalled and enjoyed in solitude.

It would be unforthcoming not to mention at this juncture the evident masturbatory echoes in this account of desire; a bank of remembered visual material wherein the poet is seen "projecting them along that substantial life," the prolonged life of fantasy, and giving fulfillment to the brief or the partial. Sam Ladkin, in an essay on Whitman and onanism, writes of the "inherent" and "contradictory" utopianism of masturbation, "the crisis caused by its own tendency towards satisfaction that models fulfilment even as it's energized by the palpable lack of that which it desires."[24] The city poems of "Calamus," traveling between the furtive and the ecstatic, satisfy themselves with generative ways of responding to lack. They make imagination interstiality's bedfellow, filling in gaps in vision or shortages of consummation with the fantasy of fulfillment, which feeds individual self-pleasure and in turn gestures to the future pleasure of the polis. Much of the work on Whitman and masturbation rightly centers the body of the poet himself as the locus of political potentiality, as in Michael Moon's classic study of the poet's "dissemination." Moon situates the "corporeal-utopian program" of Whitman's writing, its metonymic principle of substitution in disseminating its author's bodily presence, as a response to the "devaluation of bodily life that his culture was in the process of imposing on its inhabitants" in the 1850s.[25] This devaluation derived from a fear of the "imminent dangers" seen as "threatening the integrity of the American body politic.[26] Seen in the light of the anti-onanist discourses of the male purity movement, the sheer corporeality of *Leaves of Grass* becomes a reassertion of embodiment, of self-pleasure as political pleasure at the very moment of its vexation. Tropes of fluidity, and of composition as ejaculation, abound in Whitman's writing, and M. Jimmie Killingsworth reads the 1856 "Bunch Poem (Spontaneous Me)" as the author figuring his poems as ""bunches" of semen he had tossed from himself."[27] If the more obviously masturbatory poems involve an absorption in the self, whose self-pleasure is the occasion and the medium of a reader's encounter with him, the cruising poems of "Calamus" might then offer premasturbatory "glimpses" or apprehensions that reassert the role other bodies play in onanistic fantasies and illuminate the way the urban cruiser becomes attached to them as a mental activity. Conceiving of them thus is also to place them in dialogue with another strain of the Calamus sequence that has a wildly different tenor, juxtaposed with the celebrations of adhesiveness and erotic looking. The poems of the body that accompany the poems of the city, crudely categorized, echo the masturbatory resonance of Whitman's larger sense of corporeal substitution. But through this dialogue they also make apparent a darkness attending homosexual desire, and the substitution of semen for another bodily fluid, one whose extraction is a process of some violence.

Cruising for a Bruising

Whitman writes, in "Trickle Drops" (*LG*, 107):

> Trickle drops! my blue veins leaving!
> O drops of me! trickle, slow drops,
> Candid from me falling, drip, bleeding drops,
> From wounds made to free you whence you were prison'd,
> From my face, from my forehead and lips,
> From my breast, from within where I was conceal'd, press
> forth red drops, confession drops,
> Stain every page, stain every song I sing, every word I say,
> bloody drops,
> Let them know your scarlet heat, let them glisten,
> Saturate them with yourself all ashamed and wet,
> Glow upon all I have written or shall write, bleeding drops,
> Let it all be seen in your light, blushing drops.

The long lines of this poem trickle, spilling across boundaries in Whitman's peculiar lineation, such that it cannot quite be called enjambment. Its spillages of blood, and blood as ink, are not brought into structural regularity nor plugged until the poem's end, which signals its unfolding over only one sentence. As with "In Paths Untrodden" and its courting of the pastoral, this poem's anatomical texture plays a metonymic role within the Calamus sequence, concerned as it is with commenting upon the composition of "every page" and the songs that "I sing." Whitman makes a virtue of injury, as though a violence inflicted unto himself yields a greater verisimilitude; these are "confession drops" after all, falling "candid" from incisions deliberately "made" to bleed them. It seems, in fact, that at one point this schema may have taken the place of the pastoral as the sequence's presiding image. In a series of notes around 1860, the year "Calamus" first appeared in *Leaves of Grass*, the poet scribbled a list of possible titles for the section including "Drops of My Blood," "Flames of Confession," "Nature Flames" and even "Verses of Evil," seeming to take, perhaps unconsciously, a leaf out of Baudelaire's book of evil's flowers.[28]

These titles speak to a spectrum of confessional modes; a poet being bled, a poet putting forth flamboyant spectacles of confession or the revelation of his "Nature," or else one turning verses which figure evil and depravity. "Trickle Drops" brings together the first few of these textures, figured as drops of blood which "glow," their light ignited by reading. Although preoccupied by the act and tropes of writing, this poem seems at once oblivious to reading yet aware that its own drops are confessional phenomena, insofar as confession implies an interlocutor whether real or imagined. This poem's sense of confession is far different to that of the cruising poems, for its imperatives "Let them know your scarlet heat" and "Saturate them with yourself all ashamed and wet" seem directed not only at the preceding list of "page," "song," and "word" but at a distant readership, a "them." Absent here is the sense of textual indirection, replaced instead with a type of physiological nudity, "all ashamed and wet." This poem sits in a strange intratextual dialogue with "Here the Frailest Leaves of Me" (*LG*, 112), which resides later in "Calamus" and similarly transfigures the text as corporeal but instead appears anxious about the exposure of something evil, perhaps, in the poet's inner nature. It reads:

> Here the frailest leaves of me and yet my strongest lasting,
> Here I shade and hide my thoughts, I myself do not expose
>   them,
> And yet they expose me more than all my other poems.

These lines present contradictions both to the cruising poems, which wield shame and secrecy rather than bemoaning them, and to "Trickle Drops," which voices an active choice to "expose" and relishes the pain of doing so. If "Trickle Drops" gets drunk off the pain, this poem marks the hangover—frail, regretting and forgetting about the flagrancy and confessions of the night before, keen to shuffle back into the closet. At first glance this interplay between confession and shame, imagined as both wounding and textual, seems at odds with the dexterous negotiations of candor found in the cruising poems. And yet, one source of this poem's anxiety is not knowing who will come to read it, thus leaving it exposed to danger. These uncertainties possess a kinship with the anonymity of cruising and the fear that a stranger could turn on you or turn you in. Like the cautious cruiser, the poem has future woundings in mind. Implicit in Whitman's demarcation that this poem embodies him at his "frailest" is the hope that readers will invest in this metaphor to such an extent that they treat the text with the delicacy they would a frail human body, and refrain from wounding it further.

Perhaps they might even nurse it. The shared ground between candor and eroticism is not only found in these Calamus poems but emerges strangely in *Drum-Taps,* the 1865 sequence which recalls Whitman's days as a nurse in Washington during the American Civil War. A striking late stanza in the poem "The Wound Dresser" (*LG*, 261) reads:

> I am faithful, I do not give out,
> The fractur'd thigh, the knee, the wound in the abdomen,
> These and more I dress with impassive hand, (yet deep in my
> breast a fire, a burning flame.)

Amidst the discomfort of witnessing the poet eroticize the soldier's wounds is an intricate metaphorical schema which aligns those wounds with the speaker's sexual confession. Earlier in the poem the recollected space of the hospital is rendered as a unique form of refuge, a space apart from the everyday exterior where "the world of gain and appearance and mirth goes on" (260). The furtive confession of the poet's desire exists in a strange mimetic relation to the open wound he is dressing, for it too is dressed and contained within the parentheses that separate it from the site of physical contact: "These and more I dress with impassive hand, (yet deep in my breast a fire, a burning flame)"; the heat of desire, the flames of confession. The utterance "I do not give out" can mean both not to take rest, as a conscientious nurse, but also not to speak out or declare, to keep the secret desire for the soldier "deep in" his breast through punctuation just as he dresses the soldier's deep abdomen wound. In unpublished notes for a lecture on Whitman's *Drum-Taps*, J. H. Prynne notes a similar moment in the "original printing" of "A March in the Ranks Hard-Prest, and the Road Unknown" (*LG*, 256) where "the long verse lines" could "mostly not be fitted unbroken into the page format; all but the first and last (shorter) lines were broken, with justified left and right margin."[29] The "longest line of all" took up "three lines of type, and was broken by a hyphen," as here:

> At my feet more distinctly a soldier, a mere lad, in
> danger of bleeding to death, (he is shot in the ab-
> domen;)

Prynne writes that the "alert reader will notice that a small sharp piece of metal (the piece of type bearing the hyphen, made of lead like a bullet) has broken into the body of the word (the medical, not commonplace word) for this soldier's stomach, just where the enemy bullet has inflicted the death-wound."[30] Wounding becomes multiplied once again, suggested as contiguous with reading by the mimetically violent lineation that organizes that reading. The soldiers' wounds in these poems prove a canvas for Whitman to project the potentially wounding nature of his own exposure, his being read, and figured through punctuation as forms of erotic openings themselves. The wound dresser of the former poem's title is in this way seen to be dressing, or preventing, his very own wounds, as the parenthesized final lines corroborate: "(Many a soldier's loving arms about this neck have cross'd and rested, / Many a soldier's kiss dwells on these bearded lips)." Like the sense of wounding as exposure in "Trickle Drops" and "Here the Frailest Leaves," poems which frame the Calamus cluster as a form of torturous confession, the wounds of this poem also seem inflicted by the potential revelation of homoerotic desire. But "The Wound Dresser" elaborates upon the unfolding of such wounding by suggesting that in engaging in perceptual interaction with an erotic object, in this case a wounded soldier, one runs the risk of being glanced back at, a glance that could make a laceration much like the wounds in question, and just as candid and revealing; "so sickening, so offensive," or a verse of evil. Desire's ability to glance is thus related specifically to an object's capacity to incorporate and reflect back the abject or forbidden desire that the looker confers upon it; upon a vulnerable corporeal surface that in being close to death is on the very brink of animism.

While this moment of wounding erotic contact is rendered in an immediate present tense, its temporal framing as the recollection of an "old man bending" who comes "among new faces" illuminates the way that it is pains, and not just "pleasures," that "develop later" in our "inner darkroom." The gap in which such development arises might even be the pain's root, as in the way that "shame," as Michael Snediker writes in response to Sedgwick, occurs in the "distance between selves," between "a 'younger self' and the self that currently is writing," such that the "younger self might be experienced not only as having written those 'younger fictions,' but as a 'younger fiction in his own right.'"[31] The act of remembrance is also an act of composition, of writing a younger self into being through memory's unfolding, and this poem suggests that shame's inherent "after"-ness, a negative affect which always intervenes *after* the experience of a more positive one, like enjoyment, allows it to exceed the parameters of immediate or proximate succession and survive over the course of many years, perhaps even intensified by such longevity. This memory, shaped by shame, also unfolds with a proleptically cinematic quality, in "silence, in dreams' projections." This phrase frames the poem's final section, as though the conjuring of "dreams' projections" is efficacious, bringing about the act of "returning, resuming," and offers an experiential surrogate for the lingering "kiss[ses]" that dwell on the poet's "bearded lips."

The visual dimension of recollection as a form of montage enacts the possibility of return for old wounds, or memories with their own *punctums*. In "The Wound Dresser," the image as a trace of experience is intimately linked with confession and exposure, within a process of self-revelation that has the capacity to "pierce" across time and space, and which reveals something of, or to, the person in the throes of recollection. The metonymic frame of "Trickle Drops," for example, comments reflexively on the activity of "Calamus" using a painterly dimension, whereby the textual and acoustic are seen as a form of image practice made up by dripping, just as a drop only trickles after it has dropped and found a surface. "The Wound Dresser" speaks to the manner of remembrance which informs that very anxiety about confession and has a haptic dimension, of being touched or pierced by memories or sensations, which also gestures to the autoerotic imperative of touching yourself. The war on onanism bears a relation to the Civil War's battlefield in Whitman's writing, and is consonant with the trademark proximity he draws between the body and the body politic. Sam Ladkin reads the Civil War poems—alongside Rob Halpern's 2012 collection *Music for Porn,* which takes them as a chief influence—as another of Whitman's defenses of masturbation, which is seen as a form of fecundity in which the nurse's "excessive generosity" is posited as an "onanistic seed to be spilt on the territory of the Civil War dead."[32] The extended temporality of "The Wound Dresser," in which images of martial intimacy are preserved over time, speaks to the preservationist instinct of onanistic fantasy. Whitman's love for the soldiers offers him a way to sing the songs of "manly attachment" in the most politically tense of contexts, and the sensory textures of wounds and touches provide him with a vivid palette for figuring the power of shame and the release of revelation, which are matters woven throughout the prewar Calamus sequence alongside its more optimistic cruising pictures. But what the nurse and soldier dynamic of "The Wound Dresser" ultimately provides is a recuperated metaphorical portrait of the love between men as a human good, one that extends also to Whitman's relation with his reader, which I will explore at greater length later in this chapter. The Washington battlefield may at first glance feel a long way from Manhattan, the city of orgies, but correspondences between them come to light with the shared emergence of another pseudoscientific discourse. Like "adhesiveness," this discourse fascinated Whitman, and it took multiple forms as an interpersonal category of perception, an atmosphere of potentiality, and a form of occult healing all at once. Most of all, it offered a telling figuration for his own poetics.

Adhesive Magnetism

In an 1863 letter written to Le Baron Russell from Washington, two years before the first appearance of "The Wound Dresser," the poet writes that

> I feel much possessed with the wounded & sick soldiers—they have taken a powerful hold of me, & I am very happy among them—it is perhaps the greatest interchange of magnetism human relations are capable of.[33]

Whitman is here using the term "magnetism" in its connection with mesmerism, a contemporary occult practice related to hypnosis that was posited as a form of medical healing. Animal magnetism refers to "an invisible, superfine fluid existing in and around all objects of the universe," and "its proper or improper distribution within any individual explained that person's state of health or disease."[34] The magnetist conceives of the "the body as a magnet," seeking "to activate the human magnetic poles" in order to "send the fluid coursing properly" by "touching the patient," "rubbing the afflicted portions of the patient's body" or "simply by making passes in the air above them," in effect trying to approximate the "effect produced by magnets."[35] Whitman had long believed in the capacities of animal magnetism, having written an editorial in the *New York Sunday Times* in 1842 that answered affirmatively to the question of his title, "Is Mesmerism True?"[36] This later reference in the letter abstracts the word magnetism from the particulars of its practice, for rather than being a weighted dynamic between healer and patient it is here conceived of as an "interchange," one in which the patients have too "taken a powerful hold" over their healer. This is consonant with the exchange at play in "The Wound Dresser" where the eponymous healer observes his own wounds while healing those of the soldiers.

As that poem attests, there is also an erotic valence in this mutual healing, an ultimate good in "human relations" whose remit is not only spiritual but sexual. Magnetism as a personal or sexual variable is more often related to a sense of health and virility, as Whitman's other journalistic writing on this word suggests. He did not only write about the mesmeric dimension of magnetism, as in his 1842 piece, but about its more common usage as a term for mysterious individual charisma that forms attractions between people, as if a sibling to adhesiveness administered as a therapy. The guide "Manly Health and Training, with Off-Hand Hints Toward Their Conditions," serialized in the *New-York Atlas* in 1858 and published under the pseudonym Mose Velsor, was recently discovered to be written by Whitman. In it, magnetism is described as an aspirational state, as something to be attained through the physical and mental training exercises that the guide advocates. One section begins with the questions "What do you suppose is the reason that some men have so much more power over the masses than other men? —such a 'personality' that they can hardly appear in a crowd, or a room full of people, but their influence is felt?"[37] What is it "at the bottom of the curious magnetism" such men possess? The difference that training makes is what distinguishes one man from one another, or one man from his pretrained self, who is in the first instance remarkable only in his unremarkability, someone "nobody finds it a pleasure to be near" nor "feels anything like delight from the magnetism of his voice, for there is no magnetism about it—he does not attract women, nor men either," and "going up and down, through the city [...] he is without vigor, without attraction" (226).

Magnetism properly attained, Whitman goes on to write, is animal magnetism, "the indescribable charm which belongs to some of the finest and most spirited animals, with flashing eyes, fine action [...] that we see sometimes in the brutes" but "seldom see in the case of men," and the "marvellous effects" of this magnetism "play invisibly out of him, wherever he moves, upon men and women in all directions" (227). That the walk, "springy and elastic," is again taken as an exemplary gesture of magnetism makes it difficult not to think of the erotic landscape of "City of Orgies" here, the "flashing eyes" like the "swift flash of eyes" of that poem, with the "walk" a medium of expression "as I pass." Whitman's divergent uses of the word "magnetism" in his Civil War letter, his 1842 editorial, and his men's health guide illuminate a shared ground between meanings seemingly opposed. On the battlefield it is a form of healing but also, "The Wound Dresser" suggests, an attraction to the act of healing and the soldier's vulnerability. On the street it is an attraction to power and vigor, an individual charisma which nonetheless refers back to magnetism's meaning as healing, for what is made visible is a picture of health and a potentiality in "human relations." These accounts of magnetism are different ends of a spectrum upon which what is magnetic depends on an individual's sensibility about what is "attractive" and what "repulsive," and also suggest that the mesmeric and men's health definitions are not so different after all, in that they are both gesturing to some kind of "interchange."

And yet are these respective meanings simply, as it were, interchangeable? The "meeting of glances" that govern this interchange and, to return to Benjamin's scrap, the aura, operates differently in the various contexts in which Whitman mobilizes it: the street, the sick bed, and the site of reading itself. Just as "magnetism" accounts, somewhat uncomfortably, for the wounds sustained by soldiers in conflict, on the one hand, and the wounds of the confessional poet on the other, the aura lingers at a strange intersection of political and erotic meanings. Halpern, in a gloss on the "perverse social alchemy" Whitman constructs out of homoerotic battlefield "affections," writes,

> Aura concentrates in the figure of this fallen soldier *so attractive so repulsive.* Sometimes he's barely perceptible *stalking the periphery of all I see* but always available for contrary ends *fundamental ambivalence of the body.* A whole metaphorics of love and war *my phalynx of clichés* converge around his vulnerability to penetration.[38]

Animal magnetism gravitates around the actual presence of an aura, that "invisible, superfine fluid," and Halpern's account speaks to the way such a belief is abstracted as a means of describing someone's personal magnetism. The perversity of this reading lies in the way that it yokes together these meanings; the fallen soldier's magnetic aura emanates from his need of aura as a medium of healing, a sign of his evident sickness and thus vulnerability to further violation. The interpolation of Whitman's "so sickening, so offensive" from "The Wound Dresser" spells out the conflicts in this desire—attractive because it's repulsive, but also a repulsive attraction—and marks it as a fetish. The soldier, in this regard, is an apt figure for the aura's multiplicity as a phenomenon whose very endangerment as an object confers it with a capacity to retaliate and wound back.

Power is taken as ambiguous in this formulation. It is not distributed simply, or simply weighted in favor of the nursing, magnetizing, or masturbating subject; the wounded object, vulnerable to the glance of this mediating subject, still answers with a glance. The soldier, Ladkin writes, is an "obstinate figure of ambivalence, over whom (and into whom) libidinal energies run rampant."[39] Rendered in the "present" of Halpern's text he is foregrounded amid the "imaginative exploitation of a sexual fantasy, which involves the expression of the past of the masturbating subject (the reason a particular figure of lust is chosen), and the aspirant longing of the future (actually having that allegorical figure), but knows, too, that there can be no easy shift from longing through imagining to having."[40] This discomfiting slippage between wounding, yearning, and writing—all of which cohere within the oddly capacious parameters of "magnetism"—ultimately lights upon the operations of Whitman's text itself. The poet's devoted avowal of an "interchange" with his reader is simultaneous with an awareness that "there can be no easy shift from longing through imagining to having."

Like the aura, Whitman's text courts closeness and distance, and poses questions about its own reproducibility. A concern about the deadening effects of reproduction is palpable at several moments in *Leaves of Grass*; as Whitman writes in an early version of "A Song for Occupations," "I pass so poorly with paper and types, I must pass / with the contact of bodies and souls" (*LG*, 177). Such statements of aesthetic failure are counterbalanced with a belief in textual animism, and in the efficacy of the metonymic principle of substitution. And yet this latter devotion is often vexed and liquid, an anxious and masturbatory exchange between text and reader made legible through blood and semen. It is the simultaneous openness and recalcitrance of Whitman's text that makes it available to queer readings and rewritings like Halpern's. The copresence of solicitous candor and unsettling corporeality raises the stakes of Whitman's textual cruising and suggests that the temporal line the poet seeks to draw from text to reader simultaneously traces a history of violence; a queer terrain of shame and pleasure that is once again made visible with recourse to images.

Whitman in the Sheets

Magnetism, being a central tenet of Whitman's visit to Plumbe's portrait gallery in 1846, had yet another role to play in the poet's imagination. This visit demonstrated to him a certain ground shared between strangers and portraits that was later to be illustrated in the city poems of "Calamus." This gallery was a place to see both daguerreotypes and people, a place "commonly known" among the "crowds continually coming and going," and was thus also a place to *be* seen (*BDE*). Whitman begins his review with reference to

> the fashionable belle, the many distinguished men, the idler, the children—these alone are enough to occupy a curious train of attention. But they are not the first thing. To us, the *pictures* address themselves before all else.

These are two distinct forms of attention, of looking at persons on the one hand and at portraits on the other, but for Whitman they cohere in a hierarchy, where the absorption demanded by the "address" of the pictures distracts us from the hubbub of bodies and faces that surround them. Plumbe's gallery, Katsaros writes, "had become a fashionable spot for the urban flaneurs in mid-nineteenth century New York."[41] As far as it is possible to draw an equivalence to *flânerie* in New York at this time, Whitman shares in the activity of the urban physiognomist, and looks both at the figures frequenting the gallery, as above, and the cast of characters he finds in the portraits, like the "woman, perhaps just married." In describing these images thus, Whitman seeks to claim for the portraits a certain vitality, and supposes that they are no less alive than the living social types observing them. In a later paragraph he seeks to account for this potency:

> There is always, to us, a strange fascination, in portraits. We love to dwell long upon them—to infer many things, from the text they preach—to pursue the current of thoughts running riot about them. It is singular what a peculiar influence is possessed by the *eye* of a well-painted miniature or portrait—It has a sort of magnetism. We have miniatures in our possession, which we have often held, and gazed upon the eyes in them for the half-hour! An electric chain seems to vibrate, as it were, between our brain and him or her reserved so well there by the limner's cunning. Time, space, both are annihilated, and we identify the semblance with the reality. —And even more than that. For the strange fascination of looking at the eyes of a portrait, sometimes goes beyond what comes from the real orbs themselves. (*BDE*)

This "beyond" suggests some form of cognitive dissonance on the part of the viewer, who is beguiled by the interpersonal trompe l'oeil that the portraits stage such that their response exceeds what is proportional to these "orbs themselves," and thus what is art-critically orthodox. Do these eyes then also emanate "beyond" the frames which contain them, and suggest signs of life in seemingly dead objects? Unlike the "swift flash of eyes" of "City of Orgies," frequenting a gallery space or having an image in "our possession" allows the absorption of "dwell[ing] long upon them," all the better to enjoy the "electric chain" that seems to emanate from them, a "sort of magnetism." That word again. Magnetism is here made local to the eyes, to be found within a nexus of mystery and familiarity where what is magnetic is the verisimilitude of a portrait's eyes, which are engaged in a slippage between the real and the representational such that the former may even usurp the latter. And yet this magnetism is also continually cast as foreign: "strange fascination," "peculiar influence." Personal magnetism may be attained, Whitman's "Manly Guide" suggests, by training, but as an outward performance it must also remain "indescribable," must not expose the seams of its own attainment, just as the limner's creation of eyes is an act of "cunning" and concealing mediation. This mystery is a question, too, then, of life and death, and what is uncanny to Whitman is that these images are simultaneously vital and *"life-like"* while being "mute as the grave."

They are not totally mute, however, for they have a "text to preach," and arise from the magnetic "current of thoughts running riot about them." This text is not an exposition so much as an extension of the image's mysteriousness, and can be pieced together only through "inference." In the poem "Out from Behind This Mask" (*LG,* 321–22), published thirty years after this account of the visit to Plumbe's gallery, Whitman turns this "strange fascination" about portraiture toward his own visage. The poem refers to an engraving by William J. Linton, which was itself based on an 1871 photograph of the poet taken by George C. Potter, that faced "The Wound Dresser" in the 1876 edition of *Leaves of Grass.* This poem in some sense makes literal work of rendering an image as a "text to preach," and yet it is appropriately enough less a narration or explanation of that image than it is a further muddying of the waters through lyric address. At the head of an early manuscript draft of the poem, there can be seen an explanatory line, excised from the final published version, that speaks back to the sense of an arrested glance that goes "beyond" the parameters of portraiture:

(On an engraved head, a Portrait "looking
at you.")[42]

As seen on the manuscript this line seems to play the role of subtitle, written in a smaller hand and placed in parentheses underneath the title proper as if it delineates what the poem to come is "on." Nonetheless, it reads curiously: an "engraved head" seems an almost violently material description, and what of the quotation marks around "looking at you"? They suggest an elsewhere, an attribution that is other than that of the surrounding lines. Perhaps it is a form of interpolation, as though this quoted description of the way portraits look "at you" implicitly refers back to a statement the speaker once heard or read. Or perhaps these marks announce a metaphoricity, and frame this sentiment as a figure of speech: this portrait is "looking at you," as it were.

In posing this question—who said this? —and thus introducing an ambiguous note, the quotation marks recast this description as a question: can portraits look? Given its somewhat anomalous presence in an unpublished draft, this moment teases at the tensions involved in our relation to images. W. J. T. Mitchell writes of a "double consciousness" in human thought, and wonders why people "behave as if pictures were alive" while simultaneously ready to "assure us they know very well that pictures are not alive," and suggests that the "usual way of sorting out this kind of double consciousness is to attribute one side of it (generally the naïve, magical, superstitious side) to someone else and to claim the hardheaded, critical, and skeptical position as one's own."[43] Whitman's aside about portraits "looking" thus seems to posit this poem as a response to or "on" this claim, implicitly attributed to "someone else." Except there is nothing "hardheaded," "critical," or "skeptical" about this poem; in both its manuscript and published versions, "Out from Behind This Mask" is effusive about the power of images—often it "goes beyond."

Confronting his own portrait, Whitman remarks upon this "common curtain of the face contain'd in me for me, in / you for you, in each for each," which is figured numerously as "This heart's geography's map, this limitless small continent, / this soundless sea" (*LG*, 321). In the schema of this poem, the face—as captured by a portrait—is the particular site of his famous assertion in "Song of Myself" that "I contain multitudes" (*LG*, 77), a multiplicity laid out as cartography or as synecdoche, a "condensation of the universe" in the visage. This metaphysical largesse tells us little about the sense in which a portrait "looks at you," however; one can easily stare at a map without any sense of an animating force that reciprocates our glance. The sense of vitality presumed by a returned look arises not from universality but rather an unreadability thereof, rendered "soundless," with "passionate teeming plays" that are "by this curtain hid!" (*LG*, 321). Under this aspect, to contain is also to withhold, and the requisite activity of reading a face without certain answers as to its essence is what can make looking at portraits unnerving. It is felt as the sensation of being looked back at, reflecting back an uncertainty, for we are not granted possession of the image. Michael Fried writes of such a contradiction in relation to Diderot's art writing and the sense in which paintings "presuppose the existence of a beholder" and must "stop him in front of itself," holding "him there in a perfect trance of involvement," while nonetheless relying upon the beholder's negation to achieve this, for "only by establishing the fiction of his absence or nonexistence" can "his actual placement before and enthrallment by the painting be secured."[44] Fried's particular application of this contradiction to eighteenth century works focuses on subjects "engrossed or absorbed in action, activity, or state of mind," as if they are "oblivious to the beholder's presence," but it also speaks to the case of the sitter who is nevertheless aware of the beholder.[45] This subject shoots a glance "from behind" a "mask," offering an interiority that is "in mystic hand wrapt." He is a subject who does not so much negate the beholder as establish a parity with them, instantiating a precarious exchange between their respective gazes and making palpable the sense that each is as alive as the other.

Bringing together ekphrasis with the act of lyric address, "Out from Behind This Mask" enacts the portrait's capacity to return a look. The closing lines of the manuscript version read: "From these to emanate, to you, whoe'er / you are, / These burin'd eyes—a Look."[46] These are adapted in the published version to incorporate Whitman's signature reach across time, and read "These burin'd eyes, flashing to you to pass to future time […] from these/ to emanate, / To you who'er you are—a look" (*LG*, 322). The word "burin'd," as the conduit for this "flashing" across time, speaks multiply. It suggests both the tool of the engraver and the poet's pen, but it also echoes "buried," a word itself buried within this one. This latter resonance gestures not only to the metaphorical buried eyes of the text—its avowed capacity to answer with a glance—but to the relationship between inscription and death. The inscription of the poet's presence into immortality is, after all, a form of burial, and the text serves to mark out the time and space of his lost presence in the hope that a reader might look closely enough—as a diligent viewer would at a portrait in a gallery—to resurrect it. Though

"Out from Behind This Mask" is less graphic than the "wound" poems, it attests similarly to the violent and difficult aspects of representation as it is scored and "burin'd" on the page for the attention of future readers.

Another portrait of Whitman inverts this poem's optical violence and makes good upon the subtitle of its published version ("To Confront A Portrait"). This image is perhaps the best-known visual representation of Whitman, and it has been in the imaginary of his readership since it first appeared as an engraved frontispiece for the first edition of *Leaves* in 1855. In 1888, Horace Traubel reported that Whitman had the following to say of this image while discussing "portraits of himself":

> I was sauntering along the street: the day was hot: I was dressed just as you see me there. A friend of mine—Gabriel Harrison (you know him? ah! yes! —he has always been a good friend!)—stood at the door of his place looking at the passers-by. He cried out to me at once: "Old man! —old man! —come here: come right up stairs with me this minute"—and when he noticed that I hesitated cried still more emphatically: "Do come: come: I'm dying for something to do." This picture was the result.[47]

Something of the insouciance surrounding this composition is there in the image itself, in which the poet stands with a hand on his hip and the other in his pocket, though it also contains other, less casual notes. Whitman himself speaks about the different ways this image seems to be coded, explaining to Traubel that many "think the dominant quality [...] is its sadness" (506–7).

And yet, despite its well-known associations, Whitman's later comments to Traubel about this image lend it an unusual and indeed confrontational resonance:

> the worst thing about this is, that I look so damned flamboyant—as if I was hurling bolts at somebody—full of mad oaths—saying defiantly, to hell with you![48]

The way this image might flicker across the breadth of an affective spectrum—emanating sadness, flamboyance, or anger depending on the beholder—is consonant with this strand in Whitman's writing whereby a "look" is mysterious and as rich in possibility as it is short on any simple legibility. This "flamboyant" comportment, full of "mad oaths," seems more the remit of the incensed preacher than the kind of sauntering or effete charisma associated with the word flamboyance. Perhaps in this instance, then, "flamboyant" obliquely takes on its etymological relation in French to flames, which are echoed by those "hurling bolts" and the extremity of "to hell with you!"

The image's air of mystery is compounded by the fact that it was published in the 1855 edition with no name attached to it, thus approximating for its reader the sense of a chance urban encounter that was the basis of its composition. Readers would only discover that it was one "Walt Whitman" upon reading "Song of Myself," with its declarations of the author's identity. If the daguerreotype portrait is not directly illustrative of the writing it precedes per se, it nevertheless seems to offer a form of visual evidence for the subjective presence announced by the poem's opening lines: "I celebrate myself, / And what I assume you shall assume, / For every atom belonging to me as good belongs to you" (*LG,* 26). The self the poem celebrates is metaphysical and amorphous, made up of shifting atoms which share in the same phenomenal stuff as its readers, who in the process of this interaction come to assume not only the atoms of this speaker, intersubjectively, but the discursive assumptions he puts forward. In this regard, the portrait seems to provide early readers of *Leaves of Grass* with a fleshly manifestation of a subjectivity otherwise too large and inclusive to be contained; a visual anchor amid the atomic. After all, the poet writes later in "Song of Myself," "Writing and talk do not prove me, / I carry the plenum of proof and everything else in my face" (*LG,* 48).

It is telling that this "plenum" coexists, defensively, with "everything else," on a face whose daguerreotype reproduction signifies a certain multiplicity through a posture of reticence, not quite providing "proof" of one authorial affect over another. The poet's assumption that physiognomy offers a form of proof is contiguous with his interest in photography as a democratic form that can record faces with minimal embellishment, unlike the artistic mediations involved in painting. And yet the presence of "everything else" muddies the picture. The sense that contact between the leaves and their readers enacts a form of atomic communion is later developed in Whitman's text as a form of anthropomorphic presence across generations, for "this is no book / Who touches this touches a man" ("So Long!," *LG,* 424). Another Calamus poem, "Whoever You Are Holding Me Now in Hand" (*LG*, 99), casts this intimacy of touch in terms analogous to the affective mysteries of the 1855 daguerreotype:

> Whoever you are holding me now in hand,
> Without one thing all will be useless,
> I give you fair warning before you attempt me further,
> I am not what you supposed, but far different.
>
> [...]
>
> For these leaves and me you will not understand,
> They will elude you at first and still more afterward I will
>   certainly elude you,
> Even while you should think you had unquestionably caught
>   me, behold!
> Already you see I have escaped from you.

This poem offers a textual equivalent to the image of a speaker who narrates verbally his reticence to be understood or indeed read, for "in libraries I lie as one dumb, a gawk, or unborn, or dead" (99), and the reader holding his book "in hand" has little hope of unlocking his mysteries.

While the erotics of this metonymic construction are self-evident, they are made almost comically literal by Ted Genoways's discovery of certain alterations made to the 1855 frontispiece while being prepared for publication, where "small differences" between variants "all result from one major change: a significant enlargement of the bulge in Whitman's crotch."[49] The historical observation of this enlargement lends an anatomical specificity to the notion of touching a man, homing in on quite where or what the reader's hand is holding, and is consonant not only with the numerous moments in *Leaves of Grass* which worship virility, but with the "Manly Health" guide. The magnetism of shared assumption which opens "Song of Myself" inheres—his guide suggests—in the "subtle virtue of physique," the male body the site of "such a 'personality' that" its agent "can hardly appear in a crowd" without exerting some interpersonal power.[50] Physical health is touted as a clear-headed form of ostentatious masculinity, a way of attaining some "heroic presence," while simultaneously cast as "subtle," among a man's most "secret" aspirations and whose "marvellous effects play invisibly out" (227). This confused double of a "heroic" visibility and a magical furtiveness conjures an erotic sense of concealment, of presence announced through something withheld. A large part of such a connection, Whitman continues, "lies in the department of sexuality; here a fund of vigor is a main part of a manly being, through many years" (although this "very citadel of manhood" and personality is compromised, he warns, by venereal disease) (225). This "citadel" suggests the common metonymic substitution of the penis for masculinity itself, "manhood," through which the enlarged frontispiece image can be read. The poet's ambivalent expression is thus offset by his markedly less ambiguous bulge, a presence created out of what "elude[s]" and what protrudes. As with cruising, it is about showing just enough for an onlooker to invite you "right up stairs with me this minute," to bend Whitman's account of Harrison's words. Or, as Frank O'Hara's "common sense" goes, on the subject of poetic measure, "if you're going to buy a pair of pants you want them to be tight enough so everyone will want to go to bed with you" ("Personism: A Manifesto," *CP*, 498).

The prospect of consummation with Whitman's text *writ large*, then, as the sum of its various (body) parts, is characterized by an ambivalence: that it seems at once to recoil from and seduce its reader. Motifs of mystery and obfuscation are copresent with moments of direct and solicitous address, just as graphic tropes of corporeal splitting and dissemination are offset by seemingly evidentiary or synecdochic images of the poet's body. To receive the poet's advances, then, is to occupy a curious, and no doubt queer, position. Tyler Bradway's recent theorization of the affective politics of what he terms "bad reading" seeks to "uncover a broader genealogy of queer reading that pre-exists, develops alongside of, and complexly engages with the emergence of queer theory as an academic discourse."[51] Bradway chooses a number of postwar "queer writers" who use "experimental form to configure and solicit modes of bad reading [. . .] modes of reading [that] often appear degraded because they are infused by and predicated on affect, or because they invest in affects" such as "love" and "pleasure" that "simply fail to count as critical within the idioms of critical theory." But might such a queer genealogy be traced even earlier, to Whitman, whose text perhaps also "proleptically speaks to queer theory's recent reconsideration of its own reading practices" (194)? At first glance, Whitman's writing hardly seems continuous with that of the twentieth-century "experimental" writers Bradway focuses on, like Kathy Acker. (Though Whitman, at least in the context of his own historical reception, is no doubt also an "experimental" writer). Yet does Whitman's text not also seek, like these more obviously resistant texts, to "go beyond" critical orthodoxies? Though he may not be "unreadable" in a manner akin to a postmodern aesthetics of difficulty, Whitman nonetheless engages a rhetoric of unreadability that troubles the directness of his lyric address, or rather redirects his textual erotics as one of indirection (103).

This erotic resonance is derived from a poetics of touching and looking through which Whitman imagines a masturbatory relation with his reader. The potency of this eroticized model of reading to a sexually liberated gay readership would seem self-evident. Michael Moon writes compellingly of Whitman's work as a protoform of gay pornography and illuminates its pertinence as a corpus which advocates sex radicalism in the light of the HIV/AIDS crisis. He writes of the way that "the author of *Leaves of Grass*" offers himself "as imaginary lover [. . .] to the reader with a directness of appeal that I had then otherwise encountered only in relation to some of the more engaging models in the full-color nude photographs in the gay-male sex magazines I had discovered around the same time."[52] Moon incorporates into his discussion a drawing by Andy Baird of a teenage boy masturbating "as he looks down, tongue extended, at his erect penis," while "in the upper left-hand corner of the picture, beside the boy's inclined head, the artist has inscribed Whitman's famous closing words: 'Camerado, this is no book, / Who touches this touches a man.'"[53] The wit of Baird's picture lies in the visual gag that there is "no book" there, for the boy does not "read *and* masturbate." But as Moon writes, what this image "depicts is not only a boy masturbating," but a "picture of a book that is in Whitman's words 'no book,' which is not only *Leaves of Grass* but any book or text that by design negates itself in the production of some kind of bodily/erotic contact between reader and author." In other words, the preservation of some interpersonal magnetism in the reproduction of a textual object involves an act of disappearance, a simultaneous absorption in the text that demands of its reader an imaginative projection into the realm of images to consummate the fantasy of communion.

Another instance of the poet's disappearance illuminates the stakes of his textual erotics, and this takes place, not accidentally, on the street-level stage of cruising. In "Poets to Come" (*LG*, 14), a call to arms for future poets to complete his literary project, to make good on his "one or two indicative words," he writes:

> I am a man who, sauntering along without fully stopping, turns a
>   casual look upon you and then averts his face,
> Leaving it to you to prove and define it,
> Expecting the main things from you.

The directness of Whitman's erotic appeal to his readers is illustrated here with a scene resembling the beginning of a cruising encounter, which possesses a potency not only of indirection but incompletion. The "casual" and inscrutable look demands a response amounting to the work of making something *of* it, proving and defining it, thus giving some longevity to the transient temporality of an urban encounter. The teasing quality of such a look, which might be written off as merely or flimsily flirtatious, is rewritten here as a potent call to arms to be a better reader of Whitman's text, its potential for masturbatory pleasure only granted by a renewed relation to the "book" that is a "man."

"Poets to Come" offers a tantalizingly neat and self-reflexive account of magnetism, variously conceived. This poem seems to refer, intratextually, to the thread of sexual encounters in "Calamus," but it also speaks to Whitman's afterlife as a poet who is famously available for queer critics and cruisers alike. Graham Robb writes that, from "the 1860s" onwards in "Britain and America," Whitman himself became a code-word, his work the "password primeval" that could be "flashed out" to potential partners to signal mutual understanding.[54] Much more recently, in September 2020, theater critic Jesse Green noted in a magazine piece on Whitman that the poet's frontispiece portrait shows "his hips, hat and eyebrows all cocked," and "his lanky frame in a louche slouch that any gay man in Brooklyn Heights today [. . .] would take as a welcome, a come-on, a song of himself."[55] That Whitman's text and image have become in some way a part of the semiotic practice of cruising speaks to his fate as a writer whose importance pertains not only to the literary canon, but to the lived experience of his queer readers. While Whitman's text, in soliciting its reader into an affective and even sexual relation, may exemplify a queer resistance to critical elucidation or assimilation, it nonetheless still betrays a belief that such reading will be generative, even reproductive. Because the erotic resonance of "Poets to Come," which arises from a lack awaiting completion, pertains not merely to reading but to the creative continuation of Whitman's work for future generations of poets. Indeed, poets from the modern American tradition and beyond have hardly failed to follow Whitman's word, and in the next chapter he will meet, somewhat ambivalently, with the glance of Langston Hughes. Perhaps this is no great surprise for such a strange and amorphous writer. "Whoever you are," and wherever, Whitman suggests, he will be one step ahead, his face averted yet somehow still looking at you.

3

Looking for Langston Hughes

Old Walt

In a chapbook published by the *Beloit Poetry Journal* in 1954 to commemorate the centennial of Whitman's *Leaves of Grass,* the following poem by Langston Hughes appeared:

> Old Walt Whitman
> Went finding and seeking
> Finding less than sought
> Seeking more than found,
> Every detail minding
> Of the seeking or the finding.
>
> Pleasured equally
> In seeking as in finding,
> Each detail minding,
> Old Walt went seeking
> And finding.[1]

This poem, titled simply "Old Walt," was published alongside other tributes to Whitman by poets including Charles Olson, Louis Zukofsky, and William Carlos Williams. David Ignatow, the editor of the volume, writes in the foreword of the imperative to pay tribute not only to "Whitman's greatness as a poet," but "also to the man."[2] Years later, Ignatow recalled that he "invited Langston to contribute a poem" to this work and "received [back] a short, tender piece."[3] The text itself gives us pause to wonder over the kind of tribute that it constitutes, for while it does focus in on "the man," the sense in which it is "tender" is more debatable. It certainly pastiches elements of Whitman's style and has in its ears that distinctive glut of present participles, the sonic pileup of "-ing" endings that often brings Whitman's text close, or as close as it ever gets, to patterns of rhyme, as in the poem "We Two Boys Together Clinging," which begins: "We two boys together clinging, / One the other never leaving, / Up and down the roads going" (*LG*, 111). The poem's tenderness, however, depends less upon stylistic approximations than upon how to read, in the first instance, the name Hughes gives to his forebear. Is "Old Walt" merely an affectionate nickname, tender in its familiarity and its clear evocation of a patrilineage? Or does it suggest something edgier, something more along the lines of Allen Ginsberg's rendering of Whitman in his poem "A Supermarket in California," published just two years later in 1956? In Ginsberg's poem, Whitman is an abject apparition who makes good on the epithet of the dirty old man: "I saw you, Walt Whitman, childless, lonely old grubber, poking among the meats in the / refrigerator and eyeing the grocery boys."[4] As in Hughes's poem, Ginsberg's Whitman is "finding and seeking," hiding in the hyperreal aisles of a supermarket, and it is his voyeuristic eye for "grocery boys" that casts his "old"-ness as dirty and perverse. Of course, Whitman's love affairs with young men and the proximity of his sensibilities to discourses of boy-love are well documented, and Ginsberg's poem demonstrates the minimal leap it takes to conceive of Whitman's elder status as an erotic as well as historical or literary quality.

And yet Hughes's poem, on this front, remains obstinate, and in the ambiguity of the nickname around which it is structured, we might say that "Old Walt" cruises its reader. Like Whitman's own cruising poems, it leaves the space for particular kinds of readers—which is to say queer readers—to tease out and inflect its meanings. In his article "Langston Hughes on the DL," Andrew Donnelly writes:

> In this poem we have a Whitman *looking*. Looking for? Looking
> for pleasure or at least pleasured equally in the looking and the
> finding. Maybe he's just curious. [...] Because it is a riddle, the
> poem seeks out the reader who is enough in the know to solve
> it, functioning not only as a description of *looking* but its own
> form of *looking*. Looking for the reader looking for Langston,
> the reader who can, by knowing, take pleasure in not knowing.[5]

There is a unique pleasure in being left in the dark, which here, paradoxically, is also a form of feeling seen by the poem. In courting the unknowable, the poem makes itself known. It is not only the possible codes suggested by the word "old," then, but the very nature of an erotic and unresolved "looking" that here solicits the reader—as Donnelly writes in a footnote, the word looking "in the era of dating apps takes on much of the meaning that 'cruising' did in previous decades."[6] True as this is, the example of Whitman and Hughes, and the figure of Whitman as mediated by Hughes, suggests that this imbrication of looking and cruising has a much longer history, as I argue throughout this book. All of which is to say that Hughes's "Old Walt," a "short, tender piece," is itself a text which not only thematizes cruising but enacts it, by framing the reader's negotiation of it as an act of looking, a double take.

This chapter explores looking and cruising in Hughes's writing and looks back to the particular queer milieu of early twentieth-century Harlem. Although, as with Whitman, the question of Hughes's out-ness is a vexed one, as I address in the pages ahead, his writing is full of acts of "finding and seeking." Seeking, as this poem suggests, can pleasure "equally" with the "finding," and it also comes to stand in for the unresolved and unspoken threads of queer desire that can be read throughout his work. The nature of the look, once again, is bound up with photography and montage, but in this chapter I also defer to a later work to help excavate more clearly the visual textures of Hughes's queer corpus. Isaac Julien's 1989 film *Looking for Langston,* made and released at the height of the HIV/AIDS epidemic in the United Kingdom and the United States, has done more than any other text to alter and vivify the discourse around Hughes's queer legacy. Julien's film not only places the poet's queerness front and center but also, as its title suggests, illuminates looking as an optical space where the racial and interracial dimensions of desire play out. It has proven influential in visual studies for precisely this reason and features heavily in Kaja Silverman's *Threshold of the Visible World,* a study I shall return to later. Anne Borden goes so far as to suggest that Julien's reclaiming of Hughes, as one example of "the rediscovery of Hughes's work by Black gay artists," is a gesture akin to the way, in "Old Walt," that Hughes "examines poet Walt Whitman's life through the lens" of his own experience.[7]

It is the nature of this "lens," however (that undertheorized analogy so often called upon in criticism), that determines the specificity of looking and cruising in Hughes's work. Recalling Silverman's use of the Lacanian screen in her reading of Fanon, the notion of the "lens" through which Hughes apprehends Whitman reveals a nexus of considerations: Whitman's views on race, Hughes's views on Whitman, and the complex intersections between race and queer desire that are addressed specifically in Julien's film. On the surface, at least, Hughes seems like a committed disciple of the good gray poet, a primary mediator, historically speaking, between Whitman and subsequent generations of Black writers. He edited and introduced three anthologies of Whitman's poetry (although only two were published) and frequently wrote about the importance of reading him. In a 1953 column titled "Like Whitman, Great Artists Are Not Always Good People," Hughes uses the case of Whitman—who exemplified "American weaknesses in regard to race," particularly "in his workaday editorials in the *Brooklyn Daily Eagle*," where he sometimes "contradicted his own highest ideals"—to reflect upon the fact that "many great writers" and "artists" have "left, at their flaming best, a great light for others, burning even brighter perhaps from the embers of their own personal failures."[8] Hughes's reframing of a critical relation to the past as a passing of the torch speaks in telling ways to poet Lavelle Porter's recent essay on Whitman and so-called cancel culture, written at a time where we now know even more about the fact that Whitman "seems to have been seduced by the proliferation of racist pseudo-science in the post-Civil War era," in stark contrast to the democratic and equalizing call of his poetry.[9] Porter's survey of this legacy makes good upon Hughes's "great light" analogy when he writes that "there is no better place to look for nuanced critical engagement with Whitman's complicated legacy than in the work of black intellectuals." Hughes is a key figure in this regard, cognizant of Whitman's racism but simultaneously firm in the decision to "choose to keep and cherish" the "best of him [. . .] not the worst."[10]

While Hughes's public avowals of Whitman's work both emphasize and look beyond the question of Whitman's racial politics, the potential of his resonance as a queer forebear for Hughes remains unspoken, the matter of more furtive "finding and seeking." Donnelly points to a correspondence between Hughes and Alain Locke in which Hughes seems to feign ignorance about the coded meaning of Locke's phrase the "Greek ideals of life," but nonetheless plays along in asking Locke if he likes "the poems in the Calamus section," which is to say that the queerness of Whitman's text could hardly have been lost on him.[11] Whitman's text had a clear currency in the queer urban milieu of Harlem, where Hughes lived and worked. In Blair Niles's 1931 novel *Strange Brother*, for example, a predictably tragic story about a closeted man exploring what Michael Bronski describes as "Harlem's ambisexual nightclubs and homosexual milieu," reading *Leaves of Grass* is framed as a rite of passage, an induction into queer culture. In fact, "it mentions so many authors and their books [...] that it functions as a basic reading list on homosexuality."[12]

Whitman would have been a focal entry on such a reading list, and although he did not write explicitly about interracial love or erotic contact with Black men, there are clearly moments in his writing where his sexuality and racial politics are negotiated. The infamous vignette of the "Negro drayman" in "Song of Myself," which Hughes included in *Whitman's Darker Brothers*, his unpublished anthology of Whitman poems with African American and Native American themes, casts a fetishistic gaze upon the man of "ample neck and breast," with the sun falling "on the black of his polish'd and perfect limbs" while the poet "behold[s] the picturesque giant and love[s] him" ("Song of Myself," *LG*, 35). In this moment, poet Jericho Brown writes, Whitman predicts "the possibility for power in beings he can only fetishize"; this ancestral "queer poet" did not "expect," Brown continues, "my black ass to be reading and admiring and questioning" his poems, even though his "poems knew I was on the way."[13] Paul H. Outka argues that, in this moment, "Whitman looks at the drayman with the same momentarily freed erotic gaze that the female "twenty-ninth" bather has when she imagines joining the young men"—another canonical moment of looking in Whitman—and precipitates the poet's "celebration of free black labor" and "explicit declaration of love for a black man."[14] And yet, if whatever freedom this act of looking supposedly confers (both on the poet as the "freed" gazer and the man as the freed slave) can then break down "the sexualised taboo against racial amalgamation," Whitman's representation of the drayman nonetheless anticipates the twentieth-century cultural fetishism around the Black male body, captured in James Baldwin's statement that "to be an American Negro male is also to be a kind of walking phallic symbol," subject to the suspicious and fetishistic gaze of white men, both straight and gay.[15] To conceive of the lens through which Hughes sees Whitman is thus also to observe the tense interrelations of queer and interracial desires, articulated in Hughes's work—and in Julien's adaptation of it—with recourse to acts of looking. And although "Old Walt" would seem to be Hughes's most explicit nod to Whitman's sexuality, so explicit is it in its implicitness, there is another short poem written by Hughes some thirty years earlier that looks back, I will argue, to Whitman's "To a Stranger" and, in turn, to the politics of optical desire in 1920s Harlem.

Subway Faces

In the summer of 1923, twenty-one-year-old Langston Hughes set sail for Africa. He had first come to New York from Mexico two years previously to enroll at Columbia University, though his primary education during this period was in the ways of Harlem, a few blocks east of the campus. Harlem already had a reputation as a city-within-a-city, a unique hub for African Americans and the Black intelligentsia. During his student years, Hughes made a name for himself as an emerging young writer and caught the attention of figures like Alain Locke, Countee Cullen, and W. E. B. Du Bois, who edited *Crisis* magazine, an African American periodical published by the National Association for the Advancement of Colored People. Hughes's focus turned away from his schoolwork and toward poetry, and he began to publish short poems in Black magazines. By 1923, however, he desired to see more of the world; he left his studies at Columbia and boarded a ship that anchored at Jones Point, a small town in upstate New York, where he stayed for a while. In June, he found work on the *West Hesseltine,* a ship that would take him much farther afield to the Western coast of Africa. So began a nomadic period in Hughes's life, which took him to Africa and subsequently to Europe and comprised, according to Arnold Rampersad's biography, a cultural and even erotic education among sailors aboard the various ships. His time at sea was also a journeying beyond the page.[16] Although he packed a box of books to take with him on this first journey on the *West Hesseltine,* he soon decided to throw them overboard, in essence throwing away the material remains of his unhappy time as a Columbia student. But, as Rampersad writes, in an oft-repeated anecdote:

> One book only did Hughes save. He had flung overboard the symbols of his hurt. But he had also kept the symbol of his best self, and of what he hoped to be. He saved his copy of Walt Whitman's *Leaves of Grass*: "I had no intention of throwing that one away."[17]

Among the symbols Rampersad identifies in this recollection, Whitman's text provides a symbol of constancy, a trusty companion, or a guiding light (to return to Hughes's own metaphor). By the time Hughes "returned to America" in November 1924, George B. Hutchinson writes, he "had determined what his vocation would be," and his "absorption of Whitman was as thorough as that of any other North American poet of his generation."[18]

Whitman's continuing resonance for Hughes was about more than some transtemporal sense of universality, but rather suggested that Whitman's text could constantly renew itself in the light of Hughes's vocation. "*Leaves of Grass*," he wrote in a much later essay called "Walt Whitman and the Negro," is "as contemporary as tomorrow's newspaper."[19] Toward the end of 1924, not long after he returned to Harlem, where he was staying with Countee Cullen in his family home at 2190 Seventh Avenue, Hughes published "Subway Face," a poem that bore Whitman's imprint but spoke very much to "contemporary" urban experience. The poem's exact compositional history is unclear—it could have been written from a nostalgic distance or, alternately, upon Hughes's return to the city after a long period—but it appeared thus in the December 1924 edition of *Crisis*, which was itself a form of "newspaper":

> That I have been looking
> For you all my life
> Does not matter to you.
> You do not know.
>
> You never knew.
> Nor did I.
> Now you take the Harlem train uptown;
> I take a local down.[20]

The magazine, full name *The Crisis: A Record of the Darker Races*, was founded by Du Bois in 1910 as the official publication of the NAACP, with the aim of disseminating information about culture, politics, current affairs, education, and employment among African American readers. Hughes's poem appeared in the magazine at the bottom of the last page of an NAACP bulletin detailing recent civil rights cases and the arrangements for the organization's annual meeting in New York in January. Although the shift between these modes of writing—from the informative reportage authored by a collective "we" to the intimate and particularized address of Hughes's "I" and "you"—was part and parcel of the miscellany format, there is something uniquely arresting about the placement of this poem in the magazine. "Subway Face" distinguishes itself from the political content that surrounds it as if it were a furtive counterdiscourse, just as the poem's speaker establishes the poem's intimate interlocution from within the crowded quotidian space of the subway. The poem's presence in a portable publication, one that could no doubt have been read during subway journeys, lends it a metapoetic immediacy, as though it might, by chance, come to narrate its reader's own live passage through the setting it describes: a subway station in, or close to, Harlem.

Like Baudelaire's "À une passante," which Thibaudet supposed could suture the everyday wounds of urban estrangement sustained by its wandering readers, Hughes's "Subway Face" extends empathy by example, uttered by a speaker who experiences an uncanny excess of feeling toward a stranger spotted on the subway. As a portrait of a passing moment it trades in readerly relation; in the narration of an experience recognizable among many of its readers, who may or may not be encountering this poem while occupying the very space of urban encounter that it describes, as if its "I" were speaking for them, instrumentally, in paraphrasing a commonplace or everyday thought. But frequency, here, does not preclude intensity, an intensity felt in the forging of a sudden intimacy that seems both determined: "I have been looking / For you all my life," and unrequited: this "does not matter to you." The sentimental narrative of an unlived life is the incipient occasion for the poem but is quickly shot down. By the stanzaic break that separates the poem's units, the uncertain present of encounter has become an impossible and irretrievable past: "You never knew. / Nor did I."

In seeking to capture the irretrievable as a condition of the urban everyday, the poet here invests aesthetically in strangers in much the same way the photographer Walker Evans did. Evans produced his well-known series of subway portraits in New York some years after the publication of Hughes's poem, in the late 1930s and early 1940s. Evans's mode of catching a glimpse was covert and controversial; he hid his 35 mm Contax camera beneath his coat and allowed the lens to peek out in the gap between two of the coat's buttons. He kept the camera's release in his coat pocket, so that he could subtly capture shots at a moment's notice, and was often accompanied on these subway journeys by his friend Helen Levitt, who was also a photographer. The ethical murkiness of Evans's project—capturing subjects who are totally unaware that they are being photographed—is also what produces its extraordinary results. These portraits capture forms of interpersonal nudity unique to transportation like the subway. As Luc Sante writes in the published edition of these photographs, since "the protocols of subway-riding advise turning your gaze inward, you can take off the face you wear for the benefit of others," such that "the subway rider, then, is naked."[21] In his "sociology of the metropolis," Georg Simmel identifies public transportation as a disquieting forum of faciality:

> The person who sees without hearing is much more confused, more at a loss, more disquieted than the person who hears without seeing. [...] Before the development of buses, trains, and streetcars in the nineteenth century, people were not at all in a position to be able or to have to view one other for minutes or hours at a time without speaking to one another. Modern traffic, which involves by far the overwhelming portion of all perceptible relations between person and person, leaves people to an ever greater extent with the mere perception of the face and must thereby leave universal sociological feelings to fully altered presuppositions.[22]

The epistemological problem of the face in the crowd or on the train—on the one hand the symbol of a disquieting anonymity and on the other the "symbol of all that accompanies the individual as the prior condition of one's life, all that is stored up in a person"—itself provides an imaginative opportunity.[23] As in Whitman's "To a Stranger," the speaker of "Subway Face" fills in the gaps with the sensation of an unknown shared past only now made uncannily familiar, read in the lines of a strange face: you must be "he I was seeking," or, "I have been looking / For you all my life." And like Whitman's poem or indeed Evans's subway photographs, "Subway Face" implies that this dual process of looking and imagining is a process akin to ekphrasis. "Subway Face" stages a relationship between title and text; the eponymous face is rendered, in the title, as a visual object that is then not mentioned again, such that the poem proper seems to be responding to it, like an introspective caption to an image, written in the face of estrangement. The poem's brevity also lends itself to the delineated, imagistic form of the snapshot; or rather it is as if the poem were the internal soundtrack to a moment that fades from view almost as soon as it has begun, as the two strangers take trains in opposite directions.

While the title, as a compositional and aesthetic frame, lends the poem a sense of visuality, it is this interchange between Harlem and downtown that offers further details as to this scene. Although the identity of neither speaker nor addressee is established, the departure at the poem's end offers hints, with the implication of a momentary exchange between two people from different parts of the city. Brian McCammack points out that during the "quarter-century between the World Wars," public transportation such as the New York subway, which first opened in 1904, was "integral to urban culture" and enforced proximity between strangers who might never otherwise meet.[24] The "same subway platform could take a rider uptown to black Harlem and downtown to white Manhattan," and the space of the subway car itself "was often crowded and forced different races, classes, ethnicities, and genders into closer proximity than was experienced in even city streets or public park," bringing "black and white bodies closer together than any other public situation" (1074–75). The stylistic economy of Hughes's short poem thus belies the complex sociological background of the milieu in which it is uttered and suggests any number of star-crossed readings; of an erotic or affective potentiality thwarted by racial, socioeconomic, and geographic divisions.

Unlike Hughes's later poem "Subway Rush Hour," from 1951's *Montage of a Dream Deferred,* which muses upon "mingled / black and white / so near / no room for fear" (*CPLH,* 423) and points more decisively to the fact that "public transportation was not always a site for fleeting attraction" but "at times, represent[ed] an incipient interracial physical threat," "Subway Face" reflects less upon interracial tensions than upon a profound sense of division that the ephemeral proximity of a subway ride paradoxically makes legible.[25] The melancholy of the two lovers is also a melancholy of two cities, estranged, passing one another by at an interchange. "Passing," another poem from *Montage of a Dream Deferred,* eulogizes Harlem from the vantage of "the ones who've crossed the line / to live downtown," those who "miss you, / Harlem of the bitter dream, / since their dream has / come true" (*CPLH*, 417.) This conception of mobility as an ambivalent victory, a "dream [...] come true" that brings its own losses, speaks to the title's implication of passing through or passing on. And, with its focus on the implicit color "line" that divides uptown from downtown, it is hard not to think of the implications of another Harlem text with the same title. Nella Larsen's 1929 novel *Passing*—famous for, among other reasons, its "tragic mulatto" plot centered on mixed-race women who pass for white—politicizes the present participle of its title in suggesting that the act of passing is by itself imbricated with performance and the legibility of race, just as Hughes's poem registers the pathos of assimilation.

Like "To a Stranger," "Subway Face" also passes for one kind of poem about the condition of urban modernity. Although its focus on race is explicit, the ambiguity of its address renders a capacious interpretive space and makes it available to a conventional heterosexual reading; queer desire is not readily or explicitly proscribed. And yet, this unmarked and unspoken quality is itself consonant with Whitman's strategy of queer address in "To a Stranger." As Shane Vogel writes, "Hughes's 1920s poetry archives spaces and temporalities that seek to escape empirical confirmation and refuse identificatory foreclosure," such that queer meanings can be detected not according to the evidentiary burden of proof, but the conspicuous quality of that which is absent or implicit, as in Whitman.[26] While this poem's melancholic charge would seem to derive from the arbitrariness of passing, the quotidian fact of "two trains traveling in opposite directions on a fixed schedule, precluding any deeper connection," this interpersonal estrangement reads as a substitute for a deeper sense of queer love's impossibility in the glare of public life.[27] The tyranny of train timetables, an instrument of state and "straight" time, wins out in this poem against the fragile, incipient moment of connection, able to circumvent the racial, social, and sexual conventions of the commute for just an instant. And, while "Subway Face" gestures outside the here and now to an imagined past and future, it hardly glimpses, unlike Whitman's poem, at the utopic, but rather bears witness to its dissipation. The frozen image of the subway face thus lingers as a symbol of the insurmountable, a visualized monument to the could-have-been, and in turn reveals the politics of passing; the sense that the transient act of looking makes visible the various forms of social division that determine our relations with others in the space of the urban everyday. If "Subway Face" wears its queer resonance only quietly, its account of the look might then be better illuminated, as I will now explore, by a queer analytical frame that sees Hughes as a poet intimately invested in representations of Black and interracial desire and, simultaneously, in the refusal of the white gaze, with the look once again its instrument.

Isaac Julien's Langston

The first frame of Isaac Julien's 1989 film *Looking for Langston* features, not exactly the subway, but an elevated train as it speeds across a Manhattan bridge. This shot is anticipated by the ambient street noises that play over the film's opening titles, which function here like a series of dedications or epigraphs: "A Meditation on Langston Hughes (1902–1967) and the Harlem Renaissance," "With the poetry of Essex Hemphill and Bruce Nugent (1906–1987)," "In Memory of James Baldwin (1924–1987)."[28] It is immediately clear from these titles that this is a film functioning on multiple levels, temporally speaking, for it quickly establishes various dramatis personae, composed of a multigenerational list of dead queer Black writers linked to Harlem, as well as the then-contemporary D.C. poet Essex Hemphill. The opening frame, merging the sound and the image of the train and shot from below on street level, makes literal the multiple levels of the film's hermeneutic scheme while also establishing the public exterior of its Harlem setting. It soon becomes clear, when the film cuts from historical footage of Harlem to a shot of a man in black tie crying before an arrangement of carnations, with an overlay of Toni Morrison's 1987 eulogy for Baldwin, that we are at a memorial service. A Black man—Hughes, we presume, and played by Julien himself—lies in an open casket, surrounded by mourners, and Julien has recently contextualized his rationale:

> The AIDS epidemic was just reaching its height. [. . .] I was spending more and more time going to funerals, thinking about what it would be like to die in one's twenties. In *Langston* I extended this feeling to seeing how I would look in a coffin. That was also my little allusion to Roland Barthes's ideas about the

death of the author, as well as a swipe at the cult of authorship in the film industry.[29]

This troubling of authorship conditions the directionality of the film; as Kobena Mercer writes, the "film looks for Langston, but what we find is Isaac," and the film's offering of a "visual equivalent of a dialogue with […] different cultural traditions" informs the "promiscuous intertextuality which the film sets in motion," gestured to immediately in the inventory of the opening titles.[30] Such promiscuity also serves to illustrate the simultaneity of two different temporalities, both a cultural past and a morbid present, temporalities whose copresence resists the linearity of progress narratives. As the camera pans away from this funereal scene it descends, slowly, to the story below, to an ornate and cavernous room adorned with a disco ball on the ceiling. A number of men, both Black and white, are frozen in poses; some are dancing cheek to cheek, others are drinking at the bar, looking squarely at the dance floor, while another looks ahead while leaning against a pillar. A small arrangement of flowers can be seen in the bottom right-hand corner of the shot, and we are led to assume that this is a wake of some kind (not least because the dancing cast members are described in the film's closing credits as Dancers at the Wake).

For Tony Fisher, this scene typifies the film's parody of the "still photograph" through "cinematic *tableaux vivants*," but it also shows that in this film, "Hughes has entered the subterranean world of film, and like Orpheus before him, his song continues to be heard."[31] Like many of the film's images, the resonance of the wake scene, which in its dressing appears to be set in the 1920s and the 1980s simultaneously, is left to viewers' imaginations: Is this an imagined, utopic space, or the space of the afterlife? Is this the space of Hughes's "dream deferred," an incipient and yet-to-be dreamscape that is, paradoxically, located in the past? This scene catches us, Fisher suggests, in the "nexus of gazes that Julien sets up," both in this scene of looking in the "form itself," which leaves us "waiting, as in a (death) watch to see how the next shot will unfold, or who will be looking at whom," such that "the film tense we are dealing with here, therefore, is not historical but topological."[32] Just as, in "Subway Face," Hughes goes underground to picture the act of gazing, Julien introduces the film's titular motif at the level of the subterranean, in a sequence of images characterized by "their solicitation of the look" such that "it can only be the spectator's look to which these images are addressed, and which they interrogate," serving to dramatize "either what it means to look 'for' or 'against' Langston."[33]

It is tempting to account metaphorically for the film's use of aesthetic and temporal levels, to imagine its form as an architectural, multistoried framework, or as Fisher's topological network. Muñoz, on the other hand, describes the film's cinematic structure as a "transhistorical and transnational 'weavelike' texture" that "can be understood as a product of the discomfort caused by traditional Western genre constraints," and the credits of the film signal that it contains an interwoven narration of American Voices—like those of Hemphill or Toni Morrison—and a British Voice, that of Stuart Hall.[34] Indeed, to write about *Looking for Langston* today, in the light of the extensive critical work on it, is to encounter all manner of metaphors that seek to weave from the film's multiple layers and threads a sense of coherence. It is no doubt the sense of interpretive plenitude it offers that has made it a mainstay in African American studies, queer studies, and film studies departments, and the optical aspect of the title is a particularly rich site of inquiry. Julien describes, in an interview with Fisher, the film's focus on looking as bound up with his interest in "the scopic—in looking, in the visual field."[35] "I think the scopic is very important," he continues, "in relation to the construction of black gay desire. [. . .] It becomes important to visualize what the Harlem Renaissance might have looked like in relation to black gay men."[36] The film's backward glance to the era of the Harlem Renaissance—or, at least, its burlesque reconstruction of that era's aesthetic in 1980s London—shares in the erotics of the archive, of visually reanimating Black gay forebears out of physical books and photographs, while also making larger claims about the relation between Black gay desire and the scopic; its nuances, pleasures, and its potential for violence.

Kaja Silverman suggests that "the film's title promises looking without a discovery or conclusion, a looking which is more akin to browsing," but it also "indexes more even than this browsing or cultural cruising" and "designates Langston as he on whose behalf a certain kind of looking is solicited."[37] Silverman's play on the title suggests that the film looks, squarely and publicly, at Black gay desire in a way that Hughes never could, or chose not to, unlike his "out" Renaissance compatriot Richard Bruce Nugent, whose 1926 prose piece "Smoke, Lilies and Jade" is heavily quoted in Julien's film and is regularly cited as one of the first queer texts published by an African American author. Julien's film may stop short of outing Hughes in any direct way, which is to say address-ing the exact nature of his sexuality or sexual relationships, but this is because it bears an altogether different relationship to history. Unlike Arnold Rampersad's biography, published just three years beforehand and controversial for its supposedly evidence-based denial of Hughes's homosexuality, Julien's film, in his own words, was "never intended" to be "a life of Langston Hughes" but "was always going to be about his status as a cultural icon and, in terms of repressed gay desire, what that might symbolise."[38] Hughes is less the agent or object of Julien's looking than its locus: the name "Langston Hughes," shortened familiarly in the film's title, delineates as much a discursive and visual terrain for explora-tion as it does a fixed and historically identifiable figure.

Looking, then, as the rich and compelling body of work on Julien's film suggests, is itself a contested site, where the various intersections of race, performance, and desire are made visible. Silverman undertakes an extended close reading of two of the central looks in the film, which are both closely tied up with the practice of cruising, in order to expli-cate the distinction between Black love and the white gaze, opposing discourses in accounts of interracial desire and its politics. In the first of these Alex, the closest the film has to a protagonist, is "shown looking from his perch at the bar toward Beauty (Matthew Baidoo), a Black man who sits drinking at a table with a white man. Beauty, who initially has his back to Alex, turns and smiles at him with answering desire."[39] Like the sensation Benjamin describes in relation to the aura, of "eyes star-ing at one's back," this moment registers the sensation of being looked at from behind, and Silverman frames the harmonious "answering" as a form of ethical exchange in which both lookers become aware of themselves and each other as desiring subjects, provoking the jealousy of Karl, the white man at the table. Julien makes sparing use here of tra-ditional film syntax, the only "moment" in the film that has "recourse to the traditional reverse shot formation" (108). The close-up that makes visible Beauty's glance back also illuminates Baidoo's face in a soft, bright light, which not only speaks to the idealizing or exalting dimen-sion of the reciprocal glance between desiring subjects—something that is also signaled, Silverman suggests, by the recurring presence of an-gels throughout the film—but also recalls the lighting effects of portrait photography and, in particular, the black-and-white portraits of George Platt Lynes, whom Julien has cited as an influence on the film's style.

This explicit invocation of the look in relation to the image, and of cruising in relation to photography—and it is worth mentioning here that Sunil Gupta collaborated with Julien on the photographic elements of the film and took a series of stills—establishes an interweaving of aesthetic and erotic considerations that pertains throughout the film's middle section in a fluid, essayistic manner, marked as it is by visual and thematic refrains. The look between Alex and Beauty is cut short by Karl who, jealous that Beauty has literally had his head turned, bangs a champagne bottle on the table to summon him back. Alex looks on, somewhat dejected, before turning back to the bar. To put it bluntly, this optical set-to illustrates how the white gaze, here embodied by Karl, who jealously ties Beauty to him, serves to obstruct the possibility of Black love, a possibility glimpsed in this moment of the look. Immediately afterwards, however, this formulation is complicated by the entrance of another Black man called James (played by Akim Mogaji), who ascends the stairs and joins Alex at the bar. He looks flirtatiously at Karl, his lip curling slightly upwards, and in another reverse shot formation, Karl is shown to be stopped in his tracks, evidently solicited by the directness of this glance. James nods to Alex with the suggestion of complicity, as if he has taken care of something for the both of them, and Alex then turns back to the bar and sips another glass of champagne, as if freed up to imagine what comes next.

At this point Julien turns to a tableau that, in Silverman's words, "can best be described as a dream within this dream" (109). James and the white man are standing by a bed, touching one another in a fixed pose, while Alex and Beauty lie naked together on the bed. The bedroom tableau is intercut with a pastoral scene where Alex and Beauty assume a similar standing pose in a field, the former in his signature dinner suit and the latter naked, while passages from Nugent's "Smoke, Lilies and Jade"—from which the names Alex and Beauty derive—are read as a voice-over. This might seem at first like a utopic landscape, a natural elsewhere in which the Black lovers are free to look and commune away from the stratified gazes of the bar, and yet the lingering presence of Alex and the white man serves to worry this scene's happy ideality. Similarly, Silverman writes, certain visual disjunctures in this scene emphasize that "what Alex 'sees' when he thinks about Beauty is somehow in excess of that figure himself" in order "to foreground once again the investitory potential of the look" and the fact that "the body" is "not intrinsically ideal, but is rather exalted" by the "openly fantasmic" and "dramatically defamiliarizing" context into which "it is inserted" (111). This sequence, attributable perhaps to Alex's reverie, illustrates how, in the act of cruising, imagination begets imagination; how Alex's fantasy of consummation with Beauty precipitates the appearance of this pastoral and no less libidinal landscape, one akin, perhaps, to Whitman's "Paths Untrodden."

The dream sequence ends as the film returns to the funeral scene and then back underground to the wake, where footage of the bar and the dance floor is overlaid with "Blues for Langston," a song by San Francisco musician Blackberri. The song's lyrics draw upon Hughes's poetry—"Whatever happened to the dream deferred?"—and seem to apostrophize Hughes himself from within the film's transtemporal diegesis: "I've seen how far you've come."[40] These lyrics speak powerfully to the sequence that comes next, which shifts throughout between the images and vernaculars of past and present. The historical "Langston" milieu of the film is connected explicitly to contemporary cruising culture and, in turn, to the insidiousness of the white gaze, thus making use of "Langston Hughes and the black tradition as enabling texts for black gays to tell their stories," in Manthia Diawara's words.[41] A man leaves the bar for another indeterminately pastoral space, a cemetery just beyond the city limits, but this is less an ideal landscape than one imbued with the danger and excitement of public cruising. Essex Hemphill reads the poems "Where Seed Falls" and "Under Certain Circumstances," both taken from his 1986 collection *Conditions*, while a Black and a white man approach each other in the cemetery and begin to kiss, both of them dressed in the contemporary leather "clone" style.[42] Hemphill's texts evoke a landscape of shadows, of "wild lips" and "certain streets," and his words "I want to court outside the race," but "love is a dangerous word / in this small town" figure the sociological and racialized "attitudes" related to cruising that Julien engages in the scene that follows, as the film returns to the wake.[43]

In this scene, Blackberri's song "Beautiful Black Man" accompanies a scene of triangulated looking, where Julien's camera alternates between close-ups of Alex, Karl, and Marcus, played by Dencil Williams, in a series of shots where it is unclear who is looking at who. For much of the scene Karl, a dark-skinned Black man, looks down or away, while

Blackberri sings "you've been made to feel / That your beauty's not real."[44] This anthem of self-love plays over an exchange of looks that reveals the power of the look—in a community obsessed with looks and types—to diminish and belittle Black men about their appearance. This racialized dimension of the look as an element of cruising is then linked to larger questions of race and representation; first, there is archival footage of Black sculptors creating busts and statues, while Blackberri implores: "be proud of your race." Afterwards, Julien cuts to footage of Black painters at work, and a white crowd in an art gallery, while Stuart Hall's voice-over offers the following commentary:

> White patrons of the Harlem Renaissance wanted black artists and writers to know and feel the intuitions of the primitive. They didn't want Modernism. They wanted Black art, to keep art and artists in their place.

The white gaze, gestured to thus far in Julien's film as an erotic phenomenon, is here also revealed as an institutional mechanism that fetishizes a whole category—"black art"—with recourse to the same "primitive" stereotypes through which the Black male body is apprehended and viewed as hypervirile and hypersexual.

The particular fetishism for the Black male body in white gay culture is explored in the next scene of the film, which "dramatizes a look," Silverman writes, that "is the very opposite of that attributed to Alex" in his earlier exchange with Beauty.[45] The objectifying capacity of the white gaze is here signaled by an opening shot of Karl, who "looks ahead of himself at an unspecified object" while "smoke passes between him and what he sees, as if to suggest that his look is somehow mediated." Over a jazz bass-line, Essex Hemphill reads "If His Name Were Mandingo," a poem whose Black speaker clearly addresses a problematic white gay man who exploits and objectifies a Black hustler for his own pleasure: "If he's not hard on / then he's hard up / and either way / you watch him."[46] Hemphill's poem is direct in its critique and, in its eponymous invocation of the Mandingo figure, a trope which elides a West African identity with the hypersexuality of the Black phallus, recalls his own essay on the fetishistic photographs of Robert Mapplethorpe. In this rallying prose piece, titled "Does Your Mama Know About Me?," Hemphill identifies the white gay objectification of the Black body as one of the major fault-lines in the so-called gay revolutionary movement, for "the post-Stonewall gay community of the 1980s was not concerned with the existence of Black gay men except as sexual objects," and "the Black male was given little representation except as a big, Black dick," as is "strikingly revealed" by Mapplethorpe's portraits of Black men.[47] It is apt, then, that in *Looking for Langston* Karl is shown to peruse and stroke reproductions of Mapplethorpe's images, which are hung as screens within the smoky atmosphere of the film's vacant set. This moment in the film makes clear on a visual level the same process of objectification that is explicated in Hemphill's poem: the way that the immediate "look" at an erotic object, signaled by Karl's stare at the start of this sequence, draws upon preceding representations in problematic ways, bringing a visual bank of material to bear upon an immediate optical perception.[48]

Silverman writes of this scene—which culminates in Karl's flippant handing-over of cash to James, after a sexual tryst prefigured several scenes earlier—that "Karl not only apprehends the Black men who command his sexual interest through the intervening agency of the screen (foregrounded here through the smoke which mediates his vision), but that he also comfortably inhabits the viewing position that has been culturally assigned to him with respect to those men."[49] The "screen" Silverman mentions here throws into relief the look-as-photograph analogy that I draw upon throughout this book, and which is palpable here in Julien's film. The rendering of Mapplethorpe's photographs as visual screens gives concrete expression to this notion of a mediating threshold that both conditions the white man's gaze and also affirms the privilege of his vantage, and it suggests an elision between the look as induced by cruising, on the one hand, and by visual artworks on the other. Silverman expands on the notion of the screen earlier in *The Threshold of the Visible World* during her analysis of Fanon's *Black Skin, White Masks*:

> Fanon speaks again about the involuntary nature of his identification with negritude, and about the destructive effects of that identification upon what was previously his bodily ego. [...] However, in this passage, Fanon also makes clear that if he is "photographed" in this guise, this is not because of the special power and productivity of the white look with respect to the

black body, but rather because of the mobilization in the viewing situation he describes of the screen of "blackness."[50]

It is not Fanon who describes himself as "photographed" in the moment
he encounters a white onlooker. Silverman borrows this term from
Lacan to refer to the "screen," the "intervening agency" administered by
the culture at large, which shows a subject how they are viewed by others via the gaze. The screen governs the visual regime of a given culture
and is correspondingly made up of archetypal cultural matter through
which the subject is (mis)represented. For Fanon, the "screen" of his
blackness is composed of the "legends, stories, history, and above all
historicity" that are mobilized by the white gaze to frame him and, in
turn, to put him in his place.[51] The gaze and screen may be culturally
embedded phenomena, but they are experienced by Fanon with violent immediacy in the instant of the look, which is reported in his text
through the verbal hailing "Look, a Negro!" To think of this projecting look as photographic—which Silverman does by way of Lacan's
"screen" and its surrogacy in the figure of the camera—is germane, for
it captures the way in which the gaze is inflicted upon the subject with
the immediacy of a snapshot. But this analogy also speaks to the way
the screen mediates this immediacy, such that the subject is not merely
"photographed" but perceived as *already photographed,* a palimpsest or
composite of "*historicity.*"

To be an agent of the white gaze like Karl is to be given the power, at
the level of consciousness and of representation, to inscribe the nature
of your relation to the other and to the other's body. With this power,
correspondingly, comes the capacity to disappear behind your own
vantage in a way that marked bodies cannot; think again of the generic
homosexual in Bersani's psychoanalytic account of cruising, who is able
to cruise happily in a sea of identification made up of inaccurate replications. For those, on the other hand, for whom this identification is
"involuntary," and structured around a de-idealizing image that is given
"back" against their will in the moment of encounter, the "screen" is a
violent phenomenon. In this same passage, Fanon describes the moment of being looked at as a brutal fragmentation where the "corporeal
schema crumbled," and "it was no longer a question of being aware of
my body in the third person but in a triple person." The "corporeal consequences of this forced identification with an abhorrent visual imago,"

Silverman writes, manifests as "the fantasy of a body in bits and pieces, as a violent mutilation."[52] This self-splitting is not a matter of multiplication but scattering, and Fanon describes "this revision, this thematization" by the screen as "an amputation, an excision."[53] That same act of violence is also visited upon the Black male body by the excision performed in the framing of Mapplethorpe's images, which, Hemphill argues, are "insulting and endangering to Black men" because of the "*conscious* determination that the faces, heads, and by extension, the minds of and experiences of some of his Black subjects are not as important as close-up shots of their cocks."[54] While *Looking for Langston* is concerned throughout, like Hughes's "Subway Face," with faciality as the surface upon which looking is inscribed in all its ambivalence, it also illustrates here the corporeal violence of faciality's elision, its exclusion from the frame, in a process where the look becomes an exclusionary and tyrannical form of objectification.

Julien's film thus ultimately poses the question of what it means to reclaim the act of looking; to identify and reject the violence of the white gaze and wrest from it more ethical forms of interracial exchange and, in particular, forms of Black love unbothered by it. If the "Mandingo" sequence is an example of the film's critique at its highest pitch, the exact relation of this critique to Hughes's work is less clear. Yet in its collapsing of temporal and historical boundaries—it features an act of problematic looking that occurs within the diegesis of the 1920s Harlem Renaissance setting, but is off-set by 1980s artists like Mapplethorpe and Hemphill— this scene locates a politics of interracial desire in this earlier tradition, and even suggests that the white gay fetishization of the Black body is analogically equivalent to the annexing and exploitation of Black Renaissance artists by white patrons. "Things haven't changed much," Blackberri sings in "Blues for Langston," as if the film's contemporary vantage was from a culture really no more enlightened about matters of race and sexuality than that of the 1920s, perhaps even less so.[55] Hughes, on the surface at least, never explicitly engaged the issues of queer interracial desire that Julien meditates upon, but at this juncture we should perhaps heed the opening line of Blackberri's song: "Whatever happened to the dream deferred?" Hughes's late photographic works from the 1950s, like the aforementioned collection *Montage of a Dream Deferred* as well as *The Sweet Flypaper of Life*, his collaboration with photographer Roy DeCarava, ostensibly seem a world away from the queer, libidinal milieu of Julien's Harlem. But if we look again and look closer, we find parallel interrogations of the complex interplay between Black bodies and the white gaze, and between looking and desire, performed covertly among the intricate relations of text and image.

Hughes's Harlem Montages

At the end of *Looking for Langston,* a group of thugs and policemen descend ominously upon the wake and bang down the door with batons and weapons. At this point the party also revs up—glasses are broken, looks are served, and the dancing breaks out from the previously established ballroom formality into something distinctly more 1980s. Essex Hemphill reads his poem "The Brass Rail" over Royal House's track "Can You Party" while the mourners dance. The men outside continue to break down the door. When they eventually break in, clearly hungry for blood and arrests, there is no one there. This ending throws into relief the phantasmic space that governs the film while also engaging a fantasy of undetectability, where queer and subterranean acts of world-making—like those historically associated with the bars and clubs of the Harlem Renaissance—are untouched by the violent force of the law. But this ending also speaks, indirectly, to perhaps the most explicit invocation of deviant sexuality in Hughes's poetry, which can be found in the poem "Café: 3 a.m." (*CPLH,* 406), from the 1951 collection *Montage of a Dream Deferred.* It reads:

> Detectives from the vice squad
> with weary sadistic eyes
> spotting fairies.
>
>> Degenerates,
>> some folks say.
>
> But God, Nature,
> or somebody
> made them that way.
>
> Police lady or Lesbian
> over there?
>> *Where?*

The poem's title—which could equally be imagined as the name of a photograph or painting, an alternate title for Edward Hopper's iconic *Nighthawks,* for example—points to a space both vivid and nonspecific, and leaves us to imagine for ourselves the neon glow of the café. The associations of this late-night demimonde, however, are made clear from the poem's intricate vantage. Here Hughes displays, Donnelly writes, a knowingness about "what goes on at such suspicious places in the after-hours," but this poem also reveals that the "the closet is always a problematized form of knowing, in that the logic of "it takes one to know one" has an alibi when that knowledge takes the subjectivity of state surveillance," and here it is the "state and not the poetic voice that is looking for fairies."[56] Much is ambiguous in this poem, from the scene being observed to the position of the speaker, as well as the status of the "police lady" or the "Lesbian," but what is clear is the attribution of a scopic and even panoptic violence to the gaze of the state, given localized expression here in the image of police's "weary sadistic eyes."[57]

Policing has its own punitive stake in cruising—think of plainclothes officers luring gay men in public bathrooms—but it's also its own mode of looking. It may not engage in the same forms of vexed eroticizing that I have been concerned with in this chapter, but it nonetheless still defers to stereotypes to cast its judgments and suspicions. It does not so much objectify as subjectify, to recall Judith Butler's account of Althusser's notion of "interpellation," for the policeman's reprimand—embodied verbally by a phrase like ""Hey you!'"—has the "effect of binding the law to one who is hailed," one who "appears not to be in a condition of trespass prior to the call," and it is this interpellative "call" that "initiates the individual into the subjected status of the subject."[58] What Hughes's bleary-eyed tableau suggests, in its replacement of cruising with the activity of "spotting," is that the process of subjectivization which Butler characterizes as verbal, after Althusser, might also take place at an optical level, with just a look, performed by the "weary sadistic eyes" of the law. That Butler's well-known account of interpellation and its slippiness precipitates her analysis of gender subversion in Jennie Livingston's 1990 film *Paris Is Burning,* a documentary about the Harlem drag balls of the 1980s, which were contiguous with the fluid spaces of the Harlem Renaissance and contemporary with Julien's *Looking for Langston,* is no accident. Both Hughes's "Café: 3 a.m." and the ending of Julien's film imply, in more or less furtive ways, that queer people of color are particularly vulnerable to, and disproportionately affected by, the optical force of state surveillance.

The notion of the "down low" or the DL, a trope that seems to literalize the subterranean aesthetic Julien mobilizes, is one way in which Black queer sexuality is policed, but also potentially liberated. Most commonly pertaining to men of color who sleep with men without being "out," the DL flouts the logic of the closet and of coming out as an essentializing ritual of homosexuality. Although the DL may risk perpetuating stereotypes related to social and sexual wiliness and renders the down-low subject's sexuality vulnerable, in so far as it is something to be found out, the anti-identificatory element of the DL has numerous appeals and functions. Not least, as Donnelly suggests in citing the work of C. Riley Snorton, that it proposes "a racialized resistance to white universality" and its associated questions, like "why don't they just come out?," which "presume a logic of progress to individual and group development that universalizes white middle-class experience as the only—and the correct—experience."[59] Just as the scopic and transhistorical form of *Looking for Langston* lights upon a strategy for claiming him as a prophet of queer Black sexuality from the vantage of the late twentieth century, the twenty-first-century analytic of the "DL" similarly offers a way of recuperating Hughes's closetedness. Although, as Donnelly concedes in his conclusion, Hughes's "reticence remains a problem," insofar as "it lines up with homophobic silence, then and now," the "existence and persistence of structures like the DL should tell us that these are not only byproducts of that homophobia but represent a felt need on the part of many people to reorganize the way we think about sexuality" and "challenge" the "racial obliviousness of essentialized homo-, hetero- and bisexuality."[60] Hughes's reticent poetics—"Café: 3 a.m." is one of extremely few texts that explicitly refers to homosexuality—can thus be seen in the light of the DL as a strategy of resistance not only against the police state but also against the white gaze, which is by turns fetishistic and essentializing.

In both 1951's *Montage of a Dream Deferred* and 1954's *The Sweet Flypaper of Life,* Hughes's furtive or down-low solicitations of readers in the know—readers perhaps imagined, or idealized, as Black and/or queer—draw upon visuality and the intertexture of the poetic and the photographic. The look, once again, becomes multiplied as an erotic and aesthetic phenomenon, a "problematized mode of knowing" that pertains to the ways in which both persons and artworks can be both intransigent and flirtatious. The former text, Lawrence Goldstein writes, foregrounds the "notion of moving pictures" and "intends to put the reader in mind not only of jazz structure but of the fluidity of film"— another parallel between Julien's essay-film and Hughes's form—"as the poet turns his attention to one scene after another without transition or argument."[61] The numerous vignettes of *Montage* comprise a composite text that bears witness to the unpredictable undulations of daily life in what Hughes describes as "a community in transition," in an introductory note where he also suggests that "this poem on contemporary Harlem, like be-bop, is marked by conflicting changes, sudden nuances" and "sharp and impudent interjections, broken rhythms, and passages sometimes in the manner of the jam session, sometimes the popular song" (*CPLH*, 387). Although Hughes neglects to refer to the work's cinematicity here, it would appear to be coterminous with the "jam" aesthetic he describes musically, for both montage and jazz provide analogs for the jamming together of words, scenes, images, and forms, an aesthetic assemblage whose variety dons the spontaneity of session musicians improvising together.

And yet, Hughes's use of "jam" here to account for the methodology of his work as a whole also offers a more surprising resonance. In the same year that *Montage* was published, a book called *The Homosexual in America: A Subjective Approach* appeared. It was written by Donald Webster Corey, the pseudonym of the gay writer and professor Edward Sagarin, an early figure in the homophile movement. Although, as Martin Duberman notes, Sagarin later became a controversial presence in the conversations around homosexuality and argued in his later years that it should be pathologized as a form of deviance, his 1951 book was perhaps "the first full-scale nonfiction account of gay life in the United States," particularly by "an author [who] spoke as an insider, an avowed homosexual."[62] In a chapter on linguistic patterns, the author states that although "*gay* is used throughout the United States and Canada, *straight* is hardly known on the West coast," and in San Francisco "the gay circles refer to other people as *jam*: 'She's gay, but her husband's jam,' a person will say."[63] Corey concedes that the term was also used on the East Coast, if less regularly, and the OED traces usages in 1930s Massachusetts. While it is unclear whether "jam" as a gay slang term would have been in Hughes's lexicon, it does offer another kind of optic upon the aesthetic variety of his work, with the suggestion that his composite poetic-photographic texts render a hybrid sexuality, too— heterosexuality as mediated, covertly and colloquially, by a queer vision.

In this regard jam, as both a jazz term and a gay term, shares in the poetics of the DL and the fact that, as Donnelly writes, "Hughes's most erotically charged poems are heterosexual scenes" where the poet's "cross-dressing" as female speakers offers a perspective through which he "can explore masculinity as the object of desire."[64] This feature of Hughes's writing again refers back to Whitman, whose "twenty-ninth bather" in *Leaves of Grass* is the consummate example of what Michael Davidson describes as the poet's adoption of "a feminine position in order to participate erotically with other males," such that "sexual and textual acts interlinks in ways that force the reader to become, as it were, a third participant in Whitman's mediated desire."[65] This central act of looking in Whitman's text itself looks back at its readers. A version of this figure—the woman who watches from her "fine house by the rise of the bank" and "hides handsome and richly drest aft the / blinds of the window" (*LG*, 34) to first watch and then, more ethereally, to join the young men bathing—also manifests in Hughes's work. She can be found not in a poem, however, but a photograph, a Roy DeCarava image that emerges around halfway through the narrative of *The Sweet Flypaper of Life*. The photo shows a woman sitting in a window, the translucent net curtains parted above her, as she looks outside into the daylight.[66] She is facing away from the camera, with the emphasis of the photograph being upon what remains unseen, for the woman's vantage is focal to the image but inscrutable to the viewer, though we presume the aerial shot of young Harlemites walking the streets on the next page offers a glimpse at what she sees. Below the photograph, Hughes's caption reads:

> Every so often, ever so once in a while, somedays a woman gets a chance to set in her window for a minute and look out.
> New York is not like back down South with not much happening outside. In Harlem something is happening all the time, people are going every which-a-way.[67]

While the image, viewed by itself, could suggests any number of readings, from the voyeurism of female desire to the relegation of women to private and interior spaces, Hughes's narration ties it to the plot at hand. *The Sweet Flypaper of Life* is narrated by Sister Mary Bradley, an "elderly, pious and hardworking African American woman" who "tells of the various travails of her extended family, their ups and downs, their children [. . .] and through this the various vicissitudes of urban life."[68] If we attribute the gaze shown in this image to Sister Mary, as Hughes and DeCarava's photo-text instructs us to do, it becomes a proud and wholesome look upon the "every which-a-way" of daily life in Harlem, shot through with a recollection of life in the South. Her way of seeing, from one or several stories up, is ostensibly aboveboard; it may be a little nosey, but it also serves simply to celebrate the vibrancy of the Harlemites, young and old, who can be seen walking outside on the street.

Sonia Weiner suggests, however, that in his text Hughes adopted a "trickster strategy, which not only appealed to the white publishers and their readership, but also spoke to African American readers through a complex network of signifying, conveying meanings that might have escaped many non-African American readers."[69] The "trickster, who can weave a web of words in order to mask meaning" shows us that "behind or beneath every stereotypical reading of the narrative, an alternative reading exists that denies the stereotype, belies the literal meaning, and resurrects the power of the image" (156). The screen, or some form of it, is once again reclaimed in the construction of this "trickster" aesthetic: "Like a smoke screen, the words of Hughes's narrator provide a way of reading the images without actually seeing their subjects in all their complexity, paving the way for the book's publication" (162). In a series of readings of sequences in the text, Weiner argues that moments of friction between text and image open up a suggestive hermeneutic space in which the potentially stereotypical elements of the work—such as De-Carava's quasi-documentary aesthetic, which risks playing to the white pseudoethnographic gaze, and the narrative voice Hughes constructs for Sister Mary, which at times resembles the trope of the "mammy" figure—are overturned and subverted, if only for readers in the know.

If Hughes's narration proscribes a more limited and limiting narrative alongside the images, which in turn provokes us to think about the nature of Black representation itself, as Weiner argues here, I would like to build upon her work in suggesting that this quality of the photo-text similarly figures unspoken desires, which are expressed once again, as in the image of the woman behind the window reminiscent of Whitman, in terms of looking. *The Sweet Flypaper of Life* is a work concerned throughout with looking—the cover image shows a young girl's eyes looking directly out at the viewer—and the photograph of the woman looking out of the window ushers in a series of images that reflects upon the optical arena of everyday Harlem. Various street personages are shown—women, children, a man sitting with a baby on a stoop, which is the Harlem equivalent of the "front porches" common to houses in the South, as Sister Mary tells us.[70] "But almost everywhere where there's something to set on or lean on," she continues, "somebody is setting or leaning. In what few parks there is, some just set on a park bench [...] and hold their hands."[71] The photograph that accompanies this caption is of a well-dressed man sitting alone on a park bench, looking into the distance, while on the next page the same image is shown again except now as a close-up shot of his hands, in an approximation of the filmic syntax of zooming in. This pair of images is somewhat inscrutable, its exact inference unclear. Is the implication that many people in Harlem can be found "setting or leaning," which, like the figure of Sister Mary's nephew Rodney and his "lazy somewhat perfunctory lifestyle," risks "stereotyping a particular version of African American manhood"?[72] Or is the man waiting for something, or someone? The zooming in on his hands is at once leading, by suggesting a significance for this detail of his comportment, and leads us nowhere, leaving us with the lingering sense of something unspoken.

The text continues on the next double page with the sentence: "Yet there is so much to see in Harlem!"[73] The "yet" is curious, both a swift moving on but also, perhaps, an exoneration of the man from the picture before—his behavior may be strange, or sedentary, and *yet* "there is so much to see in Harlem!," so who can blame him for looking? More intriguingly still, this sentence is the caption to an image of a street with a long fence, with two men looking through holes in it like peeping toms. Although it is clearly intended for comic effect and engages in a form of visual word play, where we see that what there is "to see" is in fact people themselves trying to see something, but it also inflects this sequence of optically focused images with a sense of the scopophilic or voyeuristic. As with the image of the woman behind the curtain, we cannot see what these men see, but this time the optical scenario is in reverse, for they are looking from the vantage of a public space into a private one. Although these respective images of men looking simply pass by, giving way to images of torn down tenements and street vendors, they establish an undercurrent in which looking is felt as something furtive and mysterious. Thus, when this sequence of reflections concludes with Sister Mary's statement "Somebody always passing,"[74] which accompanies an aerial shot of a man walking the street in a suit and hat, it is hard not to think of passing's wider resonances throughout Hughes's Harlem corpus, where he "invite[s] the reader to the position" where "lines of difference [...] cross" in order to observe the "closet door as a meeting place of queer and non-queer identities."[75] Such observations are at play in a whole range of transient tableaux, from the passing moment of interracial contact on a subway platform in "Subway Face" to the issue of racial passing in the short story "Passing"[76] and the passing from uptown to downtown, as in the poem of the same name (*CPLH*, 417).

Indeed, this image of passing in *The Sweet Flypaper of Life* illuminates that Hughes's cruising of the reader through this hybrid work is often intratextual in nature, which is to say that he recovers sites and motifs from his poetic texts in order to gesture, albeit furtively, in particular directions. Another example of this is the subway sequence earlier in the book, which begins with the image of someone seen descending behind the distinctive railings of a subway entrance, with Sister Mary's reflection that "I done rid a million subway cars, and went back and forth to work a million days for that Rodney."[77] In this same passage, just above the image that immediately follows, of a subway car empty but for a lone passenger reading a paper, Sister Mary prefaces it with a quasi-imperative caption that she employs throughout the book: "Now you take the subway:" This deictic labeling of particular images not only suggests that the reader's seeing of an image is in fact a taking or a taking in, as if we ourselves possessed the capacities of a camera; this specific sentence is also almost identical, linguistically, to a line from "Subway Face": "Now you take the Harlem train uptown." The echo of that poem, with its focus on loss and transience, cannot help but inflect the solitude of this image, its almost eerie rendering of a passenger with no other subway faces to connect with. "It's lonesome at night," Sister Mary reminds us, beneath a photograph of a woman standing alone on a subway platform, "But at the rush hour—well, all it took was the Supreme Court to decide on mixed schools, but the rush hour in the subway mixes everybody—white, black, Gentile, and Jew—closer than you ever are to your relatives."[78] This caption directly recalls the compositional situation of "Subway Rush Hour," from *Montage of a Dream Deferred*. Just as that poem hints at an interracial erotics in its description of "Mingled / breath and smell / so close" (*CPLH*, 423), the double-voicedness of Sister Mary's musing similarly gets at the potentially erotic intimacy of the subway, for while being "closer than you ever are to your relatives" has a spatial and respectable meaning when uttered by Sister Mary, it simultaneously hints at a kind of closeness that exceeds the familial, like Whitman's delineation in "Among the Multitude" of a stranger "Acknowledging none else, not parent, wife, husband, brother, / child, any nearer than I am" (*LG*, 115).

The Sweet Flypaper of Life is thus a fitting title for Hughes and De-Carava's hybrid text, for flypaper, like the work itself, is palimpsestic in nature, capturing and layering the things that seek to pass it by. However gruesome this eponymous image may be, it is recuperated by the metaphorical sweetness—figured by the designed sticky sweetness of flypaper—that is conferred upon life itself, a life full of noticing and capturing, in contrast to the "bitter dream" of those who have left Harlem in the poem "Passing" (*CPLH*, 417). In fact, as works both invested in the textual and the photographic, *Sweet Flypaper* and *Montage* share a fixation upon sweetness that is bound up with questions of looking and of representation more broadly. For example "Island [2]," the final poem in *Montage* (and the second called "Island"), imagines Harlem's position "Between two rivers / North of the park" in terms of the color line, but also of taste and sweetness: "Black and white, / Gold and brown—/ Chocolate-custard / Pie of a town" (*CPLH*, 429). This conception of Harlem's multiplicity as delectable resembles one of Hughes's straightest and stickiest poems, "Harlem Sweeties," from the 1942 collection *Shakespeare in Harlem*, which is set, playfully, in the Sugar Hill area of Harlem and instructs its readers to "Cast your gims / On this sepia thrill: / Brown sugar lassie, / Caramel treat / Honey-gold baby / Sweet enough to eat" (*CPLH*, 245). Enumerating forms of "feminine sweetness" among the Black and brown women of Harlem, Hughes renders the erotic specular economy of heterosexual Harlem as a "luscious" and delectable milieu, and in so doing reclaims a fetishizing language that might merely be fetishistic and diminishing in the wrong hands, in a manner akin to the way he repurposes the potentially stereotypical nature of Sister Mary's narration to more subversive hermeneutic ends in *Sweet Flypaper.*

The *Montage* poem "125th Street" (*CPLH*, 407) similarly engages the act of linguistic reclamation in coded and confectionary terms:

Face like a chocolate bar
full of nuts and sweet.

Face like a jack-o'-lantern
candle inside.

Face like a slice of melon,
grin that wide.

Returning to the faciality of public urban space—the title could be referring to the street itself, one of Harlem's main thoroughfares, or to the
subway station of the same name—this poem evokes a veritable "jam":
crowded, "full," and "sweet." It enacts in miniature the sequence's larger
principle of montage in offering a series of faces encountered on 125th
Street and visualized as part of daily life's sweetness. While the first two
images conjure faces whose appeal lies within, either as the "nuts" in
a chocolate bar or the light inside a "lantern," the third is a face whose
appeal lies in its exteriorization, a "grin" the width of a "slice of melon."
This final image invokes erotics of the smile as a collusive and affective
gesture, like the "secrecy our smiles take on" in Frank O'Hara's poem
"Having a Coke with You" (*CP*, 360), but it also points clearly at the
politics of the watermelon as a racialized symbol. This "particular fruit,"
as Hughes himself writes in a 1944 letter, has "been used lo these many
years to make Negroes a funny picture race."[79] Indeed, the image of the
watermelon smile has continued to be a site of political wrangling for
contemporary Black poets like Terrance Hayes, whose 2002 poem "Sonnet" repeats the line "We sliced the watermelon into smiles" fourteen
times, and exposes through incantation the reductiveness of watermelon's associations to Black culture.[80]

In jamming together the various loaded matter of this poem—a
"chocolate bar," a "melon," a "grin"—Hughes's "125th Street" both creates and critiques a "funny picture." It is, in this regard, like another *Montage* poem aptly titled "Movies" (*CPLH*, 395):

The Roosevelt, Renaissance, Gem, Alhambra:
Harlem laughing in all the wrong places

      at the crocodile tears
      of crocodile art

that you know
in your heart
is crocodile:

    (Hollywood
    laughs at me,
    black—
    so I laugh
    back.)

In its critique of Hollywood's racist depictions for the pleasures of the white audiences (and indeed the word "crocodile" could easily be replaced here by the word "white"), this poem crystallizes the nature of Hughes's resistance to the white gaze. Harnessing African American clichés in his late, quasi-photographic works, Hughes "laugh[s] back" not only at Hollywood but at an entire image culture in which Black bodies are either ridiculed, exoticized, or fetishized, as if it were all just a "funny picture."[81] Hughes's riffing upon sweetness in these late works conjures images of Blackness and interraciality that elude the tyranny of the screen and thus laugh, as in this poem, "in all the wrong places." Although these images do not pertain particularly to queer desire in a manner akin to Julien's recovery of Hughes's work, they light upon a contested interpretive space where suggestive meanings emerge, and desire is made legible, out of the interplay between the visual, the verbal, and the unsaid. In looking for Langston, then, perhaps we need look no further than the closing montage of Julien's "movie," interspersed with close-up shots of its characters smiling and laughing "back" at us through the fourth wall of the camera, before they disappear entirely, ready in waiting for the "finding and seeking."

4

Frank O'Hara's Moving Pictures

Looking for Hustlers

In June 1963, Frank O'Hara went to a dinner party at the musician Charles Turner's apartment, where he met an African American hustler called Joe. As O'Hara mentions in a letter to Larry Rivers, Joe was tall and attractive and looked like singer and actor Harry Belafonte, though he described himself in conversation rather more campily, using the moniker of Hollywood icon Marlene Dietrich.[1] This quasi-cinematic figure, remembered passingly in this letter, seems a prime example of the poet's well-documented—or much-rumored— sexual preference for Black men, and for the particular kind of masculinity embodied by the figure of the hustler.[2] Hustlers, as Barry Reay argues in his history of them, are defined as "male prostitutes who paraded their masculinity and who were paid for sex with (nearly always) men" and often viewed interchangeably with "trade," those "ostensibly straight and similarly masculine men, often those in uniform, who would engage in same-sex sex."[3] O'Hara, Reay suggests, had a particular penchant for ostensibly heterosexual men and would often bring sailors back to his apartment in the 1950s.[4] And just as the inventory of New York hustler types is a capacious one—from sailors and soldiers to longshoremen from Brooklyn or laborers from New Jersey—the number of gay male New York writers who have dallied with hustlers both on and off the page is extensive. The literary history of gay New York is populated with them.

O'Hara observed his exchange with Joe in a tangible narrative context by suggesting to Rivers that it was like a scene from John Rechy's cruising novel, *City of Night*. Rechy's novel, published that same year and reviewed by O'Hara in *Kulchur* magazine,[5] tells the story of gay street life in the 1960s from the perspective of a hustler, and memorably begins with a panoptic view: "Later I would think of America as one vast City of Night stretching gaudily from Times Square to Hollywood Boulevard [. . .]. America at night fusing its darkcities into the unmistakable shape of loneliness."[6] The prevalence of the movies in the novel and in this opening reflection, where Times Square suggests the (in)famous Forty-Second Street movie theaters and Hollywood Boulevard stands in for the studio system as a whole, is pertinent. As Reay writes, it is "fitting that that temple of fantasy, the motion picture house, was so closely associated with hustler sex" and was a "primary site for homosexual contact" from the 1930s and 1940s onward.[7] In this chapter, I will argue that O'Hara's well-known love of the movies is closely related to his engagements with gay cruising. The movie theater seems a sensible place to start, not least because it appears throughout his poetry as a site of heightened sensation where cruising can happen. The poem "Ave Maria," for example, suggests that the movie theater is as good a place as any to pick up (or be picked up by) strangers, where watching a movie and an anonymous sexual encounter are simultaneous ways of being "truly entertained" (*CP*, 372). "In the Movies" puns on the simultaneous sense of location that watching a film enacts, where one is both "alone," depending upon "the screen for accompaniment," and also aboard "a voyage to Africa" (*CP*, 208), transported away from these surroundings by the visual narrative one is watching. The viewer is thus both *in* the movie theater and *in* the movie itself, splashing away "the afternoon / in the movies / and in the mountains."

In this poem such simultaneity also has erotic connotations, and the sexual potential of the movie theater is both immediate—the speaker is sat "with my own prick" and addressing the "Ushers! Ushers" who "seek me with your lithe flashlights!" (207)—but also pertains to the mediation of images, and the speaker's beguilement by the phantasmagoria of the screen and the ambiguous "point of intersection a foot in front of me" (206). Sarah Riggs writes of this poem as describing the "structure of spectatorship" and the "various sites of slippage in the flesh-to-image encounter," as though the cinema screen negotiates an "invitation to fleshly desires in the absence of a corporeal body."[8] In this sense, movie theaters are not only the site of possible anonymous sexual encounters, but the site of a more profound erotics of seeing, where the visual illusions of spectatorship in the dark involve an ambiguity that is inherently titillating in its difficulty. Darkness is variously important to this poem, with ambivalent results, for as Peter Stoneley writes, "blackness" for O'Hara "is the desired black man, but it is also dark spaces which permit the impermissible," and these meanings appear simultaneously in this poem.[9] Although there is the suggestion of a cruising or hustling encounter in the theater itself, as lines concerned with language such as "this stranger collects me like a sea-story / and now I am part of his marine slang" give way to the mention of "a poem written in blackface" (*CP*, 208), O'Hara's "invocation to black phallic being" in this poem has a "sense of quotation and refraction, in that the black figures are familiar Hollywoodized stereotypes: the slave field deep in the south, and African chiefs and princes," such that we might conceive of this encounter as one where the speaker is "spellbound by the enormities of the screen and of 'Africa.'"[10] Like Hughes's "Movies," O'Hara's poem posits the cinema as a literal iteration of the "screen" of Blackness that is described by Fanon. Mark Goble argues, in a reading of the poem "Vincent and I Inaugurate a Movie Theatre," that for O'Hara the movie theater demonstrates that "there is fantasy aplenty right in America, 'our country's black and white' past of innumerable Hollywood films replete with racist slapstick, exoticized others, and sublime spectacles of American ideology," not least the Black Mammy figure, like the maid character played by Hattie McDaniel in *Gone with the Wind,* whom O'Hara refers to in this poem, a cliché to which Hughes's Sister Mary Bradley from *The Sweet Flypaper of Life* also knowingly bears some resemblance.[11]

Both Stoneley and Goble argue that O'Hara's penchants for both Blackness and for movies are not uncritical fixations. Stoneley suggests that "O'Hara's invocation of blackness as the primitive" seems "to accept racist clichés but also to throw them into question," while Goble suggests "that O'Hara argues incessantly with the movies and in so doing makes a series of points about the relationships between language and the visual," and these "arguments with film [. . .] swerve at surprising moments into images of an America whose symbolic coherence is hopelessly intercut with images of racial difference and ideological manipulation."[12] In the light of such critical recuperations, how might we then read O'Hara's offhand description of Joe the hustler, a passage where, as in "In the Movies," the screen of Blackness has multiple meanings? Joe, who evidently embodies for O'Hara a certain kind of Black masculinity, is described as being both like camp icon Marlene Dietrich *and* popular Black entertainer Harry Belafonte. The substitution here of a Black man for Belafonte is vexing, in so far as perceptions of likeness between people of color frequently underpin offensive misapprehensions and microaggressions. This slippage between Joe and a star of the screen also speaks to a larger tendency in O'Hara's work to engage cruising as an aesthetic economy, where potential hookups are rendered in relation to photographic or cinematic likenesses and to the erotic fantasies attached to movie culture. The fantasy of sleeping with a hustler thus becomes synonymous with the fantasy of sleeping with a movie star. And such looks and hookups do not only occur at parties or in the theaters, but on the streets of a city O'Hara once called "Sodom-on-Hudson" ("Commercial Variations," *CP*, 85), where fantasies become daydreams that seek to collapse the gap between the cruiser and the stranger.

To look to O'Hara's meeting with Joe the hustler as an introductory example is to observe a mode of looking at a flippant extreme, and it also calls to mind the poet's reference to the "Negro" who "stands in a doorway with a / toothpick, languorously agitating" in the lunch poem "A Step Away from Them" (*CP*, 257). Aaron Deveson reads this moment as an example of O'Hara's tendency, shared with Edwin Denby (whose 1964 lecture "Dancers, Buildings and People in the Streets" also observes the everyday motions of sailors and African Americans, among others), toward "generalizations about ethnic and cultural difference," made legible and erotic in the glare of everyday urban space.[13] To look beyond these instances toward other examples, then, where the masculinity being "photographed" (to once again borrow Silverman's gloss of Fanon) is predominantly white working class, is not simply to exonerate O'Hara from these tendencies, but rather to identify a larger mode of erotic looking that is evidently capable of fetishization. This larger mode is given expression in *City of Night* when Rechy's narrator walks around Times Square; he notices the "racks of magazines with photographs of almost-naked youngmen like an advertisement for this street," and then, "the army of youngmen [. . .] like photographs in a strange exhibition: slouched invitingly or moving back and forth restlessly."[14] Rechy's description, which enacts a slippage between photographs and persons, and between the pages of a magazine and the cruising spaces of the street, renders the look as an instrument of visualization. In so doing, it performs exactly the kind of metaphorical work that is central to the argument of this book, and could apply equally to any of the writers I am concerned with. In O'Hara's work, however, the copresence of still and moving images—of "slouched" statues and "moving" bodies—is of particular importance, and I will thus begin by attending to one of his best-known movie texts, one that articulates the look of cinema as a vision both in, and of, motion.

Marvellous Appearances

O'Hara's 1955 poem "To the Film Industry in Crisis" is addressed to Hollywood itself and enumerates almost thirty of the industry's stars. But in its lineation, it also extends a tribute to Whitman, whose influence can be felt numerous times throughout O'Hara's work, from "memorizing Whitman" in "Dolce Colloquio" (*CP*, 150) to the sonic inheritance of "A Whitman's Birthday Broadcast with Static" (*CP*, 224). It is often as though he is tuning in to his forebear on some oblique frequency, but the particular reemergence of Whitman's long line is palpable in "To the Film Industry," which begins with an invocation that recalls the ample anaphoric constructions of "Not . . . nor . . . nor" found in Whitman. O'Hara's opening lines in turn revive the democratic objective of Whitman's syntax, the task of reevaluating received distinctions between things and persons, and his conception of a reconstructed cultural hierarchy resembles the ethos of Whitman's urban poem "City of Orgies," where it is in fact "Not the pageants [. . .] nor the bright windows, with goods in them," but the more ephemeral "flash of eyes offering me / love," which "repay me" (*LG*, 107). These negative constructions bear a peculiar stylistic function, at once lofty and cumbersome. They intensify and defer feeling simultaneously, and even mark a turn toward the grandeur of epic. In giving "credit where it's due" (*CP*, 232) to Hollywood movies, but by way of negated apostrophes to such institutions as the "Catholic Church" or the "American Legion," O'Hara's list echoes the principle of inclusion that informs much of Whitman's work, and offers an extension of his quip in "Personism" that "only Whitman and Crane and Williams, of the American poets, are better than the movies" (*CP*, 498).

Making such lists can itself be an act of love: as Wayne Koestenbaum writes, "when O'Hara makes a list of items, he adores them. Otherwise, why list them?"[15] By taking stock in this way, this poem suggests a different pace to other list-poems that seem, to Koestenbaum, "breathlessly uttered" in "long lines whose speediness announces their credo (a velocity without futurism's militaristic seriousness)."[16] Such poems, like "Poem (O sole mio, hot diggety, nix)" (*CP*, 367), may attain a certain speed in their associative randomness, but there is nothing inherently speedy about long lines themselves, even if they maintain the illusion of some proportional relation that length and quantity bear to pace, as units which can impose breathlessness upon the voice that tries to read them aloud. According to this conflation, a line may work to curtail the excitement of its passions, or it may give in to that "ecstasy of always bursting forth!" ("Meditations in an Emergency," *CP*, 197), but in either case this negotiation of containment implicitly confers momentum and can be mapped onto line endings. O'Hara's own 1957 recording of the poem plays out slowly. Commissioned for a radio show by *Evergreen Review* founder Barney Rosset, the recording also features the voice of Jane Freilicher and musical accompaniment by John Gruen.[17] Gruen has described how his "offbeat musical noodling" led to the decision to "have a piano roll be the accompaniment [. . .] a Steinway Duo-Art which played piano rolls by the hour," and which for this recording played "a popular song from the thirties" as "Frank and Jane" each read specific lines, with "wonderfully *outré*" results.[18] In choosing a song from the thirties, Gruen roots O'Hara and Freilicher's reading of the list of names in the cultural past they are largely drawn from, just as the self-playing and mechanized piano melody imitates the kind of presence that movie stars inhabit.

As phantoms of the screen, stars occupy a vexed form of liveness; they are made visible by a projector and destined for repetitions, perhaps accompanied by melodies that roll on a Steinway. This choice of the piano roll acknowledges the way that O'Hara's poem veers closely to the automated melody of the roll call. Rolling out in this way as a unique "experience," passed between two voices over music, the list's most "distinct" notes sound at once glamorous and elegiac. Enthusiasm is counterbalanced with solemnity, as if O'Hara and Freilicher are comperes introducing the stars one by one in the glittery roll call of a Hollywood pageant, or the "in memoriam" segment of an awards ceremony. These stars are after all largely those of yesteryear, drawn from the Golden Age of the Hollywood studio picture that precedes the poem's eponymous crisis of the 1950s. Koestenbaum writes of the way O'Hara's poems can stage a "time blur," an "undoing of chronology and teleology" where the poet "takes artifacts from 1930s culture and propels them forward" into the "now" of the poem as "crystallizations of unfulfilled longing."[19] The list can thus serve not so much to "blur" the present with recourse to the past entities it enumerates, but rather to name a new present which hangs suspended not only in historical time but in the temporality of the work itself, as something made up of constituent parts and read in sequence.

O'Hara's constellation of stars is temporally various in this way. It operates on Hollywood's "star system" and the "flash" that Walter Benjamin describes, and lists film actors made present to the popular imaginary not only through the rolling camera of cinema but the flash of photographic stills. Although, as Mark Goble writes, it pays to remain suspicious of the idea of "a basic equivalence between certain techniques of film editing—jump-cuts, swish pans, fade-outs, cutaways, and wipes—and some of O'Hara's signature techniques for directing readerly attention," this poem does unfold in units comparable to flashes, with each film star invoked fleetingly in a list that adheres consistently to the formula of name plus image, like the not unlike "strange exhibition" Rechy's narrator notes.[20] Each actor is recalled with the memory of a physical idiosyncrasy, like "Jeanette MacDonald of the flaming hair" or Sue Carrol sitting "for eternity" on the "damaged fender of a car" (*CP*, 232). O'Hara's list is distinguished from mere roll call by preserving each star's "particularity" and seeking in turn to grant them a sense of "eternity." It recalls these stars not only with recourse to their monikers but their motions, like the equivalent of a film-still reanimated. Even the stiller-seeming portraits or poses suggested by these images, such as MacDonald's, are cast with present participles in "flaming" vitality.

In this sense the poem reads intriguingly alongside an essay by a different McDonald, a New York film critic and contemporary of O'Hara's at Harvard, whose piece "When Words Fail" consists simply of the names of film stars (many of which overlap with this poem) arranged into alphabetized paragraphs, such as "Martin Gabel. Greta Garbo. John Garfield."[21] McDonald is writing in the 1980s and watching these stars revived by the syndication of their films on cable television's Hall of Fame, many of them by this time dead. The paradox of his essay's title—paratextually designating a failure of words as the principle of a piece made up *only* of pairs of words, of which none comprise full sentences—suggests that in the context of such retrospection, it is names in all their specificity that embody the aura of stardom, not words as generally conceived, which could perhaps only "fail" in their vagaries. O'Hara was certainly alive to encountering movie stars from his childhood as part of the then-recent advent of television, but what is curious in his poem is the feeling that even at this point in time, when many of them were still alive, these stars are firmly out of reach. That they are, in this sense, like the already dead.

The poem's address to the stars can only do so much in reviving their immediate presence, insofar as they themselves are not fixed objects for representation and are in their own way intangible and hologrammatic projections of the silver screen. That the poem can only hail these figures verbally in a loving celluloid ekphrasis further places them out of reach, and they are rendered only as imaginings or recollections of existing reproductions. At the end of the poem O'Hara instructs these "reels" to roll on "as the great earth rolls on!" (*CP*, 233), in conversation with Whitman's poem "A Song of the Rolling Earth," which itself contains the related insight that "bodies are words, myriads of words," and in the "best poems re-appears the body, man's or woman's" (*LG*, 184). O'Hara's wish that they may "illumine space with your marvellous appearances" (*CP*, 232) contains echoes of this Whitmanian sentiment; the sense that bodily presence can reappear through acts of inscription. In this sense it is like the distinction between naming a film or a star one admires on the one hand, and illustrating that admiration on the other; let me count the ways. The iteration of Sue Carrol or Jeanette MacDonald's physical presence in the poem seeks both to justify and enact their illumination of space beyond its instance on celluloid, which passes in a flash.

The transience threatening these "marvellous appearances" is not only that of the immediate unfolding of a film in time, then, but the relation of this to a graver sense of passing. A flash is neither quite fast nor slow; it simultaneously suggests the temporary or partial while providing the frame for the snapshot, an image whose ephemerality becomes a paradoxical form of lastingness, a crystallization through an aperture fixed. The film stars of this poem are captured at a unique threshold of perception; both the point in history where they face impending obsolescence, becoming passé in the context of the industry and its machinations, and a more profound sense of passing. This latter resonance touches upon a perhaps primally anxious paradox of reproduction; the sense that seeing people captured alive and in motion on-screen for all posterity is necessarily referential to their death, and that these apparitions come to acquire a particularly strange air in the wake of their referents. Images of the passed possess both a magic and a melancholy;

they intensify absence just as they can remedy it momentarily by bringing into vision an iteration of that person, such that the reproduction gains a unique resonance or iconicity in the face of paucity. Being iconic is already the remit of the movie star, whose profession at its heart involves skills of presence, a fact to which O'Hara's poem is alive. The reference to "Marilyn Monroe in her little spike heels reeling through Niagara Falls" (*CP*, 232) embodies this fragile iconicity by invoking both the girlishness of her persona and the attendant sense of vulnerability conferred by knowledge of her death seven years later, which the poem seems hauntingly to anticipate in summoning the tableau of this larger-than-life personage resting so precariously on a "little spike," swamped by the waterfall behind her.

Indeed, like the iconic candle in the wind, O'Hara's descriptions of these stars and their lives appear to flicker. It calls to mind the physical idiosyncrasies of each star at the same time as they fade from view, giving way to the next in the sequence of the list's unfolding. This poem is not explicitly about the death of movie stars, at least not in the same way that O'Hara's poems for James Dean are about his untimely demise, and yet its focus upon passing and fragile tableaux indirectly anticipates the elegiac. The metaphor of actors as stars itself seeks to recuperate them from such fading, and they are enshrined as figures who will continue to "shine" on film and remain accessible as reference points in posterity precisely because their charisma is committed to celluloid, as the saying goes. But their being awarded "eternity" surely requires other forms of commitment, lest the light of their presence be destined to shine no more brightly than that of a battery-powered tea-light, and they are fated to appear only during the graveyard time-slots of cable television, like a piano roll playing to an empty music hall. In the schema of O'Hara's movie poems, these remembered images are only made vivid, and their attendant preservation in a line of poetry is only made possible, by an initial or originary liveness. The importance of the experiential encounter between spectator and movie is foregrounded in "Ave Maria" (*CP*, 372) where O'Hara distinguishes between the vitality of a child's possible trip to the movie theater, which can nurture the "soul / that grows in darkness" (and has the added bonus of perhaps even offering their "first sexual experience"), and the stultification that would afflict the same child "old and blind in front of a TV set," watching movies they weren't allowed to watch in childhood. Alternatively, this encounter may play out in someone or other's apartment with a gathering of friends, and Joe LeSueur recalls that O'Hara would often have such movie nights with John Button and James Schuyler.[22] In either case, movies for O'Hara must offer a clear sense of occasion, must be experientially distinct from the monotony of sitting "old and blind" before a television set. Such occasion can be fulfilled through the relative liveness—of time and place, at least—that a movie theater can offer, as well as the sexual possibilities such a space can tease, or else the intimacy and shared references of a viewing with friends. Occasion is necessary to make the act of viewing worth preserving, for giving "credit where it's due."

In this vein, it is then not enough that these beloved stars are preserved on reels of celluloid but that these reels "roll on"; that Monroe "reels" on vividly by reappearing in the "now" of a poem, which thus restages that encounter in its initial immediacy. This relation to the moving image seems not only like that of the poet but the zealous fan, even the archivist. O'Hara's enthusiasm for movies and their stars is well documented; his was a form of fandom which critics have not neglected to identify as queer. Laurence Goldstein, writing of this poem's historical moment as one where "the charismatic power of the movies" is for the "first time in its brief history" felt to be approaching "the passé," suggests that it is an instance of O'Hara exemplifying the camp sensibility.[23] The gay male love of female movie stars is a well-worn trope of camp taste, and "To the Film Industry in Crisis" does appear to be steeped in such a culture. In his classic study of stars and of the relationship between Judy Garland and gay men, Richard Dyer identifies Jeanette MacDonald—O'Hara's flaming figure—as being "well established as a camp queen," such that when Garland refers to her in the opening of the song "San Francisco" in her 1961 Carnegie Hall performance, "it was enough to mention MacDonald's name to get a camp response" from her largely gay male audience.[24] But if the shared codes of camp, defined by a love of the excessive and artificial, offer one way of accounting for the gay male love of movie stars, it does not tell the whole story. Garland is a suggestive case study in that, as Dyer notes, it is not just her sense of camp or androgyny that has endeared her to gay audiences, but also her ordinariness and the "emotional quality" of her performance, which demonstrates that the "gay sensibility holds together qualities that are elsewhere felt as antithetical: theatricality and authenticity."[25] Indeed, Joe LeSueur sees "To the Film Industry" in precisely these terms, suggesting that if this poem is even camp at all, it is only of the "high" or "serious" variety, because "Frank shamelessly meant every word—*felt* every word."[26]

"Homosexuality in the movies," Vito Russo writes in his classic study *The Celluloid Closet*, "whether overtly sexual or not, has always been seen in terms of what is or is not masculine."[27] It is telling how neatly Russo's description of Hollywood cinema maps onto the realm of the street hustler once again, in a move away from a camp fixation with the female. If the interior spaces of movie-watching or movie-going are associated with certain forms of love (the last section of "In the Movies" ends with the lines "If love is born from this projection [. . .] / I love you" (*CP*, 209), while "To the Film Industry" proffers a love of the passing and the passé in the face of a crisis), the cinematic economies of affect and desire outside of such spaces are altogether different. In his essay "Leaving the Movie Theater," Roland Barthes describes the "reverie" of the movie theater experience, where the "dark" is both the "very substance" of such a state and "the 'color' of a diffused eroticism," and in his formulation the "movie house" is "a site of availability (even more than cruising)" that accommodates "the inoccupation of bodies" which "best defines modern eroticism [. . .] that of the big city."[28] For Barthes, it is "in this urban dark that the body's freedom is generated," and such freedom gives way to a porosity not unlike the situation of "idleness, leisure, free time" that prefigures the decision to go to the movies.[29] But what happens after the credits roll, and you return from the libidinal darkness to the peripatetic cruising space of the "big city"? Looking beyond O'Hara's poetry and toward his dalliances with film itself, the next section of this chapter will take such a walk.

Brandos of the Boulevard

Two film texts from the bookends of O'Hara's oeuvre invoke a cinematic mode of attention as a feature of gay cruising. One of them, the beginning "for a movie scenario," was jotted in his Harvard journal from 1948 (and published only posthumously); the other, a more complete film script in collaboration with Alfred Leslie, was still being written a few months before O'Hara's death in 1966. The Harvard scenario lays out a familiar scene, perhaps its first iteration in O'Hara's writing, which has distinctly European influences:

We are looking up a street: noon light, early spring. A row of
street lamps like sick tulips blooms metallically in the sun as
a speck on the distant stretch of sidewalk grows larger, approaches. It is a man in his early thirties wearing a restrained
simper, a lavender tie, and such an elegant stroll that he might
almost have gone to school with Harold Acton. He is humming
a song of his own composition entitled *Your Room Is Awfully
Pleasant but I Think I'll Run Along*; it is, of course, Gerard Purble,
and as his eyes roll about with what we immediately recognize
is an habitually avid curiosity the camera takes over their action,
scooting under taxicabs, into store windows, peering into faces,
down bodices, hurrying here, lingering there, distorting features
and accidentals (to be worked out in detail), etc.[30]

These images, the most narratively coherent of the "scenario," echo the
lunch-poet figure O'Hara would later come to inhabit in New York; the
man in his thirties in a tie, strolling the streets with an "avid curiosity"—
and perhaps a slightly greater sense of workday urgency—and sporting
a look inflected as queer. The layers of visual detail in this scene range
from fairly obvious associations, like that between simpering and effete-
ness, to signs that involve a more particular knowledge of the contemporary homosexual aesthetic. For one, the reference to Harold Acton, the
writer and old Etonian who provided some of the inspiration for Evelyn
Waugh's *Brideshead Revisited,* invites a whole host of associations, not
least those of the European aesthete and the age of decadence, which
are hallmarks in the homosexual imagination. Walking is cast here as a
mode of performing social class through its intersection with sexuality.
The "elegant stroll" refers back to a culture embodied by Eton College
and more broadly that of the dandy, and propels the associated qualities
of aestheticism and effeminacy into a contemporary American scene,
where the "sidewalk" replaces the pavement or boulevard.

The lavender tie offers a signal more obviously American than European in alluding to the conflation of the color with homosexuality (concealed or otherwise) that had been used since the 1920s, with one of
its earliest incarnations attributed to Cole Porter's song "I'm a Gigolo."
This phrase was to find a new and unwelcome cultural resonance as the
name for the so-called Lavender Scare that began in February 1950 with
the speech given by Deputy Undersecretary John Peurifoy to Congress.

Peurifoy warned of an infiltration of the federal government by homosexuals in the same month as Senator Joseph McCarthy's speech about such an infiltration by Communists, which ushered in the era of fear that was to form the political backdrop of O'Hara and his wider artistic community's lives in New York for several years. As David K. Johnson writes, the "Red Scare now had a tinge of lavender," as a moral panic which also marked the increasing dangers for public officials of cruising Lafayette Park, Washington's famous cruising spot.[31] Cruising, like the subcultural concealment of homosexuality that characterized its practice at this time, requires a euphemistic language and visual signals that can point in at least two directions, and it is an implicit presence in O'Hara's movie scenario. Even Gerard's "song of his own composition," *Your Room Is Awfully Pleasant but I Think I'll Run Along,* sounds like it could be the ditty of a botched cruise: a quick exit perhaps sung in the leisurely idiom of a Cole Porter musical. This utterance gestures to the camp in its effusive diction ("awfully pleasant") and limp sense of propriety ("but I think I'll run along"), and it conjures a voice equal parts stylized and repressed. In the situation it riffs upon, it also calls to mind the willful humor of contradiction on show in the entry O'Hara writes for Ronald Firbank, another intertextual presence associated with a particular stylistic excess, in his poem "Biographia Letteraria": "I will not go home with you, so perhaps I shall" (*CP*, 464). To be running along or passing by in such a scenario is to play upon the partial vision of the street—passing a desirous stranger and all the while "passing" as straight—and suggests that walking is of especial importance in this performance. In between states of "hurrying here, lingering there," and largely without recourse to the verbal, the walk performs a look which lasts a "second longer" than that of "normal people," to recall O'Hara's jesting reference to the homosexual "look." This look also often refers, like Gerard's, to the gait and gaiety of lavender figures like Acton, as though a peripatetic flamboyance is something one learns by imitation.

This early journal entry is a curious discovery, trying out in a minor key and laying out in miniature, on the streets of Cambridge, Massachusetts, an aesthetics of urban walking that is central to some of O'Hara's best-known New York poems. If sitting before the silver screen is a place to be dazzled by the more glamorous, practiced, and even esoteric motions of movie stars "reclining and wiggling" (*CP*, 232) within the worlds of their cinematic plots, the street's gesture is the walk, a performance that plays out on the sidewalk daily. This walk does not occur inside an already given narrative situation (other than that suggested by factors like the time of day or the neighborhood one is walking in) and thus becomes imaginative fodder for its observer, as a phenomenon out of which a narrative, and speculations as to personhood, might arise. This kind of attention to another's motion is thus distinct, if subtly, from the corresponding way one might catch someone's eye in an interior social setting like a bar or a party. Living openly within the parameters of his queer coterie, O'Hara not only frequented artist's bars like the Cedar Tavern and the San Remo in Greenwich Village, or jazz clubs like the Five Spot, but danced in gay bars like the Old Place, which he pays tribute to in his ebullient 1955 poem "At the Old Place" (*CP*, 223–24). Describing this bar, Joe LeSueur writes: "When I say the place was gay, I don't mean it was anything like what came later, in the sex-crazed seventies, the pre-AIDS period when you sniffed poppers, snorted coke, and had sex on the dance floors of the more raunchy queer joints. No, the Old Place was sweet and innocent, more limp-wristed than S&M or pseudo-macho."[32] O'Hara, LeSueur continues, was only in it for the dancing—"in the time I knew him" he "never cruised gay bars"—but an early work like "All the mirrors in the world," which was written during the period when O'Hara began to visit New York and eventually moved there in the fall of 1951, suggests his familiarity with the ocular mechanism of bar cruising.[33] The speaker imagines his "eyes in, say, the glass / of a public bar" as they "become a / depraved hunt for other re- / flec- tions," for anything "but the old shadowy bruising, / anything but my private haunts" (*CP*, 39), and this scene rhymes multiply ("bruising") with the phenomenon of cruising as a "hunt" in a bar, a self-reflective mirror, and a solution to the "private" pains of repression. And if gay bars were not a regular fixture for O'Hara, who traversed gay New York at a historical precipice, in those years preceding Stonewall which none- theless anticipated the "sex-crazed seventies," he certainly went to a lot of parties, no doubt full of gay men who behaved much as if they had gone to school with Harold Acton.

In the second film text, *Act & Portrait,* a rarely discussed 1966 script devised with Alfred Leslie, the act of cruising on the street is made cine- matic in a number of ways, and unfolds both *as* a film and in relation to film culture. Strangers are conceived of as cinematic characters, or as figures possessing some essence of Hollywood actors. Laying out a walk that begins on Fourteenth Street and finishes in Central Park, this script is a more complete object than the film scenario from the Harvard journal, albeit with its own complex compositional history. In the first instance it seems to share with O'Hara's earlier scenario a passing interest in European aestheticism, including an English paraphrase out of Joris-Karl Huysmans's 1884 novel *À rebours*: "I seek new perfumes, ampler blossoms (and bosoms), untired pleasures."[34] This balmy scene of erotic potential finds metaphorically consonant completion with the "cruising fairies" O'Hara encounters in the next paragraph, on "Seventh Avenue and Greenwich," and these figures invite rumination of a more overtly political nature:

> Like St. Eulalia, I looked at the cruising fairies with compassion. I definitely think that sex should be allowed between consenting adults. The only question is how to become adult. Let them worry about that as long as they're let. Of course nobody wants to be alone, maybe they need the police like Negroes need Mississippi. Consent has nothing to do with it. You look around and you can't find anything to consent to. All you can do is try to forget it. (165)

O'Hara, in his characteristically irreverent approach to political subjects, here repeats words associatively at their beginnings and ends ("consenting adults" to "adult," and "Let" to "let") such that the passage seems continually to digress. It lingers like the men themselves and puns on the sense that there are hustlers among these fairies who are "let" like rent boys. Nevertheless, cruising emerges in the process as the vexed site where a gay political struggle might play out. Such a struggle is made legible by possible forms of intimacy and companionship—"Of course nobody wants to be alone" (165)—that are then obliquely compared to the numerous civil rights struggles of African Americans in Mississippi around this time, evidenced particularly by the murder of three civil rights workers in June 1964.

This passage suggests political awareness by way of indirection, and the speaker's flippant naivety is nonetheless still alive to the sinister social reality being gestured to, even if all one can do "is try to forget about it." The next paragraph recommends as much, making reference to the fact that "Miles is now in Viet Nam. Brave stand. Where was he when the cop hit Julian over the head? Where was I?" (166). These sentences, similarly, seem barely to contain the sarcasm evident in casting Vietnam activism as "brave" just as they nevertheless foreground details of an increasingly repressive city. The vacant building of Julian Beck's Living Theatre is passed earlier in the script's walk—it "sure looks dead, yak" (164)—and Beck himself was imprisoned briefly in 1963 in a conflict with the police over the occupation of the theater space. This is the paradoxical political texture of much of O'Hara's writing; it sidesteps sincere imperatives to collective action while being palpably aware of what might be under threat. Such brushing aside is consonant with what Susan Sontag describes as camp's "comic vision of the world," a sensibility intended to "dethrone the serious" by way of "underinvolvement" and "detachment."[35] Sontag goes as far as to suggest that such a "sensibility is disengaged, depoliticized—or at least apolitical," thus reducing it to a form of complacent triviality without acknowledging the way that the "apolitical" might be performed or harnessed for resistant ends.[36] An insensitive joke might also serve as a way of being in the world: as a quietly defiant refusal to yield to the solemnity of a political reality that has been historically antagonistic toward gay men.

Act & Portrait also includes projections of foreign spaces from the historical present: "It was cold. Soft bombs are falling into our hard Arctic palmtrees. We are softly bombing our insides, our tough skin will splinter, our shell will fall away" (*AN*, 165). This passage seems both surreal and lucid, and invokes a military elsewhere that is inscrutable for being incongruous yet obvious in its reference to wars past and present, and most immediately the aforementioned conflict in Vietnam. Gay cruising is rendered as military several times in O'Hara's work, just as penetration is here made atomic in *Act & Portrait*. The poem "Grand Central" (*CP*, 168–69), which illustrates "wheels" of machinery "thundering," casts the act of fellatio in the train station's latrine thus: "He unzipped the messenger's trousers / and relieved him of his missile, hands / on the messenger's dirty buttocks, / the smoking muzzle in his soft blue mouth." Cruising in "Grand Central" constitutes a rewriting of the body through annihilation. The speaker gestures to "an anonymous body," perhaps his own, that is "reconstructed from a model of poetry" and "riddled with bullets" (*CP*, 168), and such lacerations resemble the way the subject's skin and shell are pierced in *Act & Portrait*. This texture not only gestures toward the situational pain or violence that a cruise gone wrong (or right) might incur, but a more profound sense of threat and domination figured by military conflict, one that could be fatal or indeed "terminal," another word for Grand Central's concourses. By yoking sexual acts to the potential violence—which could be that of the stranger, the police, the militarized state in conflict abroad—O'Hara recuperates the seeming insouciance of these connections by suggesting that cruising is both implicated in these larger realities and can resist them.

To cruise the latrines is also to cruise the frontline of social belonging, or to inhabit a kind of masochistic relation to the police, whom the "cruising fairies" need like "Negroes need Mississippi." Under the flippant "shell" of these instances is an acute questioning of filiation itself, soiled by "dirty buttocks," and this exploration extends further back to the foundation of belonging as constructed by the family. What O'Hara describes in "All the mirrors in the world" (*CP*, 39) as the "shadows / of my childhood" also loom large in the exposures at play in *Act & Portrait*. The sight of two nuns walking by prompts "thoughts of my childhood and dirty underwear. My socks" (*AN*, 165). This is a good example of the way O'Hara sets up the reflective only to deflate it: invoking "dirty underwear" in relation to figures of religion suggests an antagonism between the dirty sexuality of the "depraved hunt" underlying the walk and one's upbringing, until it is deflated by the clarification as "socks." These instances, in the main oblique and ambivalent, draw upon both history and humor, upon phrases torn between seriousness and parody. What is being engaged in is not a straightforwardly serious politics of cruising. Instead, these instances borrow from cruising's textures, shooting indirect glances at its experiential reality and only glimpsing what endangers it, fittingly, in passing.

At first glance, these film texts seem a great distance from the big Hollywood pictures O'Hara eulogizes in "To the Film Industry in Crisis." They are sketches of cruising scenes which range from the aestheticized to the dirty, and have largely been ignored in critical work on O'Hara, although Daniel Kane refers briefly to the "surrealist, libidinal melange" of *Act & Portrait* as "supplementary evidence of O'Hara's participation in the experimental film scene."[37] Such evidence, Kane argues, helps to "rectify the notion that his taste as cineaste was solely popular," and "the disconnect between 'mainstream' and 'avant-garde'" was one that O'Hara "worked to eliminate through his enthusiastic embrace of any number of filmic approaches."[38] Richard Moore's short *USA: Poetry* documentary on O'Hara from 1966 offers further evidence of O'Hara's desire to transgress formal distinctions. In a scene of O'Hara and Alfred Leslie walking down the street, Moore's voiceover suggests that "in part the film script" the two men are writing "is derived from [. . .] 'To the Film Industry in Crisis.'"[39] The connections between these works, an experimental short film on the one hand and a capacious, Whitmanian love letter to Hollywood on the other, are not immediately forthcoming. However, in a filmed outtake of the two men chatting about the film, and following O'Hara's adamant declaration that "I love Truffaut and that's that" (a further corrective to the notion that his love of big studio pictures precluded a leaning also toward the *auteur*), O'Hara asks Leslie, "Do you believe in the star system, Alfred?" The camera ironically moves away from the documentary's stars to focus on Leslie's cat, following its movements, as its owner replies, with an image that should by now sound familiar, "The star system? You mean the heavenly bodies that go by . . . yeah, why not."[40]

This echo of the celestial bodies who "illumine space" in O'Hara's poem speaks to a narrative interest in archetype in *Act & Portrait,* and suggests that the street might have its own star system of spotlit bodies who "go by" ephemerally. At one point, the script's speaker encounters one such body, less heavenly than it is sinister, but nevertheless referential to a "star" quality: "Guys in black leather jackets give me the creeps. Who doesn't want to be Marlon?" (*AN,* 164). Amid the film's associative momentum, with its speaker piling up details of sights, sounds, and thoughts as they appear, this Marlon-wannabe goes by quickly and is not granted a full encounter. Nonetheless, he makes an impression. Like Gerard Purble, whose walk was such that "he might almost have gone to school with Harold Acton," this figure further suggests a physiognomy of the "look" as derived through imitation, his style copied from the cultural trends ushered in by "stars" and the characters they inhabit. So much so, it seems, as to be derivative, for "who doesn't want to be Marlon?" The aura of '50s and '60s Marlon Brando, embodied chiefly by his star turn in *The Wild One* (1953) as the leather-jacketed biker Johnny Stabler and his tour-de-force performance as Stanley Kowalski in the film version of *A Streetcar Named Desire* (1951), "conveyed," Reay writes, "precisely the homoeroticism associated with trade that blended same- and opposite-sex sexualities."[41]

Just as O'Hara "illustrates" in topographical and site-specific cruising poems like "Homosexuality" and "Grand Central" that "gossip and cruising" can appear "as kindred queer practices," Chad Bennett writes, "each forms whose performance of privacy holds out the potential to remap the contours of public spaces"; gossip about the sexual orientations of male movie stars like Brando or James Dean could in turn inform the semiotics of cruising practices.[42] The association of a certain kind of masculine cool and a blue-collar authenticity with "rough trade" recalls the prototype-based "gay semiotics" identified by Hal Fischer, one in which dreaming erotically of a "cowboy" involves not the invention of a new figure but the queering of an iconic masculinity that is ubiquitous in the American imaginary from Western films, for example. Such reveries might be dreams or nightmares; tender or dangerous, and in the world of sexual desire these are not necessarily separate states. Why else does this Marlon look-alike give the speaker of *Act & Portrait,* mock-prudishly, the "creeps"? The appearance of "guys in leather jackets," while highly imitative in so far as it pertains to performing Marlon Brando performing a motorcyclist or a longshoreman, suggests both an erotic potential and a threat of danger. These contiguous variables are at once exciting and can give one "the creeps." This Brando figure exists in chorus with the later apprehension in the script of the "cruising fairies," and these constitutive "types" in cruising may be distinguished from one another according to respective performances of masculinity or effeminacy but can nevertheless cohere in one person looking to be "let." In this regard the "fairy" and the leather-jacketed Marlon belong, as simultaneous extremes, to the same form of role-play that is embodied by the "star" system in which Brando is a leading light.

Writing around the same time as Vito Russo, who in *The Celluloid Closet* traces the imbrication of masculinity and homosexuality on-screen, Boyd McDonald frames the men of the street not only as akin to those of the movies but as their substitute, and addresses what he perceives to be a contemporary lack of masculine wattage:

Motion pictures are for people who like to watch women; the men in pictures, as Bette Davis and [Pauline] Kael herself have said, are not *men.* There's better stuff on the streets, any street; the streets are my cinema, the male whores my Brandos of the boulevard, the only time I see on the streets men like those who appear in pictures—Warren Beatty, Ronnie Reagan, Robert

Taylor, Ryan O'Neal, Robert Redford and so on—is when by coincidence I pass, just as it is letting out, a dance school.[43]

McDonald is here writing of male stardom in the 1980s, although the fey elegance suggested by "dance students" (defiantly unlike "*men*") seems to speak to the sort of vintage male presence O'Hara affirms in his reference to Fred Astaire "of the feet" in "To the Film Industry" (*CP*, 232). While O'Hara displays a wider embrace of movie stars both male and female, McDonald's statement nevertheless speaks to the gendered particularities of charisma in the gay imagination. Watching "women" on-screen speaks to a camp relation to the cinema, as distinct from the more straightforwardly carnal attraction to *men,* who in McDonald's formulation are distinguished thus by eschewing the flourishes of the "men in pictures" or those at "dance school." That is not to say that the men in pictures are not ripe for gay recuperation. Just as characters can be brought into the collusive and erotic orbit of their gay viewers to "mean" a certain way, the "Brandos of the boulevard" turn tricks around others "know[ing]" what they "mean," and thus depend upon the same kinds of artifice as the fairies or queens who reperform the mannerisms of female film stars. The street as a space of trade may confer some sense of authenticity, lending the "male whores" a gritty realism, but this site nevertheless exists for McDonald in analogous relation to the "cinema," and its "whores" rely upon imitating "Brando." These men may be found on "any street" but can also be said, in this sense, to be men who "appear in pictures," who draw upon recognized codes of dress or appearance that are not merely peculiar to them but belong to a shared subterranean and semiotic vocabulary. And they can also be found elsewhere in O'Hara's writing, waiting on street corners to be looked at.

Songs and Sight Queens

Act & Portrait goes *À rebours* not only through its allusion to Huysmans but in the mode of its composition, insofar as Leslie and O'Hara's conversations suggest that the film's visual and verbal components are intended to run against one another. In Moore's documentary, O'Hara is shown sitting at his typewriter in his apartment working on the script while Leslie sits behind him discussing the accompanying images. This is a neat visual approximation of their respective roles in the making of the film, of image and text as simultaneous. O'Hara's split attention here—he also takes a phone call while writing, and includes a phrase from this conversation in the final script—is consonant with anecdotes that enshrine him as the improvisational lunch-poet, for whom writing is itself a form of multitasking. Leslie, keeping track of O'Hara's typing, observes that "We've timed this now up to here—we have 3 minutes and 40 seconds," as though the process is akin to a form of musical composition, with the image's soundtrack being constructed around a careful negotiation of timings.[44] In "Second Edition," however, the collected outtakes of the film, the relation between O'Hara's words and Leslie's images seems as much one of discord, with Leslie wanting "to keep the whole thing full of those images, just sort of write it through, and then we'll play it together, we'll play it against the picture and see what it's like, see what it feels like."[45] O'Hara responds that rehearsing this will also be "to time it, sort of." Leslie, less interested in timing all of a sudden, suggests "Well, not to time, but to see . . . if you were reading it, while you were watching the film, then you'll be able to proximate in some way how the total sense of the two levels will work." One thing upon which they agree is that they "want it to be against the movie," for "the printed dialogue" to be "against [. . .] what we're looking at in the scene."[46]

In the case of *Act & Portrait,* simultaneity is a feature of the script itself. Its attention is divided between the present-tense "quiet walk along 14th Street and 7th Avenue and 23rd Street" (*AN,* 164) and its ostensible backstory, a fraught *ménage-a-trois* between the characters of Dorothea, Miles, and John (played by their namesakes Dorothea Rockburne, Miles Forst, and John Ahearn, artist friends of O'Hara and Leslie's). Leslie describes how "at the beginning of the film Dorothea starts making love to Miles, and then John is laying there," after which point Dorothea and John are then "making love" for the "rest of the film," while in the outtakes his projection of what will be on-screen involves "the warmth of the bed, the sexuality of the scene to play something against it all the time."[47] While the script suggests the setting of the street, it would appear that the "picture" itself remains firmly in the bedroom. This can be corroborated, somewhat, by all that appears to have survived of this film (a fire in Leslie's studio in 1966 destroyed many of his prints). A 1965 film, also called *Act & Portrait,* appears to be an early attempt. It is made up of selections from ten hours of black-and-white 8 mm film shot in 1964 that came to provide the visual assets for five different shorts gathered under the title *Birth of a Nation* (1965).[48] The exact nature of the relation between these films, which largely use the same images, is complicated by the destruction of Leslie's archive, but in any case the *Act & Portrait* section corroborates what the documentary makes known about the project. It features images of three lovers in bed that are offset against a soundtrack of music and dialogue, as consistent with the other collected films, and O'Hara's script is present as subtitles, with minor variations.

In conversation with O'Hara, Leslie distinguishes between two kinds of image-making, and suggests that they "keep the whole thing [the script] full of those images" that they will then play "against the picture."[49] The film's dual image arises, in this sense, from the tense interplay between text and image, from the way the story being told through "shots" runs against the visual narrative of the walk suggested by the subtitles, thus inviting a viewer to look in several ways. These are distinct but porous forms of representation, and in plot terms inflect one another in such a way as to suggest a temporal gap. It suggests that the written walk might be taking place after a bedroom scene. The script begins with the statement "We walked [down] 14th Street. It was cold," which becomes the scene for John's inner ruminations. Several paragraphs later:

> We walked on and on, hating each other. The air was better in bed. Now my eyes hurt, I'm coughing and out of cigarettes. I looked at them on the corner of 23rd Street and Seventh Avenue. I wanted to lie down and be run over. It will come anyway. I didn't come, but it will. Miles did. Come. (*AN*, 164)

O'Hara reads from this section in Moore's documentary, holding the typescript page he has just finished. As he begins with "We walked on and on, hating each other," he turns to Leslie to explain "they're on 14th Street," bringing an urban-geographical axis of orientation to bear upon this already crowded intersection of words and pictures, as though this is one other factor in "play" to remain aware of. Following on, the script takes us in a flash to "23rd Street and Seventh Avenue," then later arrives farther south, at "Seventh Avenue and Greenwich," before finishing at "Central Park" by way of the "Plaza" Hotel and its exclusive "Oak Room" bar (a rarefied cruising spot at the time). The trajectory of this walk borrows from a cinematic grammar of movement, and the ability to cheat time and jump from one area to another in the space of a paragraph or sentence. Each mention of a new place has the feel of punctuation, which diverts the text away momentarily from John's thoughts and provides new stimuli. Yet, as here, where the street corner becomes the occasion for reflecting upon being run over (eerie in the light of O'Hara's fatal accident months later), and then upon Miles and ejaculation, the urban sights soon come to be incorporated into John's ramblings and inflected by the sexual dynamics of the threesome plot.

In its principle of accompaniment as opposition, of writing that "runs against" or "after" the film's plot, O'Hara's contribution to *Act & Portrait* is compositionally similar to his involvement in other film projects. In addition to his screenplays for Leslie and a never-to-be-realized project directed by Andy Warhol, O'Hara also played a "real role" in Rudy Burckhardt's films, "playing piano in some of Burckhardt's efforts from the 50s" and also, as Burckhardt's wife Yvonne Jaquette explains in an interview with Daniel Kane, "gave Rudy advice on what music to include [. . .]. 'Oh, try Wagner there, try Grieg there.'"[50] These musical contributions are analogously related to O'Hara's screenplays insofar as they involve tracks to "run against" a picture, and suggest a way of conceiving of his texts as a form of soundtrack, except that they do not provide sound at all and are presented in Leslie's films through subtitles. As an addition to the film's sound and image, this textual track is an interjection that further vexes sense and plot and multiplies the viewer's imaginings of what is out of frame by suggesting a voice and narrative that cannot be seen or heard. These semantic difficulties also speak to the fact that poetry and film can be strange bedfellows. O'Hara, in conversation with Moore, states:

> The reason that I'm interested in movies is not as a substitute for poetry, but who is making it. If Al is making it, then I am interested in the sense that I can understand what it's going to be, or that I know that it's at least going to be something interesting for me.[51]

This account serves to corroborate the sense that, for O'Hara, collaborating with visual artists is not something undertaken for its own sake, but rather informed by a highly personal, and even coterie-related impulse.[52] Outside of this rationale, O'Hara's "reason" seems to withhold more than explain, but it nevertheless offers the important distinction that movies are "not a substitute" for poems, and thus any account of their shared activities requires a more elastic conceptual apparatus. Film and poetry are in a crucial sense wildly different materials, demanding distinct forms of attention on the part both of their creators and their audiences. Sarah Riggs writes that when "O'Hara conflates different art forms [...] he does so not for the sake of likeness, but rather to create an effect of emergence, of what 'is,' out of the tension between media."[53]

So what "is" this film, in its whole and constituent parts? Its presence in Moore's 1966 documentary suggests that it remained of interest to Leslie and O'Hara beyond the previous 1965 segment and was set for a different and fuller realization. In the context of O'Hara's oeuvre it sits as a rarely discussed prose curio, a text unmistakably in O'Hara's voice with no discernible other incarnation. Yet this script, if at times inchoate, speaks playfully to threads that are resonant elsewhere in O'Hara's work, and suggests an interplay between text and image, walking and looking, and cruising and the movies. Quite what constitutes *Act & Portrait* is indeterminate; its only complete remnant is O'Hara's script, but the film's never-completed realization hangs over its textual iteration. *Act & Portrait* asks to be visualized, and its imagined life as a film can be composed multiply by working solely from the text, or by piecing together the documentary evidence we have of the film's creation. Leslie and O'Hara's conversations, in this regard, at least provide something of a vague blueprint for the images "against" which the text can "run."

Poems, too, invite visualizations, and O'Hara's "Song" (*CP,* 327) suggests a further sense that poems—as lines of text which are "full of [...] images"—can realize imagined filmic manifestations for which they provide a track to run against, over, or after them. The poem's compositional situation speaks both to the ambiguities of sight and materiality in "In the Movies" and to the apprehension in *Act & Portrait* of the "guys in black leather jackets." This poem's "Brando of the boulevard," to return to McDonald's phrase, "comes along," and is caught momentarily "in the city." The poem turns on—and is turned on by—a notion of dirtiness as both an urban and erotic condition:

Is it dirty
does it look dirty
that's what you think of in the city

does it just seem dirty
that's what you think of in the city
you don't refuse to breathe do you

Dirt is distributed here between surface and depth, interior and exterior: maybe it just "look[s]" dirty, or "seem[s]" dirty. This question
of materiality is figured in the poem's imperative image of thought:
"run your finger along your no-moss mind / that's not a thought that's
soot." A dirty mind names a way of looking at something, and dirt is
something you look at, or for. It is also an instrument of attraction, or
a stylistic detail through which to shoot a look. Anthropologist Mary
Douglas conceptualizes dirt and "uncleanness" as "matter out of place,"
as "that which must not be included if a pattern is to be maintained."[54]
O'Hara's poem illustrates how dirt, as an erotic variable, can nonetheless depend upon a constructed pattern of disorder. A detail "out of
place"—disheveled hair, a leather jacket slung an inch off one shoulder, a handkerchief hanging from a pocket—can be a deliberate way
of performing disorder and signaling some inner dirtiness legible to
those looking for it. The poem's initial concern for surface and visibility echoes a similar moment in *Act & Portrait*, written in the same year
as the publication of Douglas's study, where the speaker observes that
"Pollution isn't interesting, you can't even see it. I'm a sight queen, I
guess. If you can't see it, it isn't there. Until it hits you. Boom" (*AN*, 164).
Considerations of sight and pollution here collude with the bawdy gay
humor of the "size queen," and this point of intersection speaks clearly
to the process of cruising. Reading a desired stranger—what they look
like, how they "seem"—is to "see" them as though in a dirty picture, and
leads easily into the explicit fantasies of anatomy that are the remit of
the "size queen." Read him wrongly, though, and he "hits you. Boom."
    The "city" of the poem thus enables a phenomenology of encounter
that is equal parts dirty and dangerous, where questions of "sight" become a matter of sizing someone up, with the risk that they size up to
you if things go awry. This is "what you think of in the city," as in *Act &
Portrait*, where moments after seeing Marlon, O'Hara muses, "They

used to take walks to read. Monks in Cloisters, nuns in Bryant Park. Now we take walks to not talk. The air is nice, anyway. It's not Malibu it's something" (*AN*, 165). This moment reads like a clean-cut iteration of "Song," where you do "not talk" but "think," where you "read" the surface of the city and its passing strangers instead of scripture, and the "air" is consequently not "nice" but "dirty." This "Song" thus emerges as a soundtrack to a cruising scene, as though it were something like Gerard Purble's hummed "song of his own composition." Indeed, as the proverb it refers to goes, this "mind" can gather "no moss," rolling at speed through the sight queen's questions: "he seems attractive. is he really. yes. very / he's attractive as his character is bad. is it. yes" (*CP*, 327). It also recalls again Barthes's reflection upon the erotic hypnotism of both movie theaters and streets. This comparison then leads him to think "of music: isn't there such a thing as hypnotic music?," and this is a schema where a song might be both the accompaniment to and the means of the "most venerable of powers: healing."[55] O'Hara's song animates the soporific eroticism of spectating by focusing in on the way that "character" is made legible by the "look." The character's "bad"-ness also refers to the other pop form of the movies, and he is made attractive by the image of villainy or delinquency that his look suggests. The liveness of the street is enfolded into the mediations of the movies, in a poem whose title signals its live reperformance, and which narrates an act of cruising ripe for repetition in a habitual present: "that's what you think of in the city."

In its curious, even didactic deployment of the second-person to describe "what you think" in the face of gay urban masculinity, "Song" calls to mind another cruising scenario famously described by Leo Bersani, which is to say not only that it is well-known but also that it courts, in its very construction, the air of being a prolific or folkloric truth. Indeed, it is a "classic putdown":

> The butch number swaggering into a bar in a leather get-up
> opens his mouth and sounds like a pansy, takes you home,
> where the first thing you notice is the complete works of Jane
> Austen, gets you into bed, and—well, you know the rest.[56]

This quip would appear to put paid to Boyd McDonald's hard-and-fast distinction between the fey men of 1980s movies and the butch "Brandos" of the boulevard or, in this case, the leather bar. Look behind the surface of the Brando "get-up," it suggests, and you may be in for a surprise. Bersani observes that this "mockery of gay machismo is almost exclusively an internal affair, and is based on the dark suspicion that you may not be getting the real article."[57] Though the joke itself is banal, and relies upon the stereotypical assumption that any fan of Jane Austen must be a sexual bottom, Bersani's rendering of it offers other layers. D. A. Miller reads this moment in Bersani's essay as a seeming disavowal of Austen—who is associated, in the logic of the joke, with male sexual insufficiency—that is in fact a studied and clever imitation of her. This imitation ranges from:

> the confident ironic presentation of a universally acknowledged truth, to the wit that hones this truth into trenchant epigrammatic point, to the even more terrible sophistication that, while leaving its ostensible victim unaware of how he is being judged, keeps the dark cloud of shame that fails to descend on *him* hanging ominously over *us,* as our prospective downfall if we should fail, or fail to pretend, to "know the rest."[58]

The "I" of Bersani's joke, Miller suggests, transfers the desire for a masculine top—a desire that is perhaps his own, and remains embarrassingly unmet by the superficially "butch" devotee of Austen and "victim" of the joke—onto the "you" who is reading. This "I," Miller writes, has "been commuted into a generalized 'you'" and in turn this "so-called narrator has in fact faded into that universal utterance which, even in Austen's own works, we can never quite read as *hers*." This "fading somehow shifts our sexual understanding of him: from his role in the anecdote as a disappointed bottom, his accession to narration virtually refigures him into the voice of a supercilious top" or even "the general voice of heterosexuality itself, mocking the faggotry it observes" (7).

For Miller, the astuteness of Bersani's writing here is thus that it performs what he argues is a dominant principle in Jane Austen's style: a personal style which is, paradoxically, impersonal, and founded upon "*de-materializing* the voice that speaks it" (6–7). Miller's reading in fact speaks to O'Hara's "Song" in a number of ways. Firstly, there is an obvious thematic connection, in that "Song" is also animated by conjecture about outward masculinity and its codes. Indeed, it would be easy to read the poem's interrogative veering—"is it dirty […] does it just seem dirty" or "is he really. yes. very"—as arising from a similar erotic situation to the one outlined by Bersani, if we take "dirty" to mean dominant, "bad" to mean a top, and its speaker to be, perhaps, an inquisitive bottom. But more than this, O'Hara's use of "you"—there is no "I" here—along with the proverbial or aphoristic diction of "that's what you think of in the city," "no-moss mind," and "you don't refuse to breathe do you," both implicate the poem's reader in a manner akin to the impersonal style that Miller theorizes. "Song" is a poem full of desire—for rough trade, and for the interpretive work of desiring itself—but this erotic charge is displaced and depersonalized. It is attributed as much to the "you" reading the poem as the speaker who hides behind this address, and, as we shall see, the queer "look" of O'Hara's poems is structured around this same stylistic principle of indirection.

A Beautiful Walk

In another "Song" (*CP*, 367), from 1960, O'Hara imagines the gaze of the locutory scenario turned back upon himself:

> Did you see me walking by the Buick repairs?
> I was thinking of you
> having a Coke in the heat it was your face
> I saw on the movie magazine, no it was Fabian's
> I was thinking of you
> and down at the railroad tracks where the station
> has mysteriously disappeared
> I was thinking of you
> as the bus pulled away in the twilight
> I was thinking of you
> and right now

This poem crystallizes the simultaneous unfolding of thinking and seeing, stillness and motion, that have been constitutive of many of the works featured in this chapter. Thinking of "you" here takes on a cinematic grammar; the jump cut enacts transitions from the "Buick repairs" to the barren "railroad tracks" and the "bus" stop at "twilight." Similarly, its setting is shot through with the visuals of pop Americana, broad brushstrokes of the small town and the industrial suggested by these locales. Thinking of "you" also refers back to the movies; the speaker sees "your" face on the "movie magazine," and in turn a movie still of another star and purveyor of "Song[s]," the teen idol Fabian. This is a poem of absence, one where a person's presence must be conjured by the verb "to think," a verb which becomes seemingly interchangeable with "to see," and in the "right now" of the poem's iteration, "to hear." The poem's "right now" of remembrance begins in the past, and the image of its author walking thus lingers throughout.

And yet the distinction here between "me" and "you" is complicated by the unfolding of the poem's first three lines. Though the addressee is clearly demarcated, "me" and "you" risk intermixing at the moment the speaker observes that "it was your face I saw on the movie magazine." Not "I saw your face," but "it was your face I saw." This construction inevitably invites consideration of other possibilities—who else's face might it have been? —and while the poem stages a blurring between the visages of "you" and "Fabian," it also leaves room for the triangulated possibility of the speaker's own face reflected back at him. It "was your face I saw," which is to say, not mine, and the poem has already established in its opening line an act of self-spectatorship conducted through the eyes of "you." The "me" of this opening line might thus seem like Bersani's cruising homosexual, who goes "in search of objects that will give him back to himself," except here he finds instead the resemblance of a lover, who is in turn mediated by a movie star.[59] This image of the poet walking calls to mind another memory described by Joe Brainard:

> I remember Frank O'Hara's walk. Light and sassy. With a slight bounce and a slight twist. It was a beautiful walk. Confident. "I don't care." And sometimes "I know you are looking."[60]

Brainard's account of O'Hara's walk weaves verbal statements as accompaniments to motion. It imagines that the particularities of "bounce" and "twist" might be literally expressive, or soundtracked by these competing attitudes which run against each other simultaneously. The speaker of O'Hara's "Song," on the surface, seems to lack some of the assurance Brainard suggests was O'Hara's signature tune; he doesn't know if you saw him walking, and seems to care if you did. And yet the intricate overlay of address and self-spectatorship in the poem's first line—with the speaker imagining his own image as witnessed by the person he addresses—suspends the poem's "me" and "you" in relation to one another and thus trades, like the other "Song," in an impersonal interpersonality. Such a style, to return to Miller, is thus able to accommodate paradoxes; it seems to hide the person of the poem while simultaneously making him visible, and cognizant of our looking.

As Brian Glavey notes, O'Hara's disclosures of queerness are often intimately bound up with the visibility of his own image and, in turn, with moments of ekphrasis. Even "Homosexuality," in a sense his most explicit poetic description of sexual identity, began its life (according to a manuscript note) with the subtitle "Ensor Self-Portrait with Masks," which refers to a self-portrait by painter James Ensor that featured in a 1951 show at MoMA. Glavey gleans from this that "the poem can be read not only as an exchange between poet and silent interlocutor but also between a viewer and oil painting," and this "ekphrastic self-portrait [. . .] allows him to flirt with disclosure" and to "approach the love that dare not speak its name by striving toward the condition of the visual rather than the verbal."[61] O'Hara's own manifesto writings imagine the verbal exchange of poetry as a visualized erotic intermingling that Gregory Bredbeck, in a Barthesian reading of the poet's textual cruising, describes thus: "The poem becomes 'Lucky Pierre,' that is, 'the one in the middle of a threesome.' [. . .] This text, like the middle in a homosexual threesome, is both receptive and piercing; its surface can be abraded, but it can also abrade."[62] And style is frequently the "surface" upon which this exchange takes place, for it is "common sense" that "if you're going to buy a pair of pants you want them to be tight enough so everyone will want to go to bed with you" (*CP*, 498). Like many of O'Hara's quips to this effect, this latter statement is as suggestive as it is silly, a metaphor for form and content that implies the a priori existence of legs and buttocks which nonetheless need the right pants to have desired and desirous effects, and this relation could alternately be phrased as one of style and substance. Many of O'Hara's poems seem playfully to resist any suggestion of the latter, barely containing a voice that revels in adopting different styles and guises, playing out in that "scene of my selves" from "In Memory of My Feelings" (*CP*, 252), or amid the wait in "Mayakovsky" for the "catastrophe of my personality / to seem beautiful again, / and interesting, and modern" (*CP*, 202).

O'Hara often outwardly resists notions of sameness, or rather conceives of sameness as serial, such that these "proliferating likenesses might therefore be read as an effort to revise the conditions of gay visibility and legibility."[63] The challenge for the reader of O'Hara, then, becomes one of meeting his look amid replications of the self in the guise of so many images. Indeed, O'Hara's quip about tight pants lights upon a more particular methodological question about how we are to read his poems, one which speaks to the relation between liveness and its representations. In suggesting the way that content might usurp form—if you want to "go to bed" with someone, you'll need to take off their pants—this metaphor speaks to the uniquely flirtatious quality of much of his work, which invites us to go beyond the poem in pursuit of Frank O'Hara himself, imagining its creator in the act of, or as the occasion for, composition. Such readerly imaginings can be ephemeral things, corroborated by phantom documents of life and presence. Since his death, scholarship on O'Hara has to greater or lesser degrees been biographically focused, in part because of the myriad names and places interwoven into his writing and in part because of the wealth of anecdotal material about his life and person that has accumulated.

This chapter has drawn upon numerous biographical materials, from published accounts by O'Hara's friends and lovers to his own letters now stored in archives, and in concluding finds within these poems an analogy for this approach. The stylized life conjured by movies and the everyday life that plays out on the street, for example, exist in a determinate relation, not interchangeable per se, but leaving residues one on the other, hence the conceptions of a walk as cinematic, say, or a real stranger as a projected Brando, and vice versa. Similarly, to read O'Hara is to get in step not just with an imaginary poetic "I" as a theatrical construction but also as a figure in the context of his own time and hour, a conception of the poet that negotiates between these positions and is made up by the numerous descriptions and images of his person that are to hand. O'Hara seems to court this ambivalently; he "celebrates his own desirability, but, seeing himself represented as an object of other's desire, recognizes that to be figured is to forfeit his self to others, who will make of him what they will—stories, stereotypes, statues."[64] The sense that the poet "know[s]" we are looking is illuminated as "the interplay between self-love and self-loss involved in recognizing oneself represented in the public sphere," and O'Hara's poems are texts that simultaneously suggest the live act of performance while offering a picture of the world from which such acts arise (107). The tensions between liveness and representation, mappable onto those between stillness and motion or past and future, do not require resolution into a singularity.

As his poem "You Are Gorgeous and I'm Coming" (*CP*, 331) attests, such tensions might yield a form of synesthetic simultaneity; a thinking of "sounds as colored," a "concrete Rimbaud obscurity of emotion." This name-check of Rimbaud is less an invocation of that total "*dérèglement de tous les sens*" [derangement *of* all the senses] with which the French poet is associated, than it is a gesture to a happily erratic multiplicity, where a state of "obscurity" is also "simple," where "sounds" might be "colored," and where a poem to a lover is both still and moving.[65] The poem's composition as an acrostic to Vincent Warren can be illuminated, too, by its final phrase, the "captured time of our being," where the "captured" fixity of inscription—what's in a name? —meets the temporal flux of "being." These lines suggest a work that is both act *and* portrait, and reveal distinct phenomenological modes in collaboration, states gestured to by that dualism of standing still and walking in New York which lies at the heart of O'Hara's work. It is not a matter of delineating who is speaking as if it were merely a riddle: "*Je est un autre*" [I is someone else], as Rimbaud's "obscurity" has it.[66] He can't be "got at one reading" ("Personism," *CP*, 498). What O'Hara shows, in his attractive mystery, is the way that queer self-representation teeters between, and is produced by, the representational poles of "me" and "you," and the states of inference and intimacy existing between them. In O'Hara, the look is itself an act of becoming; an exchange of one to one performed by a text that is simultaneously solicitous and insouciant, open and closed. It invites us to "go to bed with" it and—well, you know the rest.

5

David Wojnarowicz's Portraits

Turning Heads

In his 1963 review of Rechy's *City of Night,* O'Hara writes that some of the novel's "best parts (especially the Mardi Gras section) seem to show an original interpretation of what Rimbaud, no less, was doing in the "parade" poems and in *A Season in Hell,* without getting into that boring avant-garde version of the French prose poem which is so ubiquitous, or was until two years ago."[1] O'Hara could perhaps not have predicted that, in the years following his own untimely death in 1966, the influence of Rimbaud's poetry and his infamously deranging celebration of "that atrocious fanfare" would extend far beyond "boring" prose poem imitations and the carnival section of Rechy's novel, which he suggests is perhaps one of "the finest and most compelling prose realization of derangement through social confrontation in American letters."[2] Rimbaud's influence could be felt among New York artists and writers throughout the 1960s and '70s in the work of poets like O'Hara and John Ashbery, but also musicians and writers like Bob Dylan, Patti Smith, Jim Morrison, Richard Hell, and Dennis Cooper, to name only a few.[3] Louise Varese's translation of Rimbaud's *Illuminations,* first published in 1946 and revised in 1957 with New Directions, brought this collection, and with it what O'Hara calls the "parade" poems, to a wider American readership.

David Wojnarowicz was one such avid reader, and in 1977, at the age of twenty-two, he published a prose poem called "Reading a little Rimbaud in a Second Avenue coffee shop" in the first and only issue of *Red M,* a small magazine he coedited with the writer John Ensslin.[4] Its title makes several readings available. On the one hand, the poem captures the speaker's reading of one particular poem, "Parade" (which is translated by Varese as "Side Show"); thus, a little bit of Rimbaud. On the other, the title speaks to the physical book itself, a compact New Directions Paperbook—or a little Rimbaud—which represents the poet's oeuvre through synecdoche, or allows the poet's vital presence to be carried in miniature. Wojnarowicz's poem, like his larger 1978–79 photographic project *Arthur Rimbaud in New York,* which will be one of the main focuses of this chapter, corroborates this sense of temporal interpenetration. It features a speaker experiencing a "lull in the body" while his "mind [is] working on" Rimbaud's poem in a Second Avenue coffee shop, such that he "can't breathe as well as before" and the air "turns thick."[5] Experiencing his body anew, the speaker sits as the world goes

> on outside the shop just rushing by in waves of sound
> & i cant do anything about it it could be nineteen twenty or
> eighteen
> sixty or now & it wouldnt make a difference except
> maybe I wouldnt
> be
> reading what i'm reading where i am what i am

This moment catches itself in the act of effacing historical "difference," experienced by a reader for whom the act of reading brings to light a foreign projected past, a "spectral past encountered in the material present as active and perceptibly current," Anderson suggests.[6] Perhaps, the poem suggests, this "I" would not be "reading" Rimbaud back in Rimbaud's time but writing him, or writing like him. In this regard "Parade" is a telling intertext as an object for imitation, for it too observes the pageantry of everyday life made infernal, like a hellish accompaniment to Whitman's "City of Orgies" in which the "*hommes murs*" ["ripe men"] are "*droles tres solides*" ["Very sturdy rogues"] and the speaker assumes the role of sensory ringleader, for "*J'ai seul le clef de cette parade sauvage*" ["I alone have the key to this savage side show"].[7] Wojnarowicz, too, is on the precipice of possessing the "clef" [key] to this moment of perception, ending the poem with the realization that "all of this must mean something." This poem both approximates in a curt American English something of Rimbaud's style in "Parade," zooming in upon the ominous and surreal potential of minutiae, and suggests that the act of personation can arise from reading as well as writing. Reading a "little Rimbaud" collapses the temporal gap between the "now" and the time of the poet's boyhood in the 1860s, while checking in with the roaring "twent[ies]" on the way.

Wojnarowicz's own little edition of Rimbaud, the one featured in this poem, brings (if only anecdotally) a literal dimension to this sense of a handed-down relation. A secondhand copy, the inside cover bears a stamp denoting that the book belonged to a Peter Kemeny, residing in Adams House, Harvard University.[8] That Wojnarowicz, who received no formal qualification beyond a high school diploma and was largely self-taught as an artist and writer, came to possess this edition speaks to a multiplicity in Rimbaud's fate as an icon both in and out of the academy, as a poet whose work was being read by Harvard undergraduates and East Village punks alike. Wojnarowicz's relation to Rimbaud situates and reperforms the poet's work in sketchy and contingent urban contexts. "For Wojnarowicz," Anderson writes, "Rimbaud's poetry permitted a reconfiguration, a mythologizing of autobiography that appealed to the young writer, who continually rewrote and reinvented the events of his own past."[9] He finds in Rimbaud a cipher for his own uninstitutional youth as a teenage hustler on the streets of New York, and reconstitutes his life in Rimbaud's image.

The first publication of the *Arthur Rimbaud in New York* images, in a June 1980 edition of the *SoHo Weekly News*, was accompanied by text that begins: "When I was younger and living among the city streets I assumed the smoking exterior of the convict. I entered the shadows of mythologies and thieves and passion."[10] This text is echoed by Wojnarowicz's later notion of the camera as an instrument which "in some hands can preserve an alternate history" ("Do Not Doubt the Dangerousness of the 12-Inch Tall Politician," *CK*, 144).[11] and this notion of photography as a medium of the marginal also reveals how these portraits of the artist as a young man depend upon the "smoking exterior" of Rimbaud as an archetype, one that gives shape and an "alternate" glamour to traumatic experience.

In the fall of 1975 Wojnarowicz did attend one class, Bill Zatavksy's free poetry workshop at St. Mark's Poetry Project in the East Village. Biographer Cynthia Carr describes this class as constituting "the whole of David's higher education."[12] Little if any attention has been paid to Wojnarowicz's unpublished poetic work from this period, perhaps because it is often perceived, Carr suggests here, as "dense if not overwritten and purplish."[13] Eileen Myles, a fellow attendee of Zatavsky's workshop, tells Carr that Wojnarowicz "used poetry as a launching pad," and "poetry is very often a plan. Like a list. At the beginning of a career, it can be a list of the directions you'd like to go."[14] Carr has noted more recently that perhaps the most "surprising thing" about Wojnarowicz's checkered and intricate life story is that "he had erased the roughly four years of his life devoted to poetry," and "certain of his poetry friends felt that this was about more than creating a persona—that he had willed himself into becoming someone else" and did away with his own rough-draft years.[15] *Arthur Rimbaud in New York,* which Wojnarowicz began working on after returning from Paris, marks his first major work as an artist and thus the end of his immersion in poetry. The curator David Breslin notes that this is not accidental, and that the "more consequential conjuring trick" of this work "was in selecting" at its center "a poet who famously had stopped writing poetry."[16] This chapter contends, in the face of Wojnarowicz's seeming disavowal of his poetic work and scholarship's following suit, that the "launching pad" of his early poems can better illuminate the implications of the *Rimbaud in New York* project as an excavation not only of Wojnarowicz's youth, but his lifelong interest in looking and cruising. While they can at times feel rough or "overwritten," Wojnarowicz's texts from this period constitute a rich "list" of images and concerns that are variously manifest in his later visual practices and written style.

Wojnarowicz's relationship to Rimbaud as an icon and surrogate for his own practice can also be illuminated by some of the material details of this edition of *Illuminations.* Most immediately apparent is the collection's cover, which was designed by collagist and mail artist Ray Johnson, a contemporary of O'Hara's. Johnson reproduced Étienne Carjat's famous 1871 portrait of the young French *poète maudit* using the Ben-Day dots screen printing process, a technique popular among artists such as Andy Warhol and Roy Lichtenstein. This adaptation put Rimbaud's image into circulation by deploying the Pop form's self-conscious iconicity and constructed a blueprint symbol of the poet's precocious and renegade sensibility, which was widely disseminated in the artistic production of New York in this era. Johnson himself returned to this image for his 1971 Rimbaud project, reproducing it in *Arts Magazine* with instructions written on the back for readers and prospective mail artists to "Detach Along Dotted Line" and "Participate by adding words, letters, colors or whatever to face."[17] This mail art project—which Johnson also replicated with an image of Paul Verlaine, Rimbaud's older lover—marks the point at which artists begin taking Rimbaud's image, quite literally, into their own hands.

Wojnarowicz's own "early adoption of collage as a way of giving visual form to his literary aspirations" can be found "on postcards sent to friends," writes David Kiehl, and along with the Rimbaud works Wojnarowicz also created "collages as homages" to Jean Genet.[18] Genet was another important French forebear whose image, like Rimbaud's, also proliferated in American artistic circles at this time, and was made ubiquitous by the presence of Brassaï's famous portrait on the cover of the 1969 Grove Press edition of *Funeral Rites*. It was Carjat's portrait of Rimbaud that Wojnarowicz, after Johnson, cut out for the famous mask at the center of his photographic project. Using a borrowed 35 mm camera, Wojnarowicz photographed his friends John Hall, Brian Butterick, and lover Jean-Pierre Delage, whom he met during an extended trip to Paris in 1978–79. They each wore the mask in numerous locales throughout Manhattan and Brooklyn, forming a narrative journey that travels between the crowded and the desolate, the built-up and the derelict. In this sense the project foregrounds the turning head as a visual effect and turns upon the nexus of meanings and associations Rimbaud's famous head calls to mind. Which is to say that this imported head also refers back to the body of writing that it famously illustrates, not least Rimbaud's short prose poem "À une raison," where the poet renders a moment of repetition as a gestural reflex, the dual motion in which "Ta tête se détourne: le nouvel amour! Ta tête se retourne: le nouvel amour!" [Your head turns away: the new love! Your head turns back: the new love!].[19] This substitution, in which Rimbaud's head appears as a shorthand for his poems themselves and illuminates their resonance in a new historical and geographical present, has further metonymic potential as a relation not only to the poet's corpus but to the body itself.

This "turn" of the "head" performed in the Rimbaud project, then, a simultaneous turn toward a cultural past and one's own artistic future, pertains equally to the more immediate turn toward strangers in the street, those possible "new love[s]" or hustling clients. The sexual fantasies of Wojnarowicz's early poems cast light upon the Rimbaud project's particular resonance as a portrait of cruising. The "conceptual economy and brilliance of the [Rimbaud] mask," Breslin writes, is its suggestion that "separation and mediation can be addressed only through the experience of *the encounter*."[20] The "face-to-face meeting with another [...] that precedes every other form of exchange or communication" is vital to "the act of cruising," in which the very "armature of society" is stripped "down to the immediacy of the encounter with another." Conceiving of *Rimbaud in New York* in dialogue with his earlier poems reveals an intersection between word and image that animates much of Wojnarowicz's artistic activity, and signals an "early desire to have both pictures and words (or at least a symbol like Rimbaud to evoke them) equally at his disposal and frequently copresent."[21] And this copresence, I will suggest, has a particular pertinence for representing the encounter between multiple present bodies; the temporally various "look" of cruising.

Juvenilia and Jerking Off

Wojnarowicz's encounter with Rimbaud in the Second Avenue coffee shop, a spatiotemporal blur intervening in an otherwise quotidian scene, locates the sensation of perceptual foreignness in the interstices between the earthly and the mental, the street and the window on to it. The interior setting speaks to the distinction between the world "going on outside the shop" and the one inside, in the coffee shop and the mind. To be on the inside looking out is to apprehend the urban scene as in a frame, as a moving tableau delimited by a window. It allows one to inhabit the position, or fantasy, even, of nonparticipation that has long attended accounts of urban experience, as in Edgar Allan Poe's 1840 story "The Man of the Crowd." The protagonist sits at the "large bow window" of a London "Coffee House," and observes "the world of light" that "flitted before the window."[22] Whether for the purposes of the flaneur's observation or a Rimbaudian reverie, such a vantage claims to offer both access to and protection from the urban spectacle. It allows recollection in relative tranquility, however ominous it may be in its own right, as signaled by the poem's suggestion of a "constant evil eye / look around the joint on the watch for gangster types."[23] The contingency of "outside" is different; the exposure of daylight may offer protection from dangerous "types," but the street has unique capacities for deviancy and alienation. *Arthur Rimbaud in New York* takes place predominantly in this exterior terrain, one where "eighteen sixty" and "now" are not interchangeable alternates in an interior reverie but are in clear visual juxtaposition, thus making the Rimbaud figure a "type" who sticks out, by turns vulnerable, desirous, and dangerous.

The *Rimbaud in New York* series contains windows of a literal kind, like the glass panes through which the Rimbaud figure is seen sitting in a diner and a late-night pizza restaurant, and another image shows Rimbaud looking into an unknown window at nighttime. The windows Wojnarowicz is chiefly drawn to in this work, however, are mental in nature, like the sensation of "something like a tiny window being opened up somewhere to the back of the head [. . .] a small distinct memory falling into place back there."[24] This account of memory, appended to the Rimbaud images in the 1980 *SoHo Weekly News* centerfold without further explanation, suggests something other than the "urban shock" of *memoire involontaire,* and instead a slow drift of approximations— "something like" and "somewhere"—that make up a "small and distinct" sensation in process at the instant of apprehension. These images stage the simultaneous turn of the head toward new objects of apprehension, as well as the past embodied by Rimbaud and the lyric past of their author illuminated somewhere in the "back," behind the scenes of its construction. This multiple temporality, in dialogue with the poems he was writing in the lead-up to the *Rimbaud in New York* project, suggests for Wojnarowicz an intricate erotics of photographic memory where preservation is also linked with masturbation. The passage that frames the *Rimbaud* centerfold, with its description of the "smoking exterior" Wojnarowicz assumed while "living on the city streets," can first be found in an earlier prose poem entitled "masturbation photo." It begins:

> In the intoxication of laying my hands to myself, I sometimes see my childhood in the company of old pederasts; elegant strangers entering the dried gardens of ~~their homes~~ low lit rooms, those of their homes. They disrobe ~~and~~ revealing the future of the flesh, that which moves ~~across~~along landscapes across years I have not slept.[25]

The framing of this recollection as a "masturbation photo" is wrong-footing if only because it suggests in the first instance an image chosen for self-pleasure, perhaps pornographic fodder, before recasting this photo as an object of involuntary memory that is "see[n]" in the sexual act, a traumatic relation that may nonetheless still be a site of pleasure.

These embodiments of an abject bodily future are recalled in the present moment of masturbation through the past lens of a child's vantage point. Wojnarowicz here offers an account of desire as it is bred and distorted by the past. He spins from these traumatic memories a pronounced visual scheme—of sordid hotel rooms cast as "dried gardens"—and in turn a certain expressive excess. The poem's images are positioned between candor and confection, and assume that slippage where remembered experiences take on the air of imagined ones. These may seem dreamed or invented, like "shadows and mythologies of thieves and passion" imported by the Rimbaud figure, and riff upon the poet's associations with dissidence and homosexuality. There is another important French forebear here, too. Genet, who appears throughout Wojnarowicz's work and in several of his photographic collages, is a poster child for erotic fantasy as a form of composition. Jean-Paul Sartre described Genet's 1943 novel *Notre-Dame-des-Fleurs* as the "epic of masturbation"; a low-life fantasy of pimps and drag queens conceived for the imprisoned narrator's own self-pleasure and animated by "reveries" and "dream words," but which begins to take on the appearance of the empirically remembered.[26] This interrelation between a fantasy conjured in the masturbatory present and the palpable sense of a past that makes up that conjuring marks the mediation involved in the act of remembering itself, where recorded material is given its fuller, later iteration with a new dimension. Wojnarowicz is often concerned, in this vein, with the visuality of memory, and in his writing itself phrases—like that of the convict's "smoking exterior"—are rehearsed in numerous guises in the form of journal entries or attempts at poems. The "shadows" one enters are after all interior spaces that are ever in dialogue with the "city streets." The lived environment of the city gives shape to the constructed "mythologies" of erotic self-realization and is thus similarly full of fodder for later pleasures; a cruising diary might read just like a dream diary.

This Genet-inspired temporality of masturbation is conceived of by Wojnarowicz as photographic—and in fact in 1983 he produced a collage work titled *Jean Genet Masturbating in Metteray Prison* in which, Anderson argues, both "Wojnarowicz and the viewer are implicated in the position of the masturbating figure."[27] This masturbatory temporality frames cruising as an apprehension that is the germ cell of fantasy. You turn your head, the new love; this phrase has a hidden future perfect, announcing a moment that will have been momentous, to be seen subsequently in a memory erotically developed. "I am to see to it that I do not lose you," in Whitman's words. Strangers seen in passing provide raw sensory material for fantasies that might be fleshed out simultaneously, which is to say at the moment of apprehension, or subsequently in tranquility, behind closed doors. As with Whitman's "faint indirections," a gesture of drawing in, cruising functions according to a certain negotiation between the known and unknown and draws energy from inference rather than information. Wojnarowicz's work is alive to the importance of this distance and conceives of interpersonal inscrutability as being companionable with the mysteries of photography. It claims, in this regard, the Rimbaud figure as the cruiser *par excellence*.

Another poem reaching back to Wojnarowicz's childhood, "Distance," ponders both the candor (or lack thereof) in photographic form alongside the masturbatory act, which is described as "the hand that one can put to themselves / while the eyes close on men miles and miles / away and the distances not measured by the map or clock."[28] It is one such distance, measurable by the "clock" but nonetheless ineffable, too, that is described at the start of this poem:

> I have in my wallet a photograph of myself at age three or four. It is not
> a very good photo because you can hardly see what I am
>   thinking...

Here Wojnarowicz betrays a conception of photography, as a document of what the subject "is thinking," which echoes the form's historic relation to revelation and the unadulterated. And yet in its value judgment of the "good" photo, Wojnarowicz's description seems "miles and miles" from his own work. These lines also refer to an implicit distinction being made between the photograph as artwork and the photograph as a personal memento. The latter kind, something kept in your "wallet," is less an object of artistry than it is of bearing witness to a moment in a life trajectory. This category of images, whose "talismanic uses [...] express a feeling both sentimental and implicitly magical," comprise an attempt to "contact or lay claim to another reality."[29] So writes Sontag, a critic Wojnarowicz once referred to irreverently as "Susan Whatsername" who said "something about photographs being like small deaths which is maybe true" ("Do Not Doubt," *CK,* 143–44.) Wojnarowicz's childhood photo is not "very good," in this regard, because it fails to approximate the kind of proximity in which its viewer can get at what this toddler is "thinking." This dynamic, of trying to get at the subject's thoughts, is described later in the poem in relation to its temporal inverse, the "times back then when I wondered what I would be thinking now and it is now." The poem's compositional moment recasts this thought experiment back across time. This return to a premasturbatory childhood summons, through a retrospective future-tense, something both irrecoverable and inevitable. It makes these child and adult selves foreign to one another even while they are inexorably bound.

These respective phenomena—a photo of a child looked at by their adult self and that child's mental projection of their future person—have something in common, for they both rely upon forms of affective conjecture. Even a photograph, the more concrete of these images, depends for its life upon an imaginative projection, or an incitement "to reverie" about its subject. To think of a photo which does not yield easily to reading as not "very good," as Wojnarowicz does here, seems somewhat at odds with the nature of its potency. It is the act of wondering—rather than merely seeing, or knowing—that produces an intimate pull between image and viewer. Barthes's *punctum,* after all, does not emanate from the immediately knowable. While "Distance" focuses on the strangeness of encountering yourself as a child, with the appearance of an uncanny distance, this strangeness also has an evident erotics pertaining to others, that "sense of the unattainable that can be evoked by photographs [and which] feeds directly into the erotic feelings of those for whom desirability is enhanced by distance."[30] This distance might be one measurable by the "map" or "clock," or one which seems to exceed such an apparatus; an intimate distance even within closeness, to recall the terms of Benjamin's "aura." In cruising, these senses of the familiar and the faraway are yielded simultaneously in the figure of a person just yards away. Recalling his hustling days in an interview with Sylvère Lotringer, Wojnarowicz describes "promiscuity" as a "vessel in which I could pour fantasy":

> The less I knew about the person I was having sex with, the more amazing it was to me. It wasn't loaded down with too much detailed knowledge—their owl collection, or their disgusting

habits—that would have made it absurd in the face of what living was for me then.[31]

The nature of this "detailed knowledge" ranges here between the bizarre and the cloyingly familiar, and such knowledge is a shorthand for the kind of domesticity that is "absurd" to the forms of "living" that both cruising and hustling constitute, in that these activities are resolutely outside of normative social belonging. But this sense of the unknown also restores a certain agency to the person facing it; the less known, the more that can be imagined, leaving more room for "fantasy" to be "pour[ed]" in. It follows that such elasticity then also prepares such encounters the better for memory, and a tryst not "loaded down" with information is riper for pleasurable rewriting.

In another interview with Nan Goldin, Wojnarowicz speaks more particularly to the indistinguishability of "fantasy and reality," which are "just as important" as each other.[32] Fantasies "were stored pieces of information that I create collages out of," and "when I start thinking of an image to jerk off to—a guy, a situation, a place, whatever—it's like 'Have I ever seen that guy in my life?'" (202). Fantasies turn on such a question; they emerge in Wojnarowicz's account as composite forms made from "fragments of memory" that prolong the life of a cruise by overlaying it with an extra, "made up" resonance. That such fantasies are intimately linked with visual culture is evident: "We carry," Wojnarowicz continues, "a whole store of genetic information that pops up like a movie screen or slide screen or something" (202–3). This tentatively drawn metaphor casts memory as cinematic or photographic or "something" similar, and this vagary speaks to the connection's own limitation, for this is not a direct and identical relation but rather an imaginative projection which brings them into dialogue. It also echoes Wojnarowicz's earlier notion of photography as an act of "collecting evidence" to make "a collage of reality."[33] As a collection of images of the male form it also recalls the "loosely conceived and never completed photographic project" referred to as the *Male Series,* composed of portraits of the male body and featuring subjects that included Peter Hujar and Iolo Carew.[34] The notion of this visual and erotically charged "store" echoes Sontag's description of the way that photographs "can abet desire in the most direct, utilitarian way—as when someone collects photographs of anonymous examples of the desirable as an aid to masturbation."[35] But the images that linger from passing encounters or a transient glance are not so readily "utilitarian" because they require a certain creative capacity. Their erotic mystery is of course different from the concrete and material form that a photograph takes, but it is precisely the latter's capacity to freeze the possibly transient that provides this conception of the mind's eye as an instrument of preservation, and brings the evanescent everyday moment into the orbit of the visual archive.

This connection, too, is not just a citation of the visual per se, but of a mediatized visual culture providing erotic titillation, and the frisson that makes up the semiotic fodder of cruising can also be rewired into historical or more traditionally literary images, like the portrait of Rimbaud. Wojnarowicz links his account of masturbatory fantasy to his "first sense of desire" as a child, "looking at a *TV Guide*" and coming

> across a soap advertisement of this guy under a stream of running water, lathering himself up. And there was something about the musculature in his chest, something about his face, his lips, his eyes, his arms, his bicep that I went into a trance.[36]

This trance of absorption accounts for that "something" which pricks, "the intoxication of laying my hands to myself" experienced as a child, prior to the advent of that act. It is also structured according to the particular mediation of the body by the advert and highlights the respective body parts of its "lathering" subject to construct a desirable image through which to sell soap. In this regard, the erotic trance that might be induced by an image arises from the coexistence between the *punctum* and the *studium,* to return to Barthes's terms. It is an experience all at once of consciously intended or constructed dimensions alongside the potent "something" that is felt to emerge more contingently. Wojnarowicz's fixation upon masturbation in these early poems and later accounts in interviews suggests an erotics that locates in the act of remembering a shared reliance upon fantasy and reality, and privileges strangeness or indirection as highly as the collage of "information" that can be inferred in a passing encounter. If this unfolds "like" a photograph or a movie, as a metaphorical conception rehearsed by these unpublished poems, then *Arthur Rimbaud in New York* constitutes the execution of such a work. Indeed Wojnarowicz's tribute to the French poet, the next section of this chapter contends, can be conceived of as a cruising montage that gives visual expression to the "new love" of the streets and piers.

Going Rimbaud

The erotic ambiguity of a photograph's address is exploited to the full in *Arthur Rimbaud in New York*. The poet's face suggests little sense of what he is "thinking" and provides little space for "detailed knowledge." Wojnarowicz's partner Tom Rauffenbart writes that this "blank, unchanging face" seems "always to be watching and absorbing sights and experiences," as if its sideways glance is caught at the moment just before the "détourne"/"retourne" that will bring to light the "new love."[37] This mysteriousness is also, Rauffenbart continues, a product of the figure's solitude. In "the end," whether on the thoroughfare of Forty-Second Street or on a deserted Coney Island beach, this figure "remains alone," differentiated from any surrounding bodies in the frame by the mask's blankness, as if this might speak to some essential solitude in Wojnarowicz himself as a "loner."[38] The image on Forty-Second Street, perhaps the series' best known, features Rimbaud standing amongst the street's bustle with his gaze fixed to the left of the frame. The figure's "blank, unchanging face" and solid stance seem particularly uncanny here because they suggest an absence of feeling or sensation even amidst the sensorium of Midtown, and he is juxtaposed with the emphatic motion of the half-jumping figure who crosses the street behind him. The mask, a photograph within a photograph, introduces a lifelessness into the frame and this cutout face, yanked from another historical time and place, highlights the action of disembodiment that has taken place. The mask may provide "relief from exposure," Olivia Laing writes regarding this work, but it is also "uncanny, sinister, unnerving."[39] It possesses what Leo Bersani, in an essay on haunting stares, describes as a "goneness"; a withdrawal that manifests as "the unfathomable sadness of an irremediable unconnectedness."[40] To return to the terms of O'Hara's "Homosexuality," being "pierced by a glance" here functions not through "taking" a mask "off" but putting one on. This glance is piercing because it suggests a subject for whom, Bersani writes, the "fully present, fully visible" world is "somehow not there"; one who is immune to the surrounding "environment's soliciting and solicitous presence."[41]

And yet could this "goneness" not itself be "solicitous," this "unconnectedness" an invitation to connection? Wojnarowicz's images figure solitude, but attending that solitude is the strange companionship that is formed between a portrait and its beholder. The images are shot through with the sense that Rimbaud knows we are looking, even if it is left unsettlingly unclear how well he himself can see through the mask's slit-cut eyes. This involvement functions according to a suspension of historical time that is already playing out in the composition of the image, merging 1872 with 1979. This temporal layering provides a certain latitude for entering the image's diegesis, as a process that reflectively casts the spectator as a character in, or just outside of, its frame. It is in this sense that the Rimbaud figure of Wojnarowicz's project—which has the sheen of the "real" conferred by photography—is not, or does not imagine himself to be, entirely alone, even in abandoned or empty urban scenes.

His gaze might then be accounted for by another passing stranger, one of any number of possible urban types: the stalker, the detective, another cruiser on the hunt for the "new love." In this regard these frozen, melancholic images court a futurity, as if they each stage the beginning of a potential erotic encounter to be multiplied or repeated across numerous New York locales. Wojnarowicz writes in his later prose piece "Losing the Form in Darkness" that these "streets were familiar more because of the faraway past than the recent past—streets that I walked in those odd times while living among them in my early teens when in the company of deaf mutes and times square pederasts [. . .] seen through the same eyes but each time with periods of time separating it" (*CK*, 13). This palimpsestic quality of place is something echoed by the Rimbaud images. The "faraway past" refers not only to Wojnarowicz's teen hustling days, which are signaled by the Times Square movie theaters in the background of the Forty-Second Street image, but the historical past of the French poet. Rimbaud, Wojnarowicz writes in a catalog for the 1990 exhibition where these photos were first shown, was not necessarily a direct surrogate of the artist himself but "a device to confront my own desires, experiences, biography and [. . .] those places that suddenly and unexpectedly revive the smell and traces of former states of body and mind long ago left behind."[42] The dead poet is thus revived here to erotic ends. As Jonathan Weinberg points out, "one of the most interesting aspects of Wojnarowicz's use of the photocopied mask" is "the way it shifts the emphasis away from Rimbaud as a poet to his representation," such that the French poet's "derangement of the senses becomes a different kind of derangement—the transformation and degrading of the image."[43] Rimbaud provides the occasion to explore one's own contingent amorous past but also cuts an archetypal figure, as a shorthand for a sexual agent living outside of the confines of respectable social practice, who is reintegrated into the visual economy of gay cruising.

Above all, however, it is the deathly anachronism of this mask which conditions the photo's gaze. This tension between the vital and the static, and between the New York settings and Rimbaud's stony, staring face, plays out according to our experience of the work, and whether we encounter it in what Bersani calls the "culturally sanctioned site of staring: the museum."[44] Besides publishing several images from it in the *SoHo Weekly News* and other small publications, Wojnarowicz did not present *Arthur Rimbaud in New York* for reception until 1990, when he printed a portfolio of twenty-five images (from a much larger pool of negatives) to display in his *In the Garden* exhibition at P.P.O.W. It was exhibited as an example of his first significant work, thus turning a retrospective glance toward his youth, and the "pictures would have been seen free of any text other than a title and the artist's statement, which viewers could read or ignore."[45] In that statement, Wojnarowicz writes that he was "attracted to the 'youth' in the series; the rock and roll do or die abandon of that period of time."[46] Imagining these photographs displayed in an exhibition space, with Rimbaud's visage multiplied throughout the room, calls to mind Whitman's description of the "phantom concourse" of the daguerreotype gallery, the sense of a "peopled word" as "mute as the grave," and the time of their presentation, just two years before Wojnarowicz's death from complications from AIDS, provides a morbid gloss on the "do or die abandon" they furtively celebrate.

Yet such a space also lends the work a new kind of vitality. In requiring its visitors to move through it, the embodied mobility of viewing these images spatially approximates something of the peripatetic experience Wojnarowicz seeks to capture in them, where the mean streets are replaced with the white cube. Your head turns away, your head turns back. The arrangement into twenty-five images also lends the project the linear force of a chronological narrative that can be walked through. It begins, according to Mysoon Rizk's reading, with "Rimbaud's imaginary arrival by sea at Coney Island" and ends with "his fatal, albeit fictive, overdose of heroin in an abandoned warehouse on a Hudson River pier."[47] This iteration was the closest Wojnarowicz got to executing the work as a cinematic montage, a possible form suggested by an unpublished 35 mm photo script that maps out Rimbaud's movements from Brooklyn to Chinatown and Times Square.[48] This script also mentions a shot of Rimbaud inside a movie theater eating popcorn and facing the screen intently. If present in the final series, this image would provide a self-reflexive gloss on the work as a whole, which depends upon that "mobilized virtual gaze," an optical relationship where viewers feel themselves immersed or transported and which is described by Anne Friedberg as a hallmark of both the cinema and the exhibition space, with its roots in nineteenth-century *flânerie*.[49] Similarly self-reflexive, if attending to *Rimbaud in New York* as a montage, is the narrative move to the dilapidated pier, where the Rimbaud figure retires from the streets and sits with a newspaper, and is then photographed masturbating in the next image. This plays out within the narrative what is implicit as a potentiality in each of the series' images, which capture discrete instances of apprehension that are made ripe for recollection in tranquility, where they provide material for self-pleasure, perhaps overlaid or further stimulated by the fodder of a newspaper.

If erotic fantasy, as a site of vision that turns both to the past of occurrence and the futurity of the potential or the yearned for, "pops up like a movie screen or slide screen or something," *Arthur Rimbaud in New York* gets close to an actualization of that "something." A screenwork that exorcises and eroticizes through reperformance some of the artist's own past demons, it spotlights in its frames the visual dimensions of memory. In this sense, the ends of this project have parallels with some of Wojnarowicz's earliest ideas for an artwork in tribute to Rimbaud, namely a series of illustrations of the poems from *Illuminations*. The line from "À une raison" with which I began sits in epigraphic relation to *Arthur Rimbaud in New York*; it narrates the "new love" of the moment of encounter, a "new love" that is after all an old one too, made in the image of an old young poet with the power to turn heads. These images also constitute quasi-illustrations of many of Wojnarowicz's early poems, at least in glimpses; rogue phrases like the "smoking exterior of the convict" travel directly from the manuscript pages of the mid-70s to the Rimbaud project, and provide a textual foundation, albeit in fairly juvenile form, through which to explicate the workings of erotic fantasy that inform these images.

Text and image are amorphous variables in Wojnarowicz's work. They are forms that refer to one another in a desirous bind. Many of his paintings, for example, foreground textual matter and typography, and just as the *Rimbaud* images are illuminated by Wojnarowicz's earlier textual or poetic experiments, which offer something of a conceptual framework, his later published prose works are steeped in consciously framed images, seeming to yearn for the slippage into visual form. Composed largely of cruising stories that take place on the streets of New York and the abandoned Hudson River piers, Wojnarowicz's prose works speak to the imagistic nature of anonymous erotic experience, and construct a textual collage of impressions at the moment of apprehending a stranger. This imagistic quality is meant less as a term for overtly descriptive prose than it is the often explicit invocation of photographic form to mediate these experiences, for Wojnarowicz frequently invokes "the temporally complex practices of photography and cinema as analogies for autobiographical strategies," as Anderson writes.[50] In this regard *Arthur Rimbaud in New York* provides a vivid precursor; a blueprint for the mode of queer temporal experience that animates Wojnarowicz's later writing, which is marked by a sustained interest in cruising and its relation to artistic practice. It is a portrait of the artist as a young man, in a frame extending beyond youth and toward death.

The Appearance of a Portrait

There is an artifice in the staging of *Arthur Rimbaud in New York*, where the protagonist's place in each image depends upon the photographer getting a clear shot, or the beholder a good look. Compositionally speaking, the "turn" of the head that conditions its phenomenology is relatively free from the contingencies or obstructions that could obscure the "new love" from view: the urban crowd, the speed of encounter, the darkness of the piers. These images execute in augmented fashion the momentary arrest, the double take that seeks to make visible something (or someone) that could easily be missed in the motion of passing by. The prose piece "Losing the Form in Darkness," as its title suggests, is structured around such perceptual obstructions, in particular the dreamlike setting of the abandoned piers, and describes the kind of first-person resources available for rescuing images from immediate experience. The piece begins in the pier's "maze of hallways wandered as in films," observing "the fracturing of bodies from darkness into light" and later describing a cruising prospect as "a passenger on the shadows" (*CK,* 9–10). In such a setting "it is the appearance of a portrait, not the immediate vision I love so much." For a shifting tableau made up of fragments drifting along like shadows, the "portrait" offers recomposure and mediates the "immediate vision." In the face of the strange or partial, portraits can reintroduce the familiar; resonances or correspondences that provide, as in Rimbaud's poem, the "*clef de cette parade.*"

The portraits Wojnarowicz enumerates transform the "immediate vision" into something stranger, and invoke "the childlike rogue slipped out from the white-sheeted bed of Pasolini; the image of Jean Genet cut loose from age and time and continent," in a similar uprooting to that of *Arthur Rimbaud in New York* (12). This is the construction of an intimacy that functions intertextually, both intensifying the sense of the fantastical (what is Jean Genet doing here?) and making it seem more real or tangible. This doubleness is after all consonant with Wojnarowicz's assertion in another piece, "In the Shadow of the American Dream: Soon All This Will Be Picturesque Ruins," that there is "no difference between memory and sight, fantasy and actual vision" (26). In this moment, "sight" arises out of cultural "memory," and "vision" out of the fantasy of resuscitation. Mapping the "immediate vision" (which is not an a priori category, but one of "disjointed observations collected and collated into the forms and textures of thought") onto the cultural field makes it memorable, in a process with equal stakes in distance and closeness. After cruising the piers during a drugs trip in "Losing the Form in Darkness," where "old images raced back and forth" like the "old senses of desire," Wojnarowicz writes of "sitting over coffee and remembering the cinematic motions as if witnessed from a discreet distance, I lay the senses down one by one" (12–13). Distance itself has a cinematic quality, as something that heightens or intervenes in "immediate vision" and confers a glamour, making matter all the more vivid for recollection over coffee. This account short-circuits the truism of memory as a distant or "discreet" iteration of what was raw and immediate and suggests that these motions were felt as "cinematic" and distant even at the moment of witnessing them. This aesthetic heightening brings a paradoxical and retrospective closeness, "lay[ing]" the memory down as if in a reverie.

Along with "Pasolini" and "Genet," Wojnarowicz also name-checks the filmmaker Tod Browning, whose notorious 1932 film *Freaks*, with its cast of deformed carnival side show performers, structures his apprehension of "a small, dwarfish man, someone out of an old Todd [*sic*] Browning image" (19). The appearance of this man is a cinematic gloss upon a tension Sontag identifies in the history of American portrait photography. The form's candid "leveling of discriminations between the beautiful and the ugly, the important and the trivial" that was inherited, Sontag writes, from "Whitman's" democratic "project," and exemplified by such photographers as Walker Evans, ultimately gave way to a darker, less generous photographic focus upon the freakish.[51] Sontag identifies this latter tendency in the work of Diane Arbus, a photographer who "chooses oddity, chases it, frames it, develops it, titles it" and found plenty of portrait subjects in "New York," a city "rich with freaks."[52] Wojnarowicz's mention of the "small, dwarfish man" blends the leveling impulse Sontag identifies in early portrait photography with the fixation upon oddness in Arbus and Browning's work. In a tape journal from 1981, Wojnarowicz himself claimed that "I like ugly people with some sense of derangement [. . .] somebody who's off in some way, somebody who's interesting, who has character, through lack of beauty or whatever."[53] Yet the man's appearance goes beyond a "lack of beauty," and Wojnarowicz lights upon his freakishness, a quality lexically recalled in the mention of Browning, and contributes to the text's larger framing of the pier as a space of a performance, where life is rendered as a sideshow, as a display of the erotic and the freakish that once again recalls Rimbaud.

These "cinematic" referents in "Losing the Form in Darkness" are more than just similes. Unlike other instances where "like" carries descriptions into the realm of comparison, like the "deaf mute" in another text who "looked like he just walked out of some waterfront in an old queer french novel,"[54] works by Genet, Pasolini, and Browning are cited as actual sources "out of" which these figures are yanked prepositionally. They are "slipped out" and "cut loose," beyond mere "like"-ness. This conflation of semblance and reality, whereby the subjects of these "portrait[s]" appear as performers uprooted straight out of cinematic works, recalls Peggy Phelan's description of the portrait as:

a developed image which renders the corporeal, a body-real, as
a real body. Uncertain about what this body looks like or how
substantial it is, we perform an image of it by imitating what we
think we look like [...]. Wanting to look like someone else,
we quote and imitate the look of the visible model.[55]

Phelan's account illuminates the conundrum of the photographed subject, for whom the corporeal and exterior shape of the "I" finds visibility
through the "them" of available cultural reference. This projection suggests that the scene of posing for a portrait—in its sense of artifice and
differentiation from everyday time—shines a light on a condition that
is also true more widely of self-presentation: namely, the question as to
whose image(s) we make ourselves, or imagine ourselves made, in. In
Phelan's words, the answer lies in "the confrontation with one's body, the
surface image upon which subjectivity is visible to the camera's eye" (37).

This "confrontation" is also true in reverse, and can be experienced
by the beholder, for whom the camera's eye is the surrogate in this formulation, if extended beyond the immediate context of posing for a portrait. If the portrait is a "developed image," produced within a duration
of exposure and composition, the performances which occur with equal
reliance upon "visible model[s]" outside such a duration—off duty, as
it were—offer an even more partial or contingent sense of our own
"body" as exterior surface, but also obscure the sought-after wholeness
of the "real bod[ies]" of others, whose "cinematic motions" we witness
perhaps only instantly. This is a parallel "uncertain[ty]" with that of the
portrait's subject, for we too only glimpse what a stranger's "body looks
like or how substantial it is" and thus "perform" its image through description, projecting upon it the imitative surface of the already existing
"visible model." Phelan's double-sided statements about the portrait are
assimilable to Barthesian terms, for both the subject and the photographer to some degree consciously intend the *studium* of the image they
create together, by wearing and teasing out the markers by which the
subject can be recognized in historical space and time. Similarly, the
photographer facilitates what will for the beholder be the image's *punctum* without meaning to, just as the subject possesses that "something"
without consciously directing it toward the gaze.

The dialogic relation between the *studium* and *punctum*, in which
the former is implicitly relegated to a lesser category of truth value with

regards to the subject being photographed, speaks to the evidently different kinds of knowledge about a person contained by a portrait, on the one hand, and a glimpse of the "real" them, at the optically brief turning point that determines the future of your relation to them. Wojnarowicz's apprehension of figures "out of" Genet and Pasolini reveals the impulse to match strangeness with *studium*, a blend of apparitional mystery and the culturally familiar. Yet these descriptions go beyond statements of resemblance and suggest figures drawn from discrete aesthetic worlds, rather than merely citing corroborable counterparts or doppelgangers. In this sense the *studium*, which goes beyond the "immediate vision" to envision and elaborate upon the nature of the stranger's "cinematic motions," becomes a powerful tool of sight in the act of cruising. It draws upon externally available fields of reference in order to get at the perceived personal essence obscured by parameters both temporal and spatial and is lent a particular erotic charge by the liveness of the apprehension itself. Any claim to knowledge of that person is simultaneously a state of possibility; an encounter that could be consummated in one way or another, where the stranger's place within a cultural repertoire becomes the basis of a sexual fantasy.

These fantasies are not only the product of an individual reverie, or a personal construction made in the rush of encounter, but refer to collective codes within the nexus of self-presentation and its particular queer inflections. To resemble, or perceive a resemblance of, a character from a work by Genet or Pasolini is to refer to something of a gay urtext, and thus to "perform" a code legible within a shared semiotic understanding among gay cruisers. The mask, like Rimbaud's face, is a product of features, like "costume and fashion," that "perfect the image stereotype" (36). And it can be a powerful invitation; the tip of an imaginative iceberg that offers some indication of the kind of sex, for example, to expect with this person. If this semiotic performance has historically been a survival tactic, arising from the necessity of concealment, as well as an expediency in gay sexual practice, it does not mean that the code is mere appendage, or a sign with only a minimal claim upon personhood. Stereotypes often, after all, have some truth. The interpersonal "image," like the look, is a gesture of both understanding and of being understood. It imagines this communion as a form of conversation. Cruising encounters are often wordless, at least at first, and this anonymous silence is often itself erotic. As such, they rely upon visual signs to approximate the verbal. The "images" exchanged by each party at the moment of apprehension are akin to a form of inquisition, a reciprocal but contingent truce which may last only a few seconds or may lead to a sexual act.

The quality of this exchange has telling parallels with Phelan's assertion that "portrait photography reflects the transference of image between the photographer and model. Like a good correspondence, the model's reply to the inquiry of the photographer is based on the quality of the photographer's question" (36). The look which initiates a cruise determines its trajectory; as an ocular "question" it must be direct enough to be legible, to elicit the like "quality" in its addressee, while furtive enough to evade the glare of the gaze. As Olivia Laing writes of Wojnarowicz's *Rimbaud* images, they simultaneously "express" a "conflict between the desire to make contact, to reach beyond the prison of the self, and to hide, to walk away, to disappear," like "a question not yet resolved."[56] The "look" of the addressee, as a stylistic term, prefigures the "question" of contact. The relation between cruisers, like that of the photographer and the subject, is one of "transference," and involves a reciprocity of visual information. The look of having "just walked out of some waterfront in an old queer french novel," say, can provide the answer that precipitates the question, and invites closer inspection.

What's in a Neck?

In "Doing Time in a Disposable Body," Wojnarowicz encounters a man "with an air of desperation and possible violence around him like a rank perfume."[57] Interrogating why "the remote edge of violence attracts" him to this man, and to seemingly dangerous men more generally, Wojnarowicz reflects:

> I associate with certain gestures or body language or scars or
> other physical characteristics an entire flood of memories and
> fictions and mythologies. It's something in the blue-ink tattoos
> or coal-scratched rubbings made in prison cells or delinquent
> basement parties. Maybe it's the sense that he could easily and
> dispassionately murder someone or rob a liquor store or a small
> roadside gas station or bang some salesman in the head at a

highway rest stop and steal his automobile; it's something about
the sense of violence carried as a distancing tool to break down
the organized world.[58]

This passage recasts the erotic "image" as an assemblage of parts; "certain" features of a stranger's countenance that summon "an entire flood"
of images. Tattoos here inscribe more than just the skin's surface. They
conjure up pulp narratives of homicide and robbery on the open road,
somewhere far away from the downtown coffee shop in which this encounter takes place. The devil is in the detail, and the breakdown of this
image into parts threatens to "break down the organized world." The
erotic aura of this figure is thus the product of an act of reading, a re-
organizing of the stranger's body into constituent parts with their own
narrative potential. These narrative projections range from the particular, "a small roadside gas station," to the more diffusely ominous, like the
"violence that floats like static electricity that completely annihilates
the possibility of future or security" that Wojnarowicz later describes
in the same passage.

The multiplicities of scale contained in this passage, which moves between the small and the big, and the specific and the general, renders the
image of cruising less as a fixed whole than as a separable ensemble of semiotic phenomena. The distance of anonymity is collapsed by Wojnarowicz's reliance upon genre tropes, like the Americana of "liquor store[s]"
and "highway[s]," as though such clichés offer a way of familiarizing the
strange. The strange here does not simply mean the unknown, but also
the specific, and specifically those discrete features of a person that seem
out of place or susceptible to imaginative probing. This passage in many
ways crystallizes Wojnarowicz's sense of cruising—its cinematicity and
its dangers—but it also reveals the importance of circumspection to
the act. Wojnarowicz's corpus is, unsurprisingly, full of anatomical features, as befits the physiognomic nature of reading strangers, but these
range from the expected to the unusual. If "blue-ink tattoos" and "coal-
scratched rubbings" are readily synonymous with a strain of dangerous
masculinity and serve to make more vivid the bodily whole, the archetypal associations of certain other body parts that appear in Wojnarowicz's writing are less immediately apparent. Take again, for example,
this moment in "Losing the Form in Darkness" (*CK*, 14–15):

He had a tough face. It was square-jawed, and barely shaven.
Close-cropped hair wiry and black, handsome like some face
in old boxer photographs, a cross between an aging boxer and
Mayakovsky. He had a nose that might have once been broken
in some dark avenue barroom in a distant city invented by
some horny young kid. There was a wealth of images in that
jawline, slight tension to it and curving down toward a hungry
looking mouth.

This passage takes in the visage of this stranger in terms of the discrete
but interrelated parts which make up the "image." It is structured around
this relation between the whole and the part and enumerates "detail[s]"
according to an order of individual features. The descriptions "square-
jawed" and "barely shaven" serve to illustrate "tough[ness]"; the addition of the "wiry and black" hair recasts this toughness as that of a
"handsome" old boxer crossed with "Mayakovsky." Those first three sentences contain miscellany enough, and the accumulating trajectory of
"tough[ness]" culminates in a surprising yoking of the vintage Americana
of "old boxer photographs" to Russian futurist Mayakovsky, famously
handsome and broadly built, who reinflects this physicality with a literary quality.

In "Cruising Ghosts: David Wojnarowicz's Queer Antecedents," the
third chapter of her study, Fiona Anderson argues that Wojnarowicz
maps his erotic "connections" with past writers "onto the bodies of
anonymous toughs, onto men with whom he shared sex, conversation, a
cheap coffee in the Silver Dollar Café," as he does here.[59] These men
are conjured or sketched out in the act of storytelling, and the backstory of the broken nose is attributed to "some young horny kid." It has
the stock feel of fantasy, taking place in a nondescript "city." Does this
"young horny kid" refer back to the young Wojnarowicz of "masturbation photo," and thus give something away of the author's own sexual
fantasies? The faint echo of Wojnarowicz's earlier writing about childhood and masturbation makes it seem as if this man could be a figment
conjured by the author's earlier self who appears in the here and now,
"cut loose" from linear temporality, as an uncanny visitor. The temporal flux underlying this fantasy presence recasts this passage as a form
of collage, marked by the way body parts are assembled in a manner
akin to that of masturbatory fantasies. Fantasies, as Wojnarowicz states

in the interview with Nan Goldin, "were stored pieces of information that I create collages out of."[60] They are "pieces" ripe for recollection, or reattachment to new facial features yet to be encountered. Conceiving of the "image" as a collage also accounts for the reliance of a style upon parts that have a life of their own, or a certain autonomy from the whole they help constitute. If this nose is capable of telling a story by itself, the same can be said for the stranger's jawline, and the passage appears to ask: what's in a jaw? The "wealth of images" contained in this jawline is connected to but separate from the "hungry looking mouth" the jaw leads "down" to. This mode of attention, with its predilection for zooming in, betrays an interest in minutiae and thus in acute anatomical images less obviously noticeable than eyes and faces. Going beyond the quasi-disembodiment of Rimbaud's "turn of the head," or Whitman's "talk of those turning eyeballs," this moment lights upon a poetics of joints found throughout Wojnarowicz's work, one marked by a particular fascination with napes and necks.

There is an image of one neck in particular that is so specific as to exceed the scene out of which it arises, and it recurs again and again throughout his writing. It is framed most comprehensively in a Super 8 script for a silent black-and-white film, never made, that follows a character simply named "Drifter" around the city. Wojnarowicz frames the first series of shots as "attempting to place on film the sexual/erotic symbols inherent in street/crowd movements flash—glimpses of strangers entering taxis, doorways, subway staircases—the wounding nature of a neck (the lines of that neck)."[61] The film also later contains a series of closeup shots of "anonymous mans [*sic*] head," "mens [*sic*] hands," "chest," "lips, noses, throats," "asses," "crotches, legs beneath trousers."[62] But the opening "neck" is the only body part of the film given such a characteristic, the capacity to be "wounding." The nature of the wound remains unspoken and has the flavor of the *punctum*'s "prick." It is a contingent feature emerging out of a visual field with the power to hurt its beholder even within its own passive and perhaps oblivious existence, and is animate only as a constituent part of the living person it has been abstracted from in Wojnarowicz's shot. While arising from a "sexual/erotic" symbol "inherent in street/crowd movements," this capacity to wound is not an "inherent" property of necks but rather reveals something of the beholder's interiority. This revelation is akin to that of the *punctum* which, in the words of Margaret Olin, is "so private" that it may not actually be "in the photograph at all," a "literary device to make us understand how he [Barthes] could feel his kind of pain [...] analogous to the smell and taste of the madeleine" in Proust.[63]

The neck for Wojnarowicz is a sign of "his kind of pain." It is related directly to his own experience, and perhaps also to "his kind" of pleasure. The recurrence of napes and necks—which are repeated throughout the sexual trysts described in his prose—also calls to mind the fetish. Freud's identification of fetishism stresses not only its basis upon object-choice, but on a particular and indeed private relation to said object that may not be readily shareable. Freud writes of a particularly "extraordinary case" in which "a young man had exalted a certain sort of 'shine on the nose' into a 'fetishistic precondition.'"[64] Caught linguistically between German and English, the young man "endowed [the nose] at will with the luminous shine which was not perceptible to others," and "the shine on the nose" was "in reality 'a *glance* at the nose.'" The fetish functions through the glance, and Wojnarowicz's "neck" shares with Freud's account of fetishism the sense of an exalting projection. The film script presents the "wounding nature of a neck" as a truism, a given endowment of necks that may not be immediately "perceptible" to those for whom they are not a fetishistic locus. Similarly in "Losing the Form in Darkness," where this opening to the film script eventually took published shape, Wojnarowicz zooms further in upon the neck within a textual montage of "old images" that "race back and forth" and incorporate the "flashes of a curve of arm, back, the lines of a neck glimpsed among the crowds in the train stations, one you could write whole poems to" (*CK*, 12.) This iteration substitutes the cinematic for the written as the locus of the neck's power, and its invocation of poetry both puns upon the "lines" of that neck and lends a literary concreteness to the fetishistic transformation of the object described by Freud. That the indeterminate "you" could write "whole poems" to this neck is cited as an indicator of its remarkableness and the sense that, like a muse, it can elicit creativity itself.

Yet the word "whole" also points to something stranger. It echoes semantically with the way the neck is described—"a neck"—such that we think of *a whole* neck. To think of body parts in terms of wholeness is to think of their disembodiment, for their entirety depends upon a degree of separation from the bodily whole they are connected to. The neck thus resonates, per se, as a free-floating erotic charge that goes beyond the bounds of its immediate urban context. Its evident relation to the city goes some way to accounting for its "wounding nature," and at the end of the film script the Drifter is shown smoking at the edge of the pier with the "suggestion of solitude among crowds. quiet feelings."[65] Within its common citational setting the neck thus becomes a figure for urban alienation, as though the "whole poems" Wojnarowicz imagines would take the form of riffs upon loneliness. This neck's melancholic reso-nance can be accounted for in one sense by the specular tableau it sug-gests. To look at someone's neck from behind becomes a figuration for estrangement because it renders that someone out of reach. The person may not be physically distant, but this posterior vantage suggests with it an elision of the face, and in turn identification itself. A neck cannot return your glance but reflects back at you your own fetishistic desire for it. It becomes a figure for all the ones that got away, those possible "new love[s]" who disappeared because their "head[s]" never turned "back," to return to the terms of Rimbaud's poem. The lines of the neck wound because they contain what Wojnarowicz describes later in "Losing the Form in Darkness" as the "slight traces that cut me with the wounding nature of déjà vu, filled with old senses of desire" (*CK*, 17). The appre-hension of the neck thus lights upon an amorous lack straddling the past, those lost and temporally distant "senses of desire," and the future, insofar as the possibility of consummation with the desired object is staged and thwarted by this moment. The city itself, with its obstruc-tions of vision and identification, provides the backdrop for the neck's symbolic resonance, and their copresence in the image of "the neck in a crowd" marks a limit point for cruising's sense of intimate possibility.

Nonetheless this neck, in its specificity, also discloses meanings that exceed the immediate situation of its apprehension. It is separated out as an art object that elicits an affective response but remains impenetrable, and as such becomes a figure for desire itself. While Freud's account of the fetish provides one optic on Wojnarowicz's fascination with necks, it cannot alone account for it, nor for its melancholic tenor, which seems at odds with Freud's suggestion that the fetish is "seldom felt" by the fetishist "as the symptom of an ailment accompanied by suffering."[66] Suffering is in some sense native to fetishism, in that the construction of the fetish frequently involves an imagined process of disembodiment. This applies in turn to fetishization, the process whereby the scopic dis-position of fetishism meets with the social hierarchization of bodies. The separating out of body parts recalls Fanon's description of fetishism's violent dismemberment, and Silverman identifies how this "obligatory identification with an intolerable imago" is "experienced through the fantasy of a body in bits and pieces, as a violent mutilation."[67] Although Wojnarowicz's "neck" scene neglects to address the power dynamics of looking, and remains coy about the exact nature or vantage of its gaze, it seems to turn the corporeal violence of fetishistic looking inward. While Wojnarowicz emphasizes the amputating frame through which the neck is apprehended, with its "lines" like forms of incision, it is he himself who is wounded by it. That Wojnarowicz seems to dwell upon and even take pleasure in this "wounding nature" is matched by the imaginative capacities induced by such moments. Body parts in Wojnarowicz are synonymous with desire because they invite an ekphrastic filling-in, as in the early poem "Auto Portrait":

> seeking something in this strangers [*sic*] forehead
> something that takes me beyond the bar, beyond the bed
> seeing photographs he makes I dream black and white
> I get tired of the silences of interior life[68]

The stranger's forehead is a space to be filled, a surface of possibility, and the hope of going "beyond" is animated by what he describes as the "photographs he makes." The photographic dream, "black and white" like those "old boxers photographs" or a film by Jean Genet, perhaps, yield the "lines" to be written "on" that forehead. This act of inscription writes this stranger into being. Yet the fantasy of the "beyond" remains ambiguous and is legible primarily as a form of negation. Wojnarowicz's dreams of escape from the alienation of the "quiet feelings" or the "silences of interior life" are frequently described as a site of desire that takes violent or annihilatory form. The erotic appeal of the tattooed man he cruises part by part in "Doing Time in a Disposable Body" is, after all, the "violence that floats like static electricity that completely annihilates the possibility of future or security." It is in this sense, then, that the neck goes "beyond" its iteration as a desirable quotidian apparition. As a haunting, oddly disembodied figuration of the erotic, this recurring neck seems eerily cognizant of an interrelation between cruising, desire, and death that, for Wojnarowicz and his peers, would soon be thrown into sharp relief.

Dead Man Walking

In November 1987, the photographer Peter Hujar died of complications related to AIDS. A mentor (and former lover) of Wojnarowicz, Hujar died in a hospital bed in the Cabrini Medical Center in Manhattan, where Wojnarowicz kept vigil. In "Living Close to the Knives," he describes Hujar's death as an image that lingers cinematically, "as if it's printed in celluloid on the backs of my eyes," and this description is not entirely metaphorical (*CK*, 103). Wojnarowicz bore witness to this moment by filming his body with a Super 8 camera and taking "portraits" with a "still camera," with the aim of capturing "his amazing feet, his head, that open eye again" (102). These portraits have gained an elegiac iconicity as documents of the HIV/AIDS crisis; "images of the deceased" that "harken back to the long-standing traditions of life and death masks, as well as casts of hands of famous artists."[69] They dwell upon Hujar's corporeality not as an entire corpse, but through a loving inventory that reinvests discrete body parts with individual character. Wojnarowicz attends at close range to the "lines" of these body parts, and attests to their "wounding nature" as reminders of loss. Death is an ultimate form of estrangement, and images of the dead can render strange the familiarity of their subject while also providing documents of idiosyncrasies which offer signs of life that might yet be easy to miss in the course of living, like "his amazing feet." These portraits cast light back upon the stranger's "neck"—an emblem which itself seems "printed in celluloid" throughout Wojnarowicz's writing—and accounts for the ambivalent meanings of its "wounding nature." Such an image, caught uncannily in a crowd, introduces a morbid quality to this "amazing" physical sight. In its disembodiment the "neck" possesses a deadness all its own and offers no futurity outside of itself. It is a strange object that is not easily forgotten.

In the Hujar photographs, Wojnarowicz's aspect shifts from that of the fetishist to that of the coroner, at least as far as body parts are concerned. The act of zooming in here constitutes a mode of elegiac tribute and seeks to provide documentary truth of Hujar's corporeal existence in its specificity, and even in its diminished and emaciated form. The mournful resurfacing here of what we might call the neck-optic of Wojnarowicz's prose, that fascination with the expressive faculties of body parts that rise out from metropolitan tableaux, in turn points to the effect of HIV/AIDS upon such faculties. With the onset of the epidemic, the annihilatory or "wounding" nature of consummatory acts was transformed from an erotic fantasy or imaginative projection into a complex and dangerous reality. In this regard the disease has obvious implications for cruising; it not only introduces anxieties around anonymous, spontaneous sex, but for cruisers with AIDS, threatens to alter one's sexual currency and appearance altogether. HIV/AIDS has rendered so many invisible to history in their early deaths, and it often fell upon artists and activists like Wojnarowicz to recuperate the memory of friends and lovers through art and resistance itself. Yet in more immediate ways, the disease has also made hypervisible the stock specter of the fragile, emaciated gay man on death's door. As Henning Bech writes, in the anxious age of HIV/AIDS, "surveillance is doubled" and "the exterior" becomes "not only a sign of homosexuality but also of death."[70]

Wojnarowicz writes about the peculiar experience of being positive but able to pass, as it were, and thus efface the latter "sign." If the experience of cruising is ultimately one of recognition, of an apprehension which takes the form of a "transference of images" between persons versed in the code, Wojnarowicz's account of a post–HIV/AIDS erotics suggests instead one of misrecognition, of being apprehended as a sexual agent one no longer believes oneself to be. This often comes to light in the changing face of minutiae, as in Wojnarowicz's lament in "Postcards from America: X Rays from Hell" that "the sexy stranger nodding to you on the street corner [. . .] reminds you in a clearer than clear way that at this point in history the virus' activity is forever" (*CK*, 118). Cruising, once everyday and repeatable, and which Wojnarowicz once described as a simultaneously transient yet lasting set of "extended seconds,"[71] now has the inflection of an unwelcome "forever." It is a reminder of the virus's spread and the danger of its consequences. The friction between "at this point in history" and "forever" in this sentence misunderstands and in turn troubles the workings of temporal measurements by mixing deictic delimitation with the eternal. It suggests not only that HIV/AIDS threatens to "forever" change the face of cruising, but that what has changed is the very meaning of "forever" at Wojnarowicz's historical moment. In erotic fantasy's projection, the transient hangs suspended in the balance of "forever," but for Wojnarowicz the virus profoundly disrupts this temporal multiplicity. Lee Edelman writes that AIDS "pervasively [. . .] reinforces an older connection, as old as the antigay reading imposed on the biblical narrative of Sodom's destruction, between practices of gay sexuality and the undoing of futurity" altogether.[72] This fatalism goes by numerous names, and harks back to Sedgwick's observation of that "peculiarly close, though never precisely defined, affinity between same-sex desire and some historical condition of moribundity."[73]

This relation between death and the visible is a contradiction for Wojnarowicz, who sees in the "sexy stranger" this "undoing of futurity," perhaps precisely because he does not apprehend Wojnarowicz as sick. In spite of William F. Buckley's barbaric call "for a program to tattoo people with AIDS," as Wojnarowicz recalls in "Living Close to the Knives," AIDS and HIV-status are not legible like a tattoo (*CK*, 107). The imaginative capacity Wojnarowicz cites in "Doing Time," where "certain [...] physical characteristics" usher in an "entire flood of memories and fictions and mythologies," is vexed in the age of HIV/AIDS because it renders the body of the cruiser an unstable hermeneutic surface. Inhabiting an HIV-positive body, for Wojnarowicz, means being aware of the lack of "certain [...] characteristics" associated with illness, which he instead experiences as an internal phenomenon amounting to a certain subjective blankness. This confrontation between one's abject body and its misrecognized exterior takes the form of a vexed portrait. In the final section of "Spiral," a late, fragmentary prose piece, Wojnarowicz writes that "Sometimes I come to hate people because they can't see where I am [...] all they see is the visual form."[74] The body has ceased to be the "surface image" which makes subjectivity visible, the surface that is the very currency of cruising, an empty visual form that is a "xerox of my former self," "a carbon copy of my form." In this state, reproduction is synonymous with a certain pallor, or a loss of proximity between the self and its image, where Wojnarowicz had once framed such repetition as a supplementarity or erotic surplus. Here there is no Genet or Pasolini to be Xeroxed, no visible model to quote and imitate. The body loses it connection with this referential field to become only a body; a disposable one that has done its time.

In "Spiral," the dying Wojnarowicz casts himself as an ultimate form of stranger. Not the stranger of cruising, whose very strangeness is an invitation to familiarity, but one made strange by a more profound sense of displacement. "I look familiar," he writes, "but I am a complete stranger being mistaken for my former selves. I am a stranger and I am moving […] I am no longer coded and deciphered […] I am an empty stranger" (60). This is a subjectivity estranged from interpersonal exchange, "empt[ied]" of erotic or affective potential. It is not only Wojnarowicz's own image that breaks down, in a process which manifests as a pallor in his "visual form"; a whole structure of vision is lost too. His "eyes," at last, "have stopped being cameras." This work marks a sobering endpoint in a writing career dedicated to thinking through the "filmic exchange" between fantasy, memory, and vision, along with its queer potential as an everyday mode of being. An earlier section of "Spiral" paints a vivid recollection of a dream which suggests not that the cameras have turned themselves off in the face of illness, but that they have been hijacked by the political reality of the epidemic. It begins with a familiar scene, "walking through this city not really sure where or why" and going "down this staircase of a subway or a hotel," and "I could sense sex as soon as I walked in" (55). Wojnarowicz proceeds to pick up a "guy in his late teens early twenties" in the cubicle, and when "his pants are down" notices a "fairly large wound on one of his thighs […]. The wound does something to me. I feel vaguely nauseous but he is sexy enough to dispell [*sic*] it."

As Wojnarowicz moves closer to the man's body to fellate him things take a turn toward the surreal, and he notices "two chrome cables with sectioned ribs pushing under the sides of flesh. Then this blue glow coloring the air above the wound," eventually seeing that "it is a miniature monitor, a tiny black and white television screen with an even tinier figure gesticulating from a podium in a vast room" (58). This vision proceeds to enumerate political figures: "the current president, smiling like a corpse in a vigilante movie," the "pope […] seated next to buckley." Gone is that "flood" of possible "fictions and mythologies" that this wound could prompt, or the enticing possibility that it's from a heist gone wrong, or a knife fight in some back alley. This is another kind of film altogether, one in which tropes like that of the "vigilante movie" still abound but which, in a hyperreal fashion, pertain to the very real and negligent decisions made by political figures in response to the HIV/AIDS crisis. The crime caper has been replaced by the geopolitical and the wound is no longer recuperable as "sexy"; it's just nauseating. The metaphorical weight of a gruesome wound as a screen for the political crisis of the epidemic is self-evident. It is the collective wound of an entire community that has been failed by the state, reducing the body to a "nauseating" and moribund form. The televisual runs throughout "Spiral" and Wojnarowicz writes, just sentences before this dream, of turning "on the television to try and get some focus outside my illness" (54). And yet the illness, "Spiral" suggests, refocuses everything "outside" of it, and colonizes even the erotic visuality that is a dominant conceptual frame in Wojnarowicz's writing. This is an illness doubly militarized, its consequences perpetuated by the heads of state and figures of "biological warfare" (58). Its bodily manifestation is felt acutely as an assault and erupts from the text accordingly, as an enraged zenith of what Hanya Yanigahara describes as Wojnarowicz's "imperfect" style, which "assaults the reader" in its "hyperactivity," "lack of deference," and "scattershot capitalizations."[75] The section ends: "THERE IS SOMETHING IN MY BLOOD AND IT'S TRYING TO FUCKING KILL ME."[76]

This exclamation echoes the mantra "Silence = Death" that was disseminated by the activist group AIDS Coalition to Unleash Power (ACT UP), with whom Wojnarowicz was involved, and also sits in melancholic counterpoint with another moment in his writing that seeks to resist silences; those of "the interior life," as in that phrase first rehearsed in the poem "Auto Portrait." In "Losing the Form in Darkness," Wojnarowicz follows the Mayakovsky-like figure deeper into the pier buildings, where the "sunlight" burns "through a window emptied of glass," and a "rusted screen" reduces "shapes and colors into tiny dots like a film directed by Seurat" (*CK,* 16). The visual stage is set for a consummation that in turn prompts another kind of vision, unfolding in montage:

> In loving him I saw men encouraging each other to lay down their arms. In loving him, I saw small-town laborers creating excavations that other men spend their lives trying to fill. In loving him, I saw moving films of stone buildings; I saw a hand in prison dragging snow in from the sill. In loving him, I saw great houses being erected that would soon slide into the waiting and stirring seas. I saw him freeing me from the silences of the interior life. (17)

This incantatory passage has a resolutely utopic tenor; a resistance to the here and now of an existence that "other men spend their lives trying to fill." This vision is not one of men behind podiums "gesticulating [. . .] in a vast room" as in "Spiral,"[77] but conversely a pacifist one of "men encouraging each other to lay down their arms." It inhabits the precarious temporality of cruising, suspending the present participle of "loving" between its own incipience and the past of completed occurrence, "I saw"; between the singularity of encounter and the repeatability of an image. As Olivia Laing writes, Wojnarowicz "rarely encountered the same men twice" but nonetheless fell "half in love with an imagined personality, a mythic being he'd conjured out of an accent or a single word," and in so doing preserved "what might have seemed even then like a transient, impossible utopia."[78] Tensions of transience and impossibility underpin utopic thinking itself, in particular the status of queer utopic thinking in relation to the "excavations" left by the HIV/AIDS crisis. Muñoz refers to utopic thinking as a mode "to conceptualize new worlds and realities that are not irrevocably constrained by the HIV/AIDS pandemic," and writes that "queer memories of utopia and the longing that structures them […] help us carve out a space for actual, living sexual citizenship."[79]

Responding to Bersani's "Cruising and Sociability" and the work of Samuel Delany, another great prophet of the piers during this period, Sarah Ensor traces cruising's efficacy for environmentalism in suggesting that, if "eroticism, sexual contact, and open expressions of desire are fundamental to the democratic potential of the spaces in which we dwell," the very ecology of cruising, then it is by "attend[ing] to the impersonal, collateral, and insistently ambient effects of casual relationships" that we can image a more disanthropocentric form of "environmentalism."[80] And cruising's ecological and ethical capacities are not only analogical, but relate intimately to the "space[s]" of Muñoz's "sexual citizenship." The piers—as liminal spaces, both urban and wild—offer up anonymous intimacy in the face of ecological ruin, and for Wojnarowicz provide a home for imagining the breakdown of the "erected" edifice of the present as a dominant mode of experience; turn your head away, toward the new love, in a suspended process of "loving" where a new kind of futurity not yet here appears. The metaphor of the ruin, as Anderson writes, "provide[s] us with a means of visualizing sexual liberation beyond a homophobic causal relation between cruising and the development of HIV/AIDS" and normative distinctions between time periods and generations, between past and present."[81] This passage from "Losing the Form in Darkness" eschews finality to dwell not only in a present tense conscious of its own passing, and retrievable in writing, but also among the physical ruins of a culture under threat. The artist's "great and enduring subjects" both "before and after AIDS" are shored up here; the "themes of encounter and precarity" and the attendant "admixture of sexuality and ethics."[82] This passage produces, at last, a moving prose portrait whose temporal moment is not restricted to the "here and now" but instead unfolds in "extended seconds," like a film directed by David Wojnarowicz.

Coda

A Click

> *Thus, it can no longer make sense, if it ever did, simply to assume that a male-centered analysis of homo/heterosexual definition will have no lesbian relevance or interest. At the same time, there are no algorithms for assuming a priori what its lesbian relevance could be or how far its lesbian interest might extend.*
>
> —Eve Kosofsky Sedgwick, *Epistemology of the Closet*

> *everyone on the app says they hate the app but no one stops*
>
> —Danez Smith, "a note on the phone app that tells me how far i am from other men's mouths"

Summer in the City

During the Fourth of July weekend in the summer of 1987, poet Eileen Myles left their apartment in the East Village to write a poem among the ruins. This poem came to be called "Hot Night," and was later published in their 1991 collection *Not Me*. Unlike the exterior of the piers, this sense of ruination was not necessary literal—although Myles does write in an essay on the poem's composition that in the "summer the city seems like a big rotten museum, or an empty abandoned culture"—as much it was metaphorical.[1] At the end of this essay, they continue:

> I was in the wreck of one culture the night I was writing this poem. All the monuments lay scattered around: the person I loved, the poet I was ten years ago, the kinds of things that were central then to my life. It's impossible to say anything new about

the East Village changing, that wreck, though my most startling experience recently was when I turned a corner on my bike early one evening and didn't recognize any of the stores and didn't know where I was. Even Little Ricky's now asks to check your bag. I walked out angry but I'm sure I'll be back because I've never been able to buy trendy postcards right downstairs before. (*NM*, 202)

Myles's recollection of heartbreak is accompanied by a description of the neighborhood that suggests a queasy double take, where commerce uncannily reinvents the city before the eyes of its inhabitants. Even Little Ricky's, the kitsch and paraphernalia store on the same street as the poet's apartment, has now adopted a sense of corporate mistrust toward loyal or local customers. Such changes are all the harder to swallow for an old hand, but the poem's speaker is emphatic about their experience in the very first lines: "Hot night, wet night / you've seen me before" (51). In a commentary on the poem Davy Knittle suggests that Myles subverts the course laid out by traditional city planning on their walk, in order to pursue a queer line of movement, one that follows the undulations of their own desires, and "resists the public-private development that has dominated the shifts in Manhattan's built environment over the arc of their writing life."[2] They observe gentrification with a cynical awareness that even complaints and critiques can eventually ossify into received or recycled narratives about the city—"it's impossible to say anything new about the East Village changing."

Instead, Myles views summer in the city in more primordial terms, finding in its trash and refuse that "big rotten museum." In recoiling from the commercialized and ever-changing face of the East Village, the poet also begins to appear distant from community itself. They dwell among the everyday ruins, which, Knittle writes, "offer Myles social experience without human interaction" and "the sense of using a shared resource," a resource that nonetheless, paradoxically, becomes their instrument of solitude.[3] "The city's outsides look like your insides if you're feeling that way," they write in the essay (*NM*, 199). The substitution of the poet's internal unrest for the exterior of the city itself, an ugly symbiosis of feeling and place, appears to depend upon a certain imaginative capacity; it will only work if "you're feeling that way." Indeed, the immanent erotic potential felt by the poet is directed not toward a possible lover but to the streets, which are described, postcoitally, as

"drenched and shimmering / with themself," and Myles makes this relation clear through apostrophe: "Impersonal street / is a lover / to me"
("Hot Night," *NM*, 51). In openly engaging and communing with the
environmental and erotic muck of the urban landscape, this moment
of the poem speaks to Sarah Ensor's call that we explore "how cruising
might inspire an ecological ethic more deeply attuned to our impersonal
intimacies with the human, nonhuman, and elemental strangers that
constitute both our environment and ourselves."[4]

This last element is crucial, for the urban night of Myles's poem feels
curiously unpopulated and "without human interaction," as Knittle puts
it, and reads rather as an erotically charged delve into the self which in
turn instantiates a form of pathetic relation to the surrounding environment. Myles characterizes the "process" in similar terms by stating their
belief that "life is a rehearsal for the poem," and continues:

> I literally stepped out of my house that night, feeling a poem
> coming on. Incidentally, it hadn't started raining yet, so I wasn't
> alone in being ready to burst. I was universally pent up [...]
> then the explosion of rain and light made it absolutely nec-
> essary to go in the deli on 6th street and buy a notebook and
> pen. I went over to Yaffa and wrote it looking out the window.
> I haven't changed a thing. (201)

Inasmuch as "Hot Night" occupies the temporality of an aftermath, composed just beyond the brink of an "explosion" and populated with refuse, it also marks a moment of becoming—a neighborhood changing, a
storm breaking, a poem arriving. The storm itself renders the street as an
ambient space—the "growling / thunder lightning / to flash and light /
up 7th" (*NM*, 51)—that offers new subjective possibilities. This "flash,"
which illuminates the scene and shapes its emerging visual landscape,
resembles the photographic flash commonly associated, via Benjamin
and Baudelaire, with urban experience itself. But it also bears a resemblance to what Eliza Steinbock has recently termed the "shimmer," after
Barthes. The concept of the shimmer has a rich history in theoretical
writing, where it is often employed as a "noun akin to sparkle or flash"
or else, in terms of "shimmering," as "a modifier to describe change in its
alluring, twinkling, flickering form" in a manner that is "politically urgent" and "breaks with binary and dialectical thinking."[5] For Steinbock,
the "shimmer" makes itself available to a trans or nonbinary ontology

precisely because it depends, as Barthes argues, on vantage, so if "trans is not identified as either/or, but depends on the 'angle' of the subject's gaze emerging in different contexts, then the slight modifications of gender could be likened to the space of the shimmer" (10). What the lighting-up of the shimmer makes possible is a body's capacity "to be one with its transitions," which bring with them "a potential change through self-multiplication across the shimmering passage of unresolvable disjunction in which we all live and breathe" (12), just as Myles's poem remains viscerally cognizant of "growling," "lightning," and the subject's own sense of becoming, of being "about to burst." The traces of this bursting are there to see on the New York streets, which are aptly "shimmering / with themself," such that we might read this phrase less as an exterior description of the sidewalk than as an investment in the "incipient subjectivity" (13) of the shimmer—a "them" self—that would appear to anticipate Myles's own coming out as nonbinary years later.

That the subjective mode of shimmering is linked, for Steinbock, to the cinematic image speaks to the photographic dimension of Myles's poem. Myles describes the poem's moment of becoming as a process wherein the aesthetic and erotic are intimately linked. "I've had this feeling before—of going out to get a poem, like hunting," Myles writes, as they describe another time they "felt 'erotic, oddly / magnetic' like photographic paper. As I walked I was recording the details. I was the poem" (*NM*, 202). Myles frames the poet as both agent and medium, the active participant in an erotic search and the surface upon which the consummatory act is developed and made legible, while photography is intimately linked to the poet's own process of self-discovery. Their full description in the poem of this photographic-erotic capacity is framed around the following scene (*NM*, 53):

> Sunday
> I photographed mounds
> of trash, finally
> turned the focus on
> me, a portrait I
> could accept. I
> feel erotic, oddly
> magnetic to the
> death of things

This moment collapses together a number of entities in a queer assemblage: trash, death, sex, the self. It reaches for a certain comic flourish, perhaps, in the succession of "trash" and "me" as chosen photographic subjects, as if there might be some self-conscious or self-flagellating relationship between the two. Trash is me and I am trash—the outsides look like your insides, if you're feeling that way. Maggie Nelson argues that Myles displays an interest in "meshing filmic devices with poetic tropes" in a manner akin to the "kinship that the first-generation New York School poets felt with Abstract Expressionist Art" and quotes their statement that "I experience writing poems as the chance to make a little movie."[6] Myles regularly posits their "speaker as a camera and the poem itself as a snapshot or collection of snapshots, complete with recurring 'clicks,'"[7] a sound that is particularly focal toward the end of "Hot Night": "used / magazines, / poetry books on a blanket, click" (*NM*, 57). The "movie" being made in "Hot Night," however, is not only about the urban environment, for the speaker's transition from forager to self-portraitist serves to reframe the poem and lends its central walk an explicit purpose, that desire to find "a portrait I / could accept."

The confluence of an erotically charged "hunting" with the photographic "click" of portraiture, as well as the "shimmering" possibilities of such a confluence, would seem to place Myles comfortably in the tradition I have identified in this book; a (mostly) poetic tradition of texts in which cruising, looking, and photographic or cinematic representations are seen to be imbricated. And yet to consider "Hot Night" a cruising poem in the way I have done other texts is to observe the ways in which it relates uncomfortably to such a categorization. As Nelson writes, "the speaker is out hunting for sex as well as a poem, and the poem concludes accordingly: "I need / whiskey sex / and I get / it," and in doing so they create "a great deal of slippage" between distinctions between male and female.[8] But "Hot Night" is also a poem vexed by questions of gender and representation. Unlike the crowded spaces of Whitman's "Among the Multitude" or the busy platform of Hughes's "Subway Face," for example, the street of "Hot Night" is, as mentioned above, curiously unpeopled, its poet-photographer dwelling in relative solitude among the garbage. "Strolling the gutters, alert to men's ever-threatening violence," writes Dianne Chisholm, Myles feels "most connected to big-city trash," a figuration for the way they have been "repeatedly 'trashed' by guardians of the all-American ideal."[9] And unlike O'Hara's "Song" or Wojnarowicz's prose dispatches from the piers, Myles's poem is not erotically oriented toward any one object or person. Cruising is instead present more diffusely, as an atmosphere. Prospective partners do not themselves emerge from the street's landscape.

As I will argue in the next section of this chapter, the photographic and curiously sepulchral qualities of Myles's poem reflect not only the particular epoch of New York in the late 1980s, in the midst of the HIV/AIDS epidemic, but also their own ambivalent position vis-à-vis a number of unfolding histories to which they might be said to belong, as both a poet and a queer person. As Davy Knittle writes, the poem's figuration of "the street as an impersonal lover echoes the practice of gay (male) public sex, a practice without a particular parallel at scale for non-male-bodied people."[10] This imbalance is no doubt exacerbated by the fact, as sociologist Denise Bullock claims, that "previous definitions of cruising have privileged the behavior of males and has been limited to an overt style of cruising for the intent of short-term sexual encounters," which has led to the perception that lesbians do not cruise, or do not engage in cruising to the same degree.[11] Rita Mae Brown, author of the runaway 1973 bestseller *Rubyfruit Jungle,* a classic of lesbian fiction, undertook practical research into gay male cruising cultures in March 1975. Venturing fully clothed into the East Village bathhouse The Club, with a mustache, squared-off nails, and a butch walk, Brown hoped that by placing herself "in an all-male situation where there is no intrusion of female sensibility" she would "learn something about that sacred cow, sexual difference."[12] Brown identifies the bathhouse as an ambivalent space, a Xanadu, or refuge, in which encounters are transactional and hierarchical, and from it draws conclusions about differences between gay and lesbian sexual cultures; the way that women "build no Xanadus because we are oppressed in a different way to the homosexual male."[13] The "anonymity" of cruising can be "undesirable and frightening" for non-male-bodied people, who are at greater risk of sexual violence and cannot "trust men sexually in an anonymous situation the way men can trust each other." The "men in the baths can walk out on the streets and reclaim all the privileges of maleness," whereas Brown "walked out of the baths as I walk out anywhere, a woman," with no such "fantasy farm" to retreat to. While the public space of the street is hardly without its dangers for gay men, the right street, in the right neighborhood, can also recreate the site of the gay bathhouse in plain sight, another "fantasy farm" of possible encounters. Myles's navigation of the street in "Hot Night" can thus be read, in this vein, as a riposte to the erasure and relative exclusion of women and nonbinary people not only from the prevailing gay male culture, but from the very cruising practices that it has traditionally monopolized.

Fully Automated and Charged Up

If the "click" toward the end of Myles's "Hot Night" registers not only the sound of the camera but also a larger sense of something climactic clicking into the place, when the speaker finally "get[s] it"—it being, variously, "whiskey," "sex," or a sense of completion—the poem makes it evident that such completion is hard won. The contingency of the "click" in Myles's poem can in fact be illuminated by an earlier "click" in the work of another downtown artist. Laurie Anderson's 1973 photo-narrative project *Fully Automated Nikon (Object/Objection/Objectivity)* was first conceived after she was approached by a woman in a seafood restaurant in Virginia who insisted that she, Anderson, was an actress from a TV soap opera. "I guess I just look like her," Anderson replied, and yet "the more I denied it, the more convinced she was of my identity," and "partly to assert myself, I asked if I could take her picture. As I shot the photograph, I realized that photography is a kind of mugging, a kind of assault. I was shooting her, then stealing something."[14] Anderson's realization of the invasive dimension of "tak[ing]" the woman's "picture" occurs here through the act of retaliation; she herself has her "identity" taken from her as a result of the woman's insistent misapprehension, and then responds in kind using her camera.

Subsequently, however, Anderson carries her aesthetic interrogation of the act of taking beyond this more or less innocuous, if frustrating, exchange and brings it to bear upon a more sinister daily reality for women in cities:

> When I got back to my neighborhood, the Lower East Side
> in New York, I decided to shoot pictures of men who made
> comments to me on the street. I had always hated this invasion of
> my privacy and now I had the means of my revenge. As I walked
> along Houston Street with my fully automated Nikon, I felt
> armed, ready. I passed a man who muttered "Wanna fuck?" This
> was standard technique: the female passes and the male strikes at

the last possible moment forcing the women to backtrack if she should dare to object. I wheeled around, furious. "Did you say that?" He looked around surprised, then defiant. "Yeah, so what the fuck if I did?" I raised my Nikon, took aim, began to focus. His eyes darted back and forth, an undercover cop? CLICK.[15]

Anderson's exchange with the stranger-subject she shoots here differs wildly from those of Sunil Gupta and Hal Fischer's work, produced later in the 1970s. But then, this exchange is not a cruise but a catcall, its participants not two men but a woman and a man. This antagonistic mode of soliciting women—which seems as invested in the assertion of power, by making someone feel unsafe, as it does in actually hooking up—has its own codes, its "standard technique." Anderson's taking "aim" with her "fully automated Nikon" disrupts the quotidian chain of events. The association of the "CLICK" with surveillance is telling, but in fact Anderson's photographic intervention in this exchange is even more discomfiting than that of the law's, because it gives visual form, and with it the implication of posterity and accountability, to the thoughtless misogyny of the passing comment.

She notes that subsequent reactions by other men, however, were the "opposite"; they acted "innocent, then offended," and by "the time I took their pictures they were posing, like taking their picture was the least I could do." The camera's exposure has a double meaning here, as it prompts these men to suddenly switch their behavior and pose as innocent in the face of potential revelation. In the exhibition photographs she displayed, Anderson placed a white strip across the eyes of the men, primarily to protect their identity, perhaps, but also to remind viewers of other contexts in which such steps are taken, as they often are with criminals or those involved with criminal activity. The mechanism of Anderson's "CLICK" is here seen to be efficacious, for the camera allows her to "object to objectification" and "glares back at the male gazing, reversing the power dynamic in which the men's behavior has placed her" and in turn "developing an aesthetics of empowerment."[16] Myles is comparably defiant in their rejection of the scopophilia of public urban spaces. In the poem "Basic August," written a year after "Hot Night," in the summer of 1988, the poet wishes they could "pull a devil mask over / my face. To be in- / visible and assertive" (*NM*, 73), and this desire soon precipitates an act of assertion on the subway:

Or I have learned from
novels that you can
stare right through a
person. All the midriffs
of men I have bored
through this summer
in the sweaty subway
which is like
an intestine. make
the beady eyes vanish
by boring through
like a train (74)

In this moment, the erotic look or leading glance is reversed, turned back upon the male gazers of the subway, running in to them like the train they cohabit for a transient moment, a hot minute. In refusing the cruising glances of men on the intestinal subway, the poet plays them at their own game, with the same affective charge of "Hot Night," where the "outsides look like your insides, if you're feeling that way." In their 2018 collection *Evolution*, Myles's poem "The City of New York" ends with a similarly sweaty vignette, half-erotic, half-comic glance shared between the poet and a woman riding the subway:

In the evening the voice
on the train was warning
us about thieves &
sexual perverts
this woman & I
started snuffling
the voice began again.
What's next we laughed.
He said thanks. The younger
woman was decidedly
cruising. The subway is hot.
I'm thinking this.[17]

Like many moments in Myles's writing, the wider implications of this scene gravitate around the pinpoint, deictic observations of present—

the here and nowness of "I'm thinking this." This recollection proceeds in a logical sequence: a train announcement, a snuffle, a laugh, a thanks, but the observation that the "younger / woman was decidedly / cruising. The subway is hot" somehow scrambles the order of the unfolding information. Privy on the page to the end of the succeeding line we might mis-hear or mis-read it at first glance as "The younger / woman was decidedly / hot." With this wrong turn the poet would tip over from mere observation into "decidedly / cruising" themself, eyeing up the hotness of a prospective partner. The *frisson* shared between the poet and this younger woman serves to undermine the subway announcement about the implied threats to women's safety, which are here laughed away not through a "click" or a reciprocally antagonistic glare, but through this furtive moment of queer solidarity.

These examples from Anderson and Myles's work illustrate how the unwelcome specular economy of the city, characterized by the predominance of the male gaze and unsolicited verbal threats, vexes the practice of cruising for women, nonbinary, and transmasculine people. Indeed, compared to the quasi-canon of gay male cruising texts, the tradition of writing about lesbian cruising is smaller and less visible, such that we gather that although Myles has "learned from / novels that you can / stare right through a person," these are not directly instrumental texts in the same manner as those in the gay male tradition. Even Audre Lorde's well-known recollection, in *Zami: A New Spelling of My Name*, of 1950s New York, passing "Black women on Eighth Street—*the invisible but visible sisters*—or in the Bag or at Laurel's," two of Manhattan's lesbian bars, is primarily about "passing in silence" and "looking the other way," hoping but also perhaps retreating from "that telltale flick of the eye, that certain otherwise prohibited openness of expression."[18] In their short story "Chelsea Girls," published in 1994 and set in the summer of 1979, Myles's auto-fictional narrator asks: "Could we possibly be two boys out cruising women together?"[19] Here Myles is referring to themself and their then-girlfriend Chris. After having dinner together, they have gone on to the Duchess, a lesbian bar in the West Village, where Myles is hoping to cruise an attractive waitress who had served them earlier at the restaurant. Although on the surface the incredulity of the question relates to the implications of sleeping with other partners for the couple's relationship, the gendering of its terms points to a larger question about whether they really could engage in the "boys" game of cruising. Although this introspective moment occurs within the (relatively) safe environs of the Duchess, its almost-ontological anxiety about the nature of lesbian cruising is anticipated by the description of the walk to the bar:

> Let's go to the Duchess I said lighting another [cigarette]. I slid my yellow bic into the small pocket of my orange painter pants. I had such faith in things. I had a little notebook in my back pocket where men carried their wallets. Firstly I was a woman, then I rolled my cash and I put it in my pocket. It was impossible to carry two square things. If you wanted anyone to see your ass. And I did but I didn't.[20]

Here Myles locates an expressive simplicity in small details, demonstrates a certain "faith in things." The presence of the notebook replaces the object of the wallet, casually gendered as male, and Myles's explanation—"firstly I was a woman"—cuts several ways. It suggests that a wallet in the back pocket is not only unfashionable for women, but unsafe. Or less safe than Myles's solution of rolling up cash and stuffing it into their pocket, which makes them less conspicuous to pickpockets and other possible menaces. Plus, it's "impossible to carry two square things"; to return to O'Hara's maxim, it's "just common sense: if you're going to buy a pair of pants you want them to be tight enough so everyone will want to go to bed with you" ("Personism," *CP,* 498). Except that Myles is ambivalent about soliciting an audience for this particular feature—"I did but I didn't"—and the use of "anyone" (akin to O'Hara's campy "everyone"), with its implication that one might be visible to *just* anyone, introduces a note of threat.

This account of the street suggests that lesbian cruising is implicated in the optical bind of male desire, and it inflects the subsequent reference to "two boys cruising." Just as Myles seeks to view themself from behind in describing the different ways that men and women wear or fill their pants, their description of "two boys cruising women" recalls, at first glance, what Laura Mulvey describes as "trans-sex identification," the process through which the "woman spectator in the cinema can make use of an age-old cultural tradition" which allows "a transition out of her own sex into another," thus coming to inhabit the "male gaze" that Mulvey theorized in "Visual Pleasure and Narrative Cinema."[21] Myles's example, however, lends this motif of spectatorship a queer resonance, where the assumption of boyhood is linked closely with lesbian desire. It is thus more in line with Steinbock's contribution to theories of looking via "the field of transgender studies," an aspect shift that involves moving away from what they describe as Mulvey's "spurious" and heavily psychoanalytical concept toward an acknowledgment that such cross-identification is neither "uncommon" nor binary, and encompasses a whole range of "threshold embodiments groping toward social identities."[22] One such identity might be that of the butch, although Myles is clear in distinguishing between butch-ness and boyishness in their recollection that "Christine was the boy in our relationship. Not the butch. No Chris was the pain in the neck little teasing boy."[23] This distinction further complicates the tone of Myles's phrase "two boys cruising" because it suggests an elision of gay cruising with a boyish petulance, giving way to a pejorative summoning of the male gender, like the inverse of what George Chauncey identifies as the gay male adoption of "women's names and pronouns,"[24] which is often to campy, collusive, or antagonistic ends.

Myles's offhand invocation of cruising's gender thus lights upon a mode of identification that exceeds singular categories and speaks to what Prudence Bussey-Chamberlain identifies as their multitudinous "category habitation," their "self-describing" variously "as a dyke, a butch, as a man or a guy (in some of their work)" and their "ultimately coming to apply a gender-neutral pronoun to themself outside the page."[25] Inasmuch as their work displays an awareness of the dangers of the street for non-male-bodied people, their own mythos as a lesbian poet is largely structured around a punk defiance against gendered limitations. That their notebook in "Chelsea Girls" is presented as an object, if not of rebellion, then of distinction from men, speaks to one such defiant moment in "Hot Night," a poem in which the process of writing on the hoof is central. Indeed, "Hot Night" gives a different meaning to the notion of the cruising poem insofar as its author is cruising *it*. It is, after all, the poem itself that the poet is on the hunt for when they write that they

> pick up "you" like
> my midnight
> rattle I shake
> at the devil

of the night
that does not
scare me.

(*NM, 56–57*)

Yoking together the language of the sexual pickup or the midnight encounter with the "rattle," Myles constructs an intricate triangulation.
As they write in the accompanying essay, "there's a welter of 'you's in
the work"—of which this instance is the "most poetic"—where "I'm
addressing my romantic obsession and the gesture or the whole performance of writing a poem" (200). This eroticized apostrophe to the
creative act is harnessed against the night's diabolical landscape in the
figure of the rattle, which could either be a physical, talismanic object or
a quick-fire succession of sound, like Myles's own "poetic" take, perhaps,
on Whitman's famous "barbaric yawps" (*LG,* 77). In an earlier part of the
poem, Myles makes use of other kinds of weaponry against the night's
malevolence: "I think I / need a bowie / knife, a / pistol, a squealing /
horn" (51). Consistent with the sense of emotional nihilism they felt on
the night of the poem's composition, Myles's enumeration of defense
mechanisms manifests as murderous and substitutes defiance for fear—
they have been "hardly ever as / charged up as / now" (52).

The sense of the deathliness that runs throughout the poem, the
speaker's feeling of being "filled / with the death / of the streets," the
streets that are themselves "wit- / ness to the death of my innocence"
(52), is thus illuminated by their speaker's destructive bent. But this invocation of the "death / of the streets" in New York City in the year
1987 surely also points to a larger cultural referent. "Hot Night" figures a
landscape that is more diffusely morbid than it is elegiac, and although
Myles frames their account of the poem around the cultural and personal wreckage they found themself in that night, the metaphorical porosity between the wasteland of the streets and the ongoing deathliness
of the city, which is weathering one of the largest public health crises
in its history, remains unspoken. Among the kinds of culture Myles
discusses in the essay, from their private museumlike "culture of one"
to "some new, larger one out there which I suspect exists" (202), there
is one community in particular that remains unacknowledged, at least

explicitly, though it is there in the poem "At Last," when the speaker stands outside the Gay Community Center and muses: "We live / in a culture of / vanishing men" (46).

Myles has written and spoken extensively about HIV/AIDS and many of their poems, like "At Last" and Hot Night," either directly or indirectly address the atmosphere of this period, when "people [...] began dying too of AIDS" and there was "this new kind of wealth and a baroque puffy quality" sitting "right next to the poverty and the stink of shit in the subway and in the streets."[26] But HIV/AIDS also appears to be a contested site for Myles, one that makes legible their sense, as they write in "Hot Night," that "I / do & do not / belong" (*NM*, 53). In "At Last," this ambivalence is given expression in the poem's opening reflection on time and the blood drive. "I always fall in love with tired / women," the poem begins, "It seems I have the / time" (46), and continues:

> On the blackboard
> at the Gay Community
> Center it said:
> Ladies, we need your
> blood. Afterwards
> come to the Women's
> Coffee House and
> have a cup of
> coffee. Donation
> $1.00

The political riskiness of the poet's statement that "I have the / time," surrounded as they are by "vanishing / men" living on borrowed time, is offset by the reference to the paltry thanks women receive for giving blood and, symbolically, this moment suggests, for remaining present and able to contribute, nurture, and sustain the imagined queer blood line of the dying.

In "The Lesbian Poet," a talk given at the St. Mark's Poetry Project in 1994, Myles theorizes the unique position and plight of the queer woman poet, and in so doing makes clear that it is not only straight men that stand in their way. When it comes to "poetic models," Myles writes, "I've actually got many more fathers" than women forebears, and this rumination on the gender of their ancestry is earlier anticipated by the following reflection:

> As a literary lesbian vis à vis gay men I'm more alone than ever before. The awesome mortality AIDS conjured up leaves fags ever more protective of their lineage. Melvin Dixon pleading at the 1992 Outwrite conference in Boston, "Who will call my name when I'm gone." We will, I whisper but I've never been so aware of the conversation between lesbians and gay men, not going on. Men want to be remembered by men. When a man dies, it's the need to be valued by men, not women, that counts. History, and we still know who keeps that.[27]

In this critique of the maleness of queer lineage, Myles is paraphrasing from a talk given by the Black poet and professor Melvin Dixon, who died from AIDS-related complications just a few months after he delivered it at the Outwrite conference in Boston in 1992. Where Myles sees Dixon as a spokesperson for masculinist coterie, a man writ large, Dixon begins his written talk, titled "I'll Be Somewhere Listening for My Name," with a more intersectional awareness, writing that as "gay men and lesbians, we are the sexual niggers of our society. Some of you may have never before been treated like a second class, disposable citizen. Some of you have felt a certain privilege and protection in being white."[28] Dixon's reflections upon the racial inequities of the queer community lead to an elegiac acknowledgment of his own fate, and the talk ends with a self-elegizing call:

> I may not be well enough or alive next year to attend the lesbian and gay writers conference, but I'll be somewhere listening for my name.
> I may not be around to celebrate with you the publication of gay literary history. But I'll be somewhere listening for my name.
> [...] You, then, are charged by the possibility of your good health, by the broadness of your vision, to remember us.[29]

It appears to be Dixon's potent, mournful apostrophe here that occasions Myles's sense of being "more alone than ever." "Hot Night," I have been arguing, comprises a radical response to this estrangement; it is a poem that sees Myles writing themself into a landscape they appear to be excluded from. In this poem, it is creation itself that offsets loneliness, as when they sardonically write that their

> poetry is here
> for the haul
> the lonely woman's
> tool—we have
> tools now, we
> have words &
> lists, we have
> real tears now,
> absence, rage
>
> (*NM*, 55–56)

This is a poem that harnesses rage and loneliness to forge an unsentimental path through a cultural wasteland of broken hearts, dead gay forebears—Hart Crane is namechecked—and the seething wreckage of the city. But the crucial distinction between the way the poem's speaker is "charged / up" here, on the one hand, and Dixon's charging of his audience to "remember us," on the other, reveals a palpable fissure in the queer community even at a time of crisis. Myles's "charged / up" poem is particular to a time and place and presents, I have been suggesting, a radical variant of the cruising poem that thinks through various forms of gendered exclusion, not least the exclusion of non-male people from the preempted legacies arising from the HIV/AIDS crisis. The insistence with which Myles seems to position Dixon as the mouthpiece of such exclusion, however, neglects to address the matter of race and thus the particular vantage of their own whiteness in relation to such questions. All of which is to say, it seems curious to choose a Black gay poet, giving a speech just months before he died, as the symbolic agent of institutional male power. Myles has revived this critique in recent years, recalling in a 2015 interview:

> He was incanting the names of all these male poets, and there wasn't one woman in there. I was sitting there thinking, "We're

going to be your legacy." Here I am right now talking about
Melvin Dixon. Why won't you let us call your name? That's the
fucked position of women-in-poetry lineage.[30]

"Hot Night" is a "charged / up" poem, uttered by a speaker who finally
"get[s]" what it is they desire, but the refusal to hear Dixon's elegy on its
own terms also leaves us wondering, from today's vantage, who else is
excluded from the picture.

Looking for "Right Now"

If it is fair to argue, as Sedgwick does in this chapter's epigraph, that
"there are no algorithms" for determining a priori the commonalities
between gay and lesbian worlds, it seems a continuous fact that the al-
gorithmic iteration of gay male cruising, as exemplified by an app like
Grindr, bears no direct or automatic comparison with lesbian sexual
cultures. After all, no such mediating app for lesbians has presumed as
much intracultural visibility or predominance. (And it is worth noting
that the term algorithm, in Sedgwick's foundational study from thirty
years ago, possesses none of its ambivalent, contemporary tint as a de-
scriptor of social media's apparatus.) This is not to say, however, that
there can't be a generative dialogue between erotic scenarios and snapshots that feature differently gendered agents. In the final section of this
coda to the book, I will explore how some of the questions Myles's work
raises regarding exclusion and representation can illuminate the poetics
and politics of cruising "right now," in a politically ambivalent age of
gay app culture, same-sex marriage, and the advent of preventive HIV
medication like PrEP.

A version of the affective and atmospheric scenario of "Hot Night"
reemerges in Myles's 2018 collection *Evolution* and illustrates this sense
of historical distinction. Indeed, scenes, figures, names, and titles con-
stellate throughout their work, like the subway exchanges found in both
"Basic August" and "The City of New York," and suggest a kind of tense
continuity, a picture of the city that is multiple and viewed from the vantage of historical moments. In the 2018 poem "The City" (and there are
at least three poems with this title throughout Myles's oeuvre), the poet
observes an urban landscape that sounds familiar: "juicy and bloody at

night / stabbing my eyes," a "city / at night / all its empty wares / are everywhere."[31] This hot night is witnessed in the wake of the Occupy Wall Street protests (the poem is dedicated to poet and activist Stephen Boyer) as its speaker muses once again on solitude and the erotic and gendered aspects of their body in space:

> my loneliness an illustrious
> path a screen
>
> I shoot these themes
> themes
> I mean my
> jism
> that look on your face
> is covered
> with my thought[32]

Here Myles imagines the poem as a site of interpersonal relation; the poet, engaged in their signature act of compositional spontaneity, "shoot[s]" from the hip and riffs on themes in an almost pornographic exchange where the matter of erotic consummation (transfigured as male) and the "look on your face" are brought graphically together. But the word "shoot" might equally be read as photographic, the poet as a fully automated camera "shoot[ing]" their themes, at least before it is linked with ejaculation, and the presence of "a screen" as a form of "path" inserts into the poem an intervening visual surface.

In a collection frequently concerned with digital culture and published in tandem with an exhibition of Myles's Instagram photographs at Bridget Donahue Gallery in New York in 2018–19, the word "screen" here cannot help but emanate a particular meaning, suggesting the familiar glow of an iPhone, the go-to and charged-up mechanization of the temporary gaze. In the artist statement for the exhibition, which was simply titled *poems,* Myles speaks to the sense of poetry and photography as a shared impulse in describing walks with their dog Honey where "together we explored what lower Manhattan had become. This bliss of geometry, trash: instantaneous configurations [. . .]. I write poems, I write about art & these photos I take I think are a similar kind of gathering—truncated places with words & writing that just trace a buzzing passage on Earth."[33] Here Myles posits their phone "screen" as an ecological tool, an appendage to their "passage" through the world, or "a path," as they put it in "The City." Screens can both compound and suppress our collective "loneliness"; they place us before the agency of a virtual world, at one further remove from the ambient one around us, and yet their mechanisms can equally revive or repurpose our relations to that world, for the poetic-photographic capacity Myles so often proffers is after all the "lonely woman's / tool." Screens also navigate as well as capture our experience, leading us via GPS to our chosen destinations.

Or, indeed, to our nearest available hookup. Although Myles doesn't explicitly invoke dating app culture, the intersection of erotic, interpersonal, and mediatized surfaces staged in this poem calls to mind cruising's contemporary iterations via the visual technologies of geosocial media, where the "click" becomes the tap. In the words of Shaka McGlotten, these "now not so new virtual intimacies encounter and rework historical antecedents particularly to queer, especially gay male, sociality: chiefly cruising and hooking up," though they are constitutively distinct.[34] Take Grindr, for example, whose "virtual" grid of user profiles bears a referential relation to the structure of lived urban (and suburban) space, of which Manhattan's grid system would seem the iconic exemplar. Moving through or within the actual space of the latter also conjures up a phantom image of the structural whole, such that orientation becomes a suspension between the lived and the virtual. As Rem Koolhaas writes, in a formulation that might equally describe acts of looking, browsing, or cruising, the "city becomes a mosaic of episodes, each with its own particular life span, that contest each other through the medium of the grid."[35] The "life span" of Grindr's "episodes" similarly involves a reification of cruising's temporality, where the phrase "Right Now," with its false promise of instant immediacy, describes both the projected teleological end of the hookup as well as the suspended tense of the search itself.

While cruising may be historically associated with a radical and democratic mode of sexual freedom—even if, as the examples of this book have shown, this is often not true in practice—cruising's translation into new media limits it, McGlotten continues, "to the context of personal choices and consumerist self-styling," and "cruising apps reduce social worlds to public sex to bad faith erotic free markets; they are in bad faith because like the neoliberal markets in which they are situated, the benefits of the market tend to accrete to the very few—namely, well to do, young, and very often white, men."[36] Tom Roach similarly begins his interrogation of digital queer intimacies by stating: "Everything you may have heard about online dating is true: It is steeped in a consumerist logic. It substitutes algorithms for pheromones. It instrumentalizes intimacy and mechanizes the wily ways of desire."[37] The novelist Garth Greenwell writes at length about this substitution in aesthetic and ethical terms:

> Physical cruising, as I experience it, is more valuable, richer both sensually and ethically than online cruising. If the kind of cruising I grew up with is poetry, then Grindr isn't just prose, but Strunk and White, prose stripped to function. The circulation of bodies in physical space allows for a greater possibility of being surprised by desire, of having an unexpected response to the presence of another. In online cruising, as in pornography, the reality of another's body is to a very great extent erased in its reduction to an image. When I cruise in real life, a man whose framed torso might have seemed unremarkable catches me by the way he moves, or the way he smells, or by the tone of his voice or heat of his glance or by any other of the million other traits we lose when we reduce ourselves to a short list of stats, a little boxed image on a screen.[38]

Greenwell captures the peculiar glassiness of the grid, an assemblage of curated images that can seem by turn unreal and unremarkable and, in Roach's words, "are ultimately flattened into a sea of similitude."[39] Greenwell's description of the "framed torso" recalls Myles's lines from "At Last" that describe "the midriffs / of men I have bored / through this summer" but gives them a different intent and emphasis, in that Grindr often feels like a sea of men's "midriffs," and the "boredom" of browsing is one of its primary effects. Greenwell's argument that the focality of images in online cruising, its visual culture, ultimately yields a loss, a reduction of subjective and interpersonal exchanges that is performed through virtualization. And there are probably very few users—or cruisers?—of an app such as Grindr, whether infrequent, casual, or regular, who would not recognize some part of Greenwell's critique, who would not see it in some essential truth about the mechanization of desire.

And yet. In a recent study composed primarily of interviews with Grindr users, researchers reflected upon the fact that "online space has historically been thought of as virtual or less real than actual encounters," but this "appears to be contradicted in the way participants talked about their experiences."[40] Greenwell's distinction between analog and online cruising as poetic and prosaic, respectively, is an appealing one, but might the use of such loaded aesthetic terms risk, even from the candid vantage of his admittedly first-person reflection, performing a form of gatekeeping that misses something about user experiences? Indeed, both Roach and McGlotten's work on virtual intimacies take surprising turns toward hope and possibility. Roach announces his novel intent from the beginning of his article when he argues "in contrast to the chorus of techno-pessimistic voices that holds the Internet responsible for the death of a public queer sex culture" and suggests that the ends of both analog and online cruising "are generally the same, that is, connection, hooking up."[41] He goes on to locate "an ethical commonality spanning public cruising and private browsing," the Foucauldian and "queer practice of shared estrangement," the sense in which Grindr's "senseless blather and crass self-interest might also be an active creation of an antirelational discourse."[42] Similarly, McGlotten states from the outset of his critique that "there's room yet for optimism" insofar as "virtuality" is not necessarily "opposed to the real; virtuality refers to immanence, capacity, and potentiality," but also because "intimacy is already virtual in the ways it is made manifest through affective experience."[43] As I have hoped to show in this book, the predominance of images on Grindr, and its proffering of a kind of visual cruising, is not exceptional or unprecedented. Cruising has long been a visually mediated phenomenon, an erotic exchange whose immediate optical iteration—the look between two strangers—implicates the visual and even the "virtual," the realm of cultural and archetypal matter that shapes our individual and collective desires.[44]

This is not to say that the flattening out of cruising's contingency and sensory immediacy online, and the reduction of a living, breathing person to "a little boxed image on a screen" is not a legitimate cause for lamentation, but rather that it is infelicitous to claim that cruising hasn't always, in some sense, involved the mediation of "a screen." In other words, we must interrogate where a critique of the present ends and a nostalgia for an imagined past begins, a "longing for a past when people supposedly had more authentic connections with one another," when in fact in the "1970s, anonymous sex was often experienced and described as dehumanizing, in much the same way that cybersex is denounced now."[45] Roach writes, in 2015, that "the virtual grid of the MSM [men-seeking-men] hookup app is hardly the picture of Whitmanesque camaraderie."[46] Bersani writes, in 1987, that "I do not, for example, find it helpful to suggest, as Dennis Altman has suggested, that gay baths created 'a sort of Whitmanesque democracy, a desire to know and trust other men.'"[47] Whitman's work is a telling intertext for the utopic bluster of this imaginative projection of an egalitarian cruising community, but it too registers the darker aspects of such desires.

That the qualities of Grindr's "Right Now" bear at least some continuity with the mediated and visualized world of historical cruising does not mean that its de facto privileging of whiteness is any less troubling, but rather that it presents the issue of racial inequities in the queer community via a new interface, one that presents its own set of complications. For the final part of this coda, I want to ask, after Greenwell's framing of Grindr as "prose stripped to function": what might a poetics of Grindr look like? And how might poetry carve out a space of gathering and critique, to offer forms that register the losses, the gains, the nuances, to give voice to affects like the "anxiety" and "paranoia" which, McGlotten argues, "organize many of the processes and relations in these online queer spaces in ways that resemble prior and contemporaneous forms of racial injury?"[48] Indeed, one of the blind spots of Myles's continued critique of Melvin Dixon is their inability to imagine the ways in which new generations of queer Black poets will remember Dixon's name. And if the burgeoning category of the "Grindr poem" can be said to exist, the most compelling examples of it are by queer poets of color reckoning with the peculiarities of online cruising and lighting through lyric form upon questions of liveness, intimacy, and visuality.

Danez Smith, for example, a Black, queer, poz writer and performer from Saint Paul, Minnesota, rethinks their own relation to the queer bloodline in the poem "gay cancer," which appears in their 2020 collection *Homie*. In this poem Smith enumerates their ancestors, Melvin Dixon, Essex Hemphill, and Assotto Saint, draws a lineage between them through the virus that "grew / in me too," and establishes a sense of transtemporal presence: "my wrist to my ear / you're here."[49] Here, Smith makes various work of the bloodline metaphor in suggesting that these poets constitute a lineage in multiple ways, both as literary fore-bears but also as preceding carriers of the blood-borne virus. They are there, painfully, hopefully, audibly, in Smith's veins. This poem also has a particular contemporary resonance in pointing to the fact that HIV continues to disproportionately affect the Black community, and in this regard the poem recalls Smith's moving, imaginary letter to Essex Hemphill, written around the time of the Stonewall 50 festivities in 2019:

> It worries me, Essex. How many people consider the epidemic over now that PrEP is here, even though more and more black people find themselves stunned in the midst of their own bodies? How many people fell off the queer liberation train when they got the right to marry and divorce?[50]

Both the sexual freedoms offered by PrEP and the so-called homo-normative forms of assimilation offered by same-sex marriage risk pre-cluding, Smith suggests, a continued solidarity with those not served by the advent of these things, which is to say, broadly speaking, those who are not middle class, cisgendered, or white. There is a not "uncom-mon (albeit ill-informed) opinion," C. Riley-Snorton writes, that "if the crisis is not over, it is nearing its conclusion," yet such an "apocryphal ending can only be narrated in terms of containment—an investment in pharmaceutical management (and even prevention)," and thus belies the fact that the end of "HIV/AIDS has only meant the redistribution of crises."[51]

Questions of race, healthcare, and the discriminate implications of the ongoing crisis haunt one of Smith's cruising poems from the same collection. This poem's title, "all the good dick lives in Brooklyn Park," refers to a suburb of Minneapolis and immediately calls to mind the location function of hookup apps in its geographical delineation. What constitutes good dick in this poem is mediated, once again, by the screen, and the poem's first few stanzas illustrate how desire for a certain race, in this case a particular form of Black masculinity, is enfolded with aspects of place. In the part of Brooklyn Park the speaker arrives at, the lack of a grocery store and the presence of successive liquor stores signifies to them the sexual prowess of their prospective partner.[52] This section of

Smith's poem is self-aware and critical about the elision of good dick with a certain kind of neighborhood. It exposes through repetition the stereotype of the "mandingo myth" that circulates around "project dick. section 8 inches," and this last detail puns on the government-funded housing program for low-income citizens and the detail about dick size you might expect to find on a Grindr profile.[53]

The poem makes clear that it is an ode to the "hood" guys the speaker sleeps with, but it takes an unexpected turn in the final stanzas, when the speaker reveals that their lover is HIV-positive and unable to afford the appropriate medication. Suddenly and soberingly, the specter of inequality and of this man's inability to afford HIV medication enters the picture. This moment illustrates the heady affective mix, where humor quickly gives way to solemnity, that so often characterizes Smith's work, and their earlier play with stereotypes soon gives way to a tender act of solidarity where "i kiss him with the pill coming apart on my tongue," hoping it can "fill both of us out." In two poems from their previous collection *Don't Call Us Dead,* the hookup similarly becomes an occasion for reflecting upon queer Black intimacy in the face of inequality, the "ordinary microaggressions as well as overt or structural forms of racism" that McGlotten supposes "online spaces reproduce and perhaps even heighten."[54] The poems, which are printed on facing pages, come as a pair, their titles running in to one another: "a note on the phone app that tells me how far i am from other men's mouths" and "& even the black guys's profile reads *sorry, no black guys.*" In the first poem, the speaker sees:

headless horsehung horsemen gallop to my gate
dressed in pictures stolen off Google

men of every tribe mark their doors in blood
No Fats, No Fems, No Blacks, Sorry, Just a Preference :)[55]

The app's visual landscape seems variously apocalyptic and tribal, marked by the insidious banalities of "preference" that in fact bespeak deep-set gendered and racial prejudices, and the poem's speaker offers their "body" anonymously, even ominously, "to pictures with eyes."[56] Different body types suggest entirely different discourses and visual vocabularies; the men who "say they weigh more than 250 pounds / fill their profiles with pictures of landscapes, sunsets / write lovely sonnets about their lonely & good tongues" while "men with abs between their abs write *ask* or *probably not interested in you.*"

As well as representing this ruthless image economy, Smith also interpolates what Roach describes as the "blather" of app culture, the "introductory interpellations, 'hey,' ''sup,' 'woof'" and the "inevitable request for pics" which "reduce dialogue to a series of churlish grunts and crass propositions—a nightmare (or perhaps a respite) for those who pride themselves on eloquence, wit, or emotional expressivity."[57] A nightmare and a respite: "everyone on the app says they hate the app but no one stops," the poet writes, "i sit on the train, eyeing men, begging myself / to talk to them." Smith's poem gives voice, ultimately, to this sense of an expressive lack, a breakdown in language and in the ability to "talk," and in so doing it draws attention to its own vocal aspects. Although the imitation of "ThIs OnE gUy WhO sPeLlS EvErYtHiNg LiKe ThIs" is a textual joke about so-called text language, the sporadic capitalization calls to mind the shouting associated with capital letters, and Smith's own live delivery of this line—yelling out the inexplicable anger suggested by this typography—enriches its humor.

The performative resonance of the poem's final line—"i sing a song about being alone"—maps the poem's ambivalent account of life on the "phone app" onto the larger aesthetic matters of liveness and performance, and suggests that the interplay between the textual reproduction, on the one hand, and the live or oral instant of iteration, on the other, might bear an analogous relation to online cruising's reification of queer intimacy's liveness. In this regard, the poem also resembles Jericho Brown's poem "Host," which too interpolates Grindr-speak through the mouthpiece of a demanding collective "we": "We want pictures of everything / Below your waist, and we want / Pictures of your waist."[58] The question of the voice is revived in the poem's final lines, where the collective speaker, seemingly a couple on an app, state: "We can host, but we won't meet / Without a recent pic and a real name / And the sound of your deepest voice."[59] Brown's satirical edge is hard to read singularly here, for these lines present but also mock this dogmatic desire for the "real," the evidentiary, and the live "voice" amid the app's economy of artifice. The phrase "deepest voice" also gestures to the prejudicial nature of preference in its summoning of a stereotypical and audible form of masculinity, one that is often enfolded with race, as McGlotten shows in the case study of one of his interviewees, a Black man who recalls once affecting a "higher-pitched, 'white' voice" in order to reveal and challenge the assumptions made by his white hookup partner.[60]

What these contemporary Grindr poems thus make clear is the continued predominance of the screen, both the physical surface upon which we access apps and the visual mediation through which archetypal desires are made legible. Inasmuch as cruising has largely moved online, its fundamental questions remain the same; namely, what does it mean to truly look at another person, to wrest from that look—in the "right now" of an encounter—a form of intimacy that may be contingent, transient, or even estranging? Apps open up a new space for enquiry into the optical and visual dimensions of desire. Critics and poets alike, as I have shown in short here, have already marked it as a space of intense ambivalence, but one we nonetheless must look to in the name of futurity, in order to consider the possibilities of other erotic or affective worlds that lie not only beyond the stratified and oppressive instruments of heteronormative capitalism, but the gendered and racialized forms of exclusion that are evidently reproduced in and by queer communities as well.[61] The matter of what you see when you look, either at another (an other) or at yourself (your self), is vital to this imaginary. It is apt, then, that Smith's second app poem apostrophizes queer Black readers and advocates self-love with recourse to a dreamlike ekphrasis: "imagine a tulip, upon seeing a garden full of tulips, sheds its petals in disgust."[62] The poem's visual minimalism, gravitating as it does around a "look in the mirror," gives way to an unambiguous moment of lyric intimacy between poet and reader: "you are beautiful & lovable & black & enough & so—you pretty you—am i."[63] Cruising, after all, should feel good for both parties.

Acknowledgments

Cruising is nothing if not experiential. The opportunity to spend an extended period in New York for archival research during this project, the city that is in some sense its muse, was a novel and necessary jolt in the academic process—energizing, consuming, sometimes distracting. It was rather through distraction that I learned about cruising. Much of *The Poetics of Cruising* in its initial form was written during long days spent in Ninth Street Espresso in Alphabet City, and many of its underlying motivations were forged and tested at night on the streets and in the bars nearby. When it came to writing over the course of the following year, it was the mental archive of memories I had made (and sometimes lost) in the city, the traces of names I had remembered, forgotten, or never learned, and the weight of a long-distance love jeopardized and then regained, that kept me going.

I am very grateful to the University of Minnesota Press for publishing this book, and I thank Leah Pennywark, Anne Carter, and Jason Weidemann in particular for their guidance and support. The book began life as a doctoral thesis at Cambridge University and was completed during a postdoctoral fellowship at Oxford. There are therefore several funding bodies to whom I extend thanks: the Cambridge AHRC DTP for funding the thesis project; the RTSG committee for providing funding toward my stay in New York in 2017; and the English Faculty, Cambridge, for funding a month-long exchange at Harvard University in 2018. Thanks to the staff members at the archives I visited during these research trips to the United States: the Berg Collection, New York Public Library; the Fales Collection, New York University; the Rare Book and Manuscript Library, Columbia University; the Museum of Modern Art Archives, New York; the Thomas J. Dodd Research Center, University of Connecticut, Storrs; and the Houghton Library, Harvard

University. I would also like to acknowledge University College, Oxford, where I have held the Stevenson Junior Research Fellowship in English. The warm welcome and support of my colleagues in English at Univ, Joe Moshenska, Laura Varnam, and Nicholas Halmi, have been a great help while I've worked on adapting the thesis into a book.

At Cambridge, I give thanks to Drew Milne for his support and suggestions as an adviser to this project, and to Alex Houen for his feedback as a secondary adviser. Thanks in particular to my viva examiners, John David Rhodes at Cambridge and Michael Snediker at the University of Houston, for their invaluable feedback on this project. The book's adapted form as a work of queer studies is shaped by their generous and penetrating insights about the project's structure and theoretical framework. And thanks to Michael Bronski and Olivia Laing for supporting my work and for reading some of this material in its earlier iterations.

I'd like to dedicate this book to a number of educators, all of whom I owe so much to. Without them, a path into writing and academia would not have seemed conceivable. To my English teacher, Karen Dean, for her inspiring, formative teaching and continued friendship and support, and to my Drama teachers, Sarah Addison and Jonathan Akin, for the confidence their teaching instilled in me. To Deborah Bowman, an inspirational teacher and interlocutor. My undergraduate years as a nervous state-school student at Caius College under your tutelage opened my mind to new ways of thinking and totally changed my life. And to Anne Stillman, "Gisel," my supervisor, collaborator, and confidante. Our many conversations over the years have been vital to this project, and our adventures with Mary, my Coney Island and "Dancing Queen" partner, are unforgettable. As our Frank puts it on John Button's birthday: "That's friendship / for you."

Lastly, a thank you to all of the friends who provided companionship, levity, and support during the PhD. A special shout out, in Cambridge, to Adelais Mills, for the years of friendship, solidarity, and writing sessions, and to Jasmine Cooper and Katie Pleming, or "Queernam," for reading chapters of the thesis at crunch-time, for the loud and magical nights off at Novi, and for many other things besides. And to my sister Hannah, my best friend, and Linda and Martin, the best parents I could ask for. I can't put into words how much their love and faith has meant to me on the long and shared journey to get here—it is what has made any of this possible.

Notes

Introduction

1. Sunil Gupta, *Christopher Street, 1976* (London: Stanley/Barker, 2018), blurb.

2. Gupta, "Christopher Street Revisited," interview by Jesse Dorris, *Aperture,* May 30, 2019, https://aperture.org/blog/sunil-gupta-christopher-street/.

3. Gupta, "Do You Have Place?," talk/interview delivered at the conference Cruising the Seventies: Imagining Queer Europe, Then and Now, University of Edinburgh, March 14–16, 2019.

4. Leo Bersani, "Sociability and Cruising," in *Is the Rectum a Grave? and Other Essays* (Chicago: University of Chicago Press, 2010), 57.

5. Gupta, "Do You Have Place?"

6. Gupta, "Christopher Street Revisited."

7. Hal Fischer, *Gay Semiotics: A Photographic Study of Visual Coding among Homosexual Men* (San Francisco: NFS Press, 1977), 22.

8. Fischer, *Gay Semiotics,* 15.

9. Fischer, *Hal Fischer: The Gay Seventies,* ed. Griff Williams and Troy Peters (San Francisco: Gallery 16, 2019), 78.

10. Fischer, *Gay Semiotics,* 15.

11. Jonathan Weinberg, *Pier Groups: Art and Sex along the New York Waterfront* (University Park: Pennsylvania State University Press), 16.

12. Fiona Anderson, *Cruising the Dead River: David Wojnarowicz and the New York Waterfront* (Chicago: University of Chicago Press, 2019), 24.

13. Douglas Crimp, "On Alvin Baltrop," in *The Life and Times of Alvin Baltrop,* ed. Antonio Sergio Bessa (Skira Editore: Milan, 2019), 10.

14. Antonio Sergio Bessa, "Into the Mystic: Pier 52 through the Lens of Alvin Baltrop," in *The Life and Times of Alvin Baltrop,* 56.

15. Crimp, "On Alvin Baltrop," 10.

16. Anderson, *Cruising the Dead River,* 13.

17. Mia Kang, "Things That I Considered Beautiful: Reflections on the Alvin Baltrop Archive," in *The Life and Times of Alvin Baltrop,* 79–80.

18. Kang, "Things That I Considered Beautiful," 80.

19. Anderson, *Cruising the Dead River*, 8.

20. Weinberg, *Pier Groups*, 17.

21. Bersani, "Is the Rectum a Grave?," in *Is the Rectum a Grave? And Other Essays* (Chicago: Chicago University Press, 2009), 3–31.

22. Grindr removed its ethnicity filter function in June 2020, as an expression of support for the Black Lives Matter movement in the wake of George Floyd's murder by a police officer in Minneapolis. The opportunism of this gesture of solidarity, the time it had taken for such a gesture to be made (the app was launched in 2009), as well as the converse benefits of such a filter for users of color seeking to avoid racist microaggressions, did not go unremarked on social media.

23. Doug Ireland, "Rendezvous in the Ramble," *New York*, May 21, 2008 [July 24, 1978], https://nymag.com/news/features/47179/.

24. Walter Holland, "The Calamus Root: A Study of American Gay Poetry since World War II," *Journal of Homosexuality* 34, no. 3/4 (1998): 9.

25. George Chauncey, *Gay New York: Gender, Urban Culture, and the Making of the Gay Male World, 1890–1940* (New York: Basic Books, 1994), 188.

26. Rebecca Zurier, *Picturing the City: Urban Vision and the Ashcan School* (Berkeley: University of California Press, 2014), 6–7.

27. John Boswell, *Christianity, Social Tolerance and Homosexuality* (Chicago: University of Chicago Press, 1980), 42.

28. Leo Bersani, *Homos* (Cambridge, Mass.: Harvard University Press, 1995), 3.

29. Mark W. Turner, *Backward Glances: Cruising the Queer Streets of New York and London* (London: Reaktion, 2003), 45.

30. John Champagne, "Walt Whitman, Our Great Gay Poet?," *Journal of Homosexuality* 55, no. 4 (2008): 648–64.

31. Chauncey, *Gay New York*, 14.

32. Bersani, *Homos*, 2.

33. Sarah Schulman, *The Gentrification of the Mind: Witness to a Lost Imagination* (Berkeley: University of California Press, 2012).

34. Christopher Castiglia and Christopher Reed, *If Memory Serves: Gay Men, AIDS and the Promise of the Queer Past* (Minneapolis: University of Minnesota Press, 2012), 84.

35. Walt Whitman, "Crossing Brooklyn Ferry," *Leaves of Grass and Other Writings,* ed. Michael Moon (New York: Norton Critical Editions, 2002), 137. Moon's text is based on the 1891–92 "deathbed" edition of *Leaves of Grass.* Further references to this edition are given with quotations in the text with the abbreviation *LG.* References to earlier editions of *Leaves of Grass* will be indicated by a separate reference.

36. Jonathan D. Katz and David C. Ward, *Hide/Seek: Difference and Desire in American Portraiture* (Washington, D.C.: Smithsonian Books, 2010), 14.

37. Brian Glavey, *The Wallflower Avant-Garde: Modernism, Sexuality and Queer Ekphrasis* (New York: Oxford University Press, 2016), 6.

38. David Wojnarowicz, "Losing the Form in Darkness," in *Close to the Knives: A Memoir of Disintegration* (New York: Vintage, 1991), 13–14. Further references to this edition are given with quotations in the text with the abbreviation *CK*.

39. Glavey, *The Wallflower Avant-Garde*, 6.

40. Frank O'Hara, "Personism," in *The Collected Poems of Frank O'Hara*, ed. Donald Allen (Berkeley: University of California Press, 1995), 498. Further references to this edition are given with quotations in the text with the abbreviation *CP*.

41. Rita Felski, "Context Stinks!," *New Literary History* 42, no. 4 (Autumn 2011): 574.

42. Walter Benjamin, "What Is Aura?," in *Walter Benjamin's Archive: Images, Texts, Signs*, ed. Esther Leslie, trans. Ursula Marx (London: Verso, 2007), 45.

43. Alfred Gell, *Art and Agency: An Anthropological Theory* (Oxford: Clarendon Press, 1998), 15.

44. Glavey, *The Wallflower Avant-Garde*, 3.

45. Kevin Ohi, *Dead Letters Sent: Queer Literary Transmission* (Minneapolis: University of Minnesota Press, 2015), 29.

46. Elizabeth Freeman, *Time Binds: Queer Temporalities, Queer Histories* (Durham, N.C.: Duke University Press, 2010), xiii.

47. José Esteban Muñoz, *Cruising Utopia: The Then and There of Queer Futurity* (New York: New York University Press, 2009), 24.

48. Paul K. Saint-Amour, "The Literary Present," *ELH* 85, no. 2 (Summer 2018): 385.

49. Saint-Amour, 368.

50. Muñoz, *Cruising Utopia*, 4.

51. Tyler Bradway, *Queer Experimental Literature: The Affective Politics of Bad Reading* (New York: Palgrave Macmillan, 2017), xxxi.

52. Bradway.

1. Passing Strangers

1. Walter Benjamin, "What Is Aura?," in *Walter Benjamin's Archive: Images, Texts, Signs*, ed. Esther Leslie, trans. Ursula Marx (London: Verso, 2007), 45.

2. "The person we look at, or feels he is being looked at, looks at us in turn. To experience the aura of an object we look at means to invest it with the ability to look back at us." Walter Benjamin, "On Some Motifs in Baudelaire," in *The*

Writer of Modern Life: Essays on Charles Baudelaire, ed. Michael Jennings, trans. Howard Eiland et al. (Cambridge, Mass.: Belknap Press of Harvard University Press, 2006), 204.

3. Benjamin, 204.

4. Miriam Bratu Hansen, "Benjamin's Aura," *Critical Inquiry* 34, no. 2 (Winter 2008): 342.

5. Charles Baudelaire, "À une passante," in *Les Fleurs du Mal,* ed. Claude Pichois (Paris: Gallimard, 1972), 127. The English translation is my own.

6. Mark W. Turner, *Backward Glances,* 34.

7. Janet Wolff, "The Invisible Flaneuse: Women and the Literature of Modernity," *Theory, Culture and Society* 2, no. 3 (1985): 42.

8. Benjamin, *The Arcades Project,* trans. Howard Eiland and Kevin McLaughlin (Cambridge, Mass.: Harvard University Press, 2002), 985.

9. Benjamin, "Über einige Motive bei Baudelaire," in *Gesammelte Schriften,* ed. Rolf Tiedemann and Hermann Schweppenhäuser, 7 vols. (Frankfurt am Main: Suhrkamp, 1972–1989), 1: 647.

10. Eduardo Cadava, *Words of Light: Theses on the Photography of History* (Princeton, N.J.: Princeton University Press, 1997), 21–22.

11. Timothy Raser, *Baudelaire and Photography: Finding the Painter of Modern Life* (Leeds: Legenda, 2015), 95.

12. Baudelaire, "The Salon of 1859: The Modern Public and Photography," in *Art in Theory 1815–1900: An Anthology of Changing Ideas,* ed. Charles Harrison, Paul Wood and Jason Gaiger (Oxford: Blackwell, 1998), 668.

13. Benjamin, "The Work of Art in the Age of Mechanical Reproduction," in *Illuminations: Essays & Reflections,* ed. Hannah Arendt, trans. Harry Zohn (London: Cape, 1970), 221.

14. Benjamin, 224.

15. Benjamin, "On Some Motifs," 175–78.

16. Dianne Chisholm, *Queer Constellations: Subcultural Space in the Wake of the City* (Minneapolis: University of Minnesota Press, 2005), 41.

17. Clive Scott, *Translating Baudelaire* (Exeter: University of Exeter Press, 2000), 99.

18. Scott, 98.

19. Benjamin, "The Paris of the Second Empire in Baudelaire," in *The Writer of Modern Life: Essays on Charles Baudelaire,* ed. Michael Jennings, trans. Howard Eiland et al. (Cambridge, Mass.: Belknap Press of Harvard University Press, 2006), 77.

20. Philip Auslander, *Liveness: Performance in a Mediatized Culture* (London: Routledge, 1999), 55.

21. Susan Sontag, *On Photography* (London: Penguin Books, 1979), 55–56.

22. Laura Mulvey, "Visual Pleasure and Narrative Cinema," *Screen* 16, no. 3 (Autumn 1975): 6–18.

23. Sontag, *On Photography,* 55–56.

24. Sontag, 56.

25. Kaja Silverman, *The Threshold of the Visible World* (New York: Routledge, 1996), 97.

26. Marcel Proust, *Sodom and Gomorrah,* trans. John Sturrock (New York: Penguin, 2005), 27–28.

27. See Susan Blood, "The Sonnet as Snapshot: Seizing the Instant in Baudelaire's 'À une passante,'" *Nineteenth Century French Studies* 36, no. 3-4 (Spring-Summer 2008): 255–69.

28. James Elkins et al., "The Art Seminar," in *Photography Theory,* ed. James Elkins (New York: Routledge, 2007), 159.

29. Roland Barthes, *Camera Lucida: Reflections on Photography,* trans. Richard Howard (New York: Hill and Wang, 1981), 18–19.

30. Silverman, *Threshold of the Visible World,* 97.

31. Albert Thibaudet, *Intérieurs: Baudelaire, Fromentin, Amiel* (Paris: Plon-Nourrit, 1924), 23.

32. Blood, "The Sonnet as Snapshot," 266.

33. Silverman, *Threshold of the Visible World,* 172.

34. Benjamin, "Central Park," in *The Writer of Modern Life: Essays on Charles Baudelaire,* ed. Michael Jennings, trans. Howard Eiland et al. (Cambridge, Mass.: Belknap Press of Harvard University Press, 2006), 162.

35. See Betsy Erkkila, *Walt Whitman among the French: Poet and Myth* (Princeton, N.J.: Princeton University Press, 1980).

36. Anthony Vidler, *Warped Space: Art, Architecture and Anxiety in Modern Culture* (Cambridge, Mass.: MIT Press, 2000), 68.

37. Turner, *Backward Glances,* 118.

38. Cited in Vidler, *Warped Space,* 70.

39. Benjamin, *The Arcades Project,* 462–63.

40. Benjamin, "What Is Aura?," 45.

41. Walt Whitman, *Daybooks and Notebooks,* ed. William White, 3 vols. (New York: New York University Press, 1977), 1: 229–30.

42. Anne Dufourmantelle, *In Praise of Risk,* trans. Steven Miller (Bronx, N.Y.: Fordham University Press, 2019), 14.

43. Mary Ann Doane, *The Emergence of Cinematic Time: Modernity, Contingency, The Archive* (Cambridge, Mass.: Harvard University Press, 2002), 217.

44. Robert Richardson, *Literature and Film* (Bloomington: Indiana University Press, 1969), 24; Barry K. Grant, "Whitman and Eisenstein," *Literature/Film Quarterly* 4, no. 3 (Summer 1976): 264.

45. Richardson, 26–27.

46. Walt Whitman, "No One of the Themes," in *Notebooks and Unpublished Prose Manuscripts*, ed. Edward F. Grier, 6 vols. (New York: New York University Press, 1984), 4: 1523–24.

47. Silverman, *Threshold of the Visible World*, 102.

48. Wolff, "The Invisible Flaneuse"; Deborah L. Parson, *Streetwalking the Metropolis: Women, the City and Modernity* (Oxford: Oxford University Press, 2000).

49. Bersani, "Sociability and Cruising," 58.

50. Michael Foucault, "Friendship as a Way of Life," trans. John Johnston, in *Ethics: Subjectivity and Truth,* ed. Paul Rainbow (London: Allen Lane, 1997), 136.

51. Tom Roach, *Friendship as a Way of Life: Foucault, AIDS, and the Politics of Shared Estrangement* (Albany: SUNY Press, 2012), 124.

52. Robert C. Doty, "Growth of Overt Homosexuality Provoking Rising Concern," *New York Times,* December 17, 1963, 33.

53. Laud Humphreys, *Tearoom Trade* (London: Duckworth, 1970), 64.

54. Otto Fenichel, "The Scopophilic Instinct and Identification," in *The Collected Papers of Otto Fenichel,* ed. Hanna Fenichel and David Rapaport (London: Routledge & Kegan Paul, 1954), 389.

55. Turner, *Backward Glances,* 148.

56. Bersani, "Sociability and Cruising," 57.

57. Bersani, 60.

58. Bersani.

59. Sara Ahmed, *Queer Phenomenology: Orientations, Objects, Others* (Durham, N.C.: Duke University Press, 2006), 172.

60. Bersani, "Sociability and Cruising," 60.

61. Bersani, 60.

62. Bersani, "Is the Rectum a Grave?," 12.

63. Bersani, "Sociability and Cruising," 61.

64. Turner, *Backward Glances,* 59.

65. Michael Snediker, "Whitman on the Verge: Or the Desires of Solitude," *Arizona Quarterly* 61, no. 3 (Autumn 2005): 29.

66. Wayne Koestenbaum, "In Defense of Nuance," in *My 1980s & Other Essays* (New York: Farrar, Straus & Giroux, 2013), 54.

67. Hugh Ryan, *When Brooklyn Was Queer: A History* (New York: St. Martin's Press), 20.

68. Ryan, 21.

69. Bersani, "Is the Rectum a Grave?," 12.

70. Silverman, *Threshold of the Visible World,* 173.

71. Jonathan Beller, "*Camera Obscura* After All: The Racist Writing with Light," *S&F Online,* Summer 2012, http://sfonline.barnard.edu/feminist-media-theory/camera-obscura-after-all-the-racist-writing-with-light/.

72. Silverman, *Threshold of the Visible World,* 184.

73. Beller, "*Camera Obscura* After All."

74. Beller.

75. Beller.

76. Nicholas Mirzoeff, *The Right to Look: A Counterhistory of Visuality* (Durham, N.C.: Duke University Press, 2011), 2.

77. Frantz Fanon, *Black Skin, White Masks,* trans. Charles Lam Markmann (London: Pluto Press, 2008), 84–85.

78. Mirzoeff, *The Right to Look,* 1.

79. Untitled script, MSS 092, Box 6, Folder 271, David Wojnarowicz Papers, Fales Library and Special Collections, New York University, New York.

2. Walt Whitman, Looking at You

1. Emory Holloway, "Whitman's Embryonic Verse," *SWR* 10 (July 1925): 30. This was the first appearance in print of this poem. It was published subsequently by Holloway as a stand-alone edition, *Pictures: An Unpublished Poem* (New York: The June House, 1927).

2. Cited in Holloway, 29.

3. Holloway, *Pictures,* 10.

4. Eve Kosofsky Sedgwick, *Epistemology of the Closet* (Berkeley: University of California Press, 1990), 128.

5. Christopher Ricks, "American English and the Inherently Transitory," in *The Force of Poetry* (Oxford: Oxford University Press, 1984), 426.

6. Alice Ahlers, "Cinematographic Technique in *Leaves of Grass,*" *Walt Whitman Review* 12, no. 4 (December 1966): 93–94.

7. Whitman, "Visit to Plumbe's Gallery," July 2, 1846, the *Brooklyn Daily Eagle,* not paginated. Hereafter abbreviated *BDE.*

8. Cited in Holloway, "Whitman's Embryonic Verse," 29.

9. Thomas E. Yingling, *Hart Crane and the Homosexual Text: New Thresholds, New Anatomies* (Chicago: University of Chicago Press, 1990), 6.

10. Michael Snediker, "Whitman on the Verge," 28.

11. Walt Whitman, *Daybooks and Notebooks,* 3: 729.

12. Cited in Graham Robb, *Strangers: Homosexual Love in the Nineteenth Century* (London: Picador, 2003), 172.

13. Laure Katsaros, *New York-Paris: Whitman, Baudelaire, and the Hybrid City* (Ann Arbor: University of Michigan, 2012), 35–36.

14. Katsaros, *New York-Paris.*

15. David S. Reynolds, *Walt Whitman's America: A Cultural Biography* (New York: Knopf, 1995), 33.

16. Whitman, "Democratic Vistas," in *Walt Whitman: Complete Poetry and Collected Prose,* ed. Justin Kaplan (New York: Library of America, 1996), 973. For critical work on Whitman and race, see Lavelle Porter, "Should Walt Whitman Be #Cancelled?," JSTOR Daily (April 17, 2019), https://daily.jstor.org/should -walt-whitman-be-cancelled/; and *Whitman Noir: Black America and the Good Gray Poet,* ed. by Ivy G. Wilson (Iowa City: University of Iowa Press, 2014).

17. Georg Simmel, *Sociology: Inquiries into the Construction of Social Forms,* ed. and trans. Anthony J. Blasi, Anton K. Jacobs, and Mathew Kanjirathinkal, 2 vols. (Leiden, the Netherlands: Brill, 2009), 2: 571.

18. Michael Moon, *Disseminating Whitman: Revision and Corporeality in Leaves of Grass* (London: Harvard University Press, 1991), 160.

19. John Hicks, "Whitman's Lyrics?," *Thinking Verse* 4, no. 1 (2014): 93.

20. Berlant and Warner, "Sex in Public," *Critical Inquiry* 24, no. 2 (Winter 1998): 558.

21. Folder 50, MSS 3829, Papers of Walt Whitman, Albert and Shirley Small Special Collections Library, University of Virginia, Charlottesville.

22. Michael Davidson, *Guys Like Us: Citing Masculinity in Cold War Poetics* (Chicago: University of Chicago Press, 2004), 101–2.

23. Davidson, *Guys Like Us.*

24. Sam Ladkin, "The "Onanism of Poetry": Walt Whitman, Rob Halpern, and the Deconstruction of Masturbation," *Angelaki* 20, no. 4 (2015): 133.

25. Moon, *Disseminating Whitman,* 8.

26. Moon, 19.

27. M. Jimmie Killingsworth, *Whitman's Poetry of the Body: Sexuality, Politics and the Text* (Chapel Hill: University of North Carolina Press, 1989), 123.

28. Cited in Roger Asselineau, *The Evolution of Walt Whitman: The Creation of a Book,* trans. Roger Asselineau and Burton L. Cooper, 2 vols. (Cambridge, Mass.: Harvard University Press, 1962), 2: 119.

29. J. H. Prynne, "Poetry and Truth: An Example from Whitman," unpublished notes (dated 2010), MS Add.10144/2, J. H. Prynne Papers, Cambridge University Library, Cambridge.

30. Prynne.

31. Michael Snediker, *Queer Optimism: Lyric Personhood and Other Felicitous Persuasions* (Minneapolis: University of Minnesota Press, 2009), 18.

32. Ladkin, "The "Onanism of Poetry," 135.

33. Walt Whitman to Le Baron Russell, December 3, 1863, in *The Correspondence,* ed. Ted Genoways, 7 vols. (Iowa City: University of Iowa Press, 2004), 7: 21.

34. Janet Oppenheim, *The Other World: Spiritualism and Psychical Research in England, 1850–1914* (Cambridge: Cambridge University Press, 1985), 210.

35. Oppenheim.

36. For a discussion of this article, see Catherine Waitinas, "'Animal Magnetism': The 'Contemporary' Roots of Whitman's 'Is Mesmerism True?,'" *Walt Whitman Quarterly Review* 34, no. 1 (Summer 2016): 55–68. For a cultural history of mesmerism, see Emily Ogden, *Credulity: A Cultural History of US Mesmerism* (Chicago: University of Chicago Press, 2018).

37. Mose Velsor (Walt Whitman), "Manly Health and Training, with Off-Hand Hints Toward Their Conditions," ed. Zachary Turpin, *Walt Whitman Quarterly Review* 33 (2016): 223.

38. Rob Halpern, *Music for Porn* (New York: Nightboat Books, 2012), 55–56.

39. Ladkin, "The "Onanism of Poetry,"137.

40. Ladkin.

41. Katsaros, *New York-Paris*, 32.

42. Whitman, "Out from Behind This Mask," *The Walt Whitman Archive*, ed. Ed Folsom and Kenneth M. Price, http://whitmanarchive.org/manuscripts/figures/bpl.00001.001.jpg.

43. W. J. T Mitchell, *What Do Pictures Want: The Lives and Loves of Images* (Chicago: University of Chicago Press, 2005), 7.

44. Michael Fried, *Absorption and Theatricality: Painting and Beholder in the Age of Diderot* (Chicago: University of Chicago Press, 1980), 100.

45. Fried.

46. Whitman, "Out from Behind This Mask."

47. Horace Traubel, *With Walt Whitman in Camden*, ed. Sculley Bradley et al., 9 vols. (Boston: Small, Maynard, 1906–1996), 2: 506.

48. Traubel, 4: 150.

49. Ted Genoways, "'One goodshaped and wellhung man': Accentuated Sexuality and the Uncertain Authorship of the Frontispiece to the 1855 Edition of *Leaves of Grass*," in Leaves of Grass: *The Sesquicentennial Essays*, ed. Susan Belasco, Ed Folsom, and Kenneth M. Price (Lincoln: University of Nebraska Press, 2007), 98.

50. Mose Velsor, "Manly Health and Training," 223.

51. Tyler Bradway, *Queer Experimental Literature*, 193.

52. Moon, "Rereading Whitman," in *The Continuing Presence of Walt Whitman: The Life After the Life*, ed. Robert K. Martin (Iowa City: University of Iowa Press, 1992), 53–54.

53. Moon, 57.

54. Robb, *Strangers*, 144.

55. Jesse Green, "Walt Whitman, Poet of a Contradictory America," *T: The*

New York Times Style Magazine, September 14, 2020, https: //www.nytimes
.com/2020/09/14/t-magazine/walt-whitman-cover.html.

3. *Looking for Langston Hughes*

1. Langston Hughes, "Old Walt," *The Collected Poems of Langston Hughes,*
ed. Arnold Rampersad (New York: Vintage Editions, 1995), 446. Hereafter abbreviated *CPLH.*

2. David Ignatow, "Foreword," *Walt Whitman: A Centennial Celebration,*
Beloit Poetry Journal 5, no. 1 (January 1954).

3. David Ignatow, "Memories of Langston," *The Langston Hughes Review*
13, no. 2 (Winter/Summer 1995): 7.

4. Allen Ginsberg, "A Supermarket in California," in *Howl* (San Francisco:
City Lights, 1956), 23.

5. Andrew Donnelly, "Langston Hughes on the DL," *College Literature* 44,
no. 1 (Winter 2017): 45.

6. Donnelly, 54.

7. Anne Borden, "Heroic 'Hussies' and 'Brilliant Queers': Genderracial
Resistance in the Works of Langston Hughes," *African American Review* 28, no.
3 (Autumn 1994): 343.

8. Langston Hughes, "Like Whitman, Great Artists Are Not Always Good
People," *Chicago Defender,* August 1, 1953, 11.

9. Lavelle Porter, "Should Walt Whitman Be #Cancelled?"

10. Hughes, "Like Whitman," 11.

11. Donnelly, "Langston Hughes on the DL," 43–44.

12. Michael Bronski, *A Queer History of the United States* (Boston: Beacon
Press, 2011), 126. George Chauncey also mentions Niles's *Strange Brother* in
Gay New York, 285.

13. Jericho Brown, "If God Is Love," *Mentor & Muse: Essays from Poets to
Poets* (2018), https: //mentorandmuse.net/if-god-is-love/.

14. Paul H. Outka, "Whitman and Race ('He's Queer, He's Unclear, Get
Used to It')," *Journal of American Studies* 36, no. 2 (August 2002): 316–17.

15. James Baldwin, "The Black Boy Looks at the White Boy," in *Collected
Essays,* ed. by Toni Morrison (New York: Library of America, 1998), 269–70.

16. Arnold Rampersad, *The Life of Langston Hughes,* 2 vols. (New York: Oxford University Press, 1986), 1: 73–99.

17. Rampersad, 1: 72.

18. George B. Hutchinson, "Langston Hughes and the 'Other' Whitman,"
in *The Continuing Presence of Walt Whitman: The Life After the Life,* ed. Robert K. Martin (Iowa City: University of Iowa Press, 1992), 20.

19. Langston Hughes, "Walt Whitman and the Negro," in *The Collected*

Work of Langston Hughes, 18 vols. (Columbia: University of Missouri Press, 2002), 9: 348.

20. Langston Hughes, "Subway Face," *The Crisis: A Record of the Darker Races* 29, no. 2 (December 1924): 71. See also *CPLH,* 40.

21. Walker Evans, *Many Are Called* (New Haven, Conn.: Yale University Press, 2004), 12.

22. Georg Simmel, *Sociology,* 1: 573.

23. Simmel, 1: 572.

24. Brian McCammack, "'My God, They Must Have Riots on Those Things All the Time': African American Geographies and Bodies on Northern Urban Public Transportation, 1915–1940," *Journal of Social History* 43, no. 4 (Summer 2010): 1073.

25. McCammack, 1075.

26. Shane Vogel, "Closing Time: Langston Hughes and the Poetics of Harlem Nightlife," in *Criticism* 48, no. 3 (Summer 2006): 400.

27. McCammack, "My God, They Must Have Riots," 1073.

28. Isaac Julien, director, *Looking for Langston* (1989; London: BQHL, 2006), DVD.

29. Isaac Julien, "Mirror," in *Isaac Julien: Looking for Langston* (London: Victoria Miro, 2017), 11.

30. Kobena Mercer, "Dark and Lovely Too: Black Gay Men in Independent Film," in *Queer Eyes: Perspectives on Lesbian and Gay Film and Video,* ed. Martha Gever, Pratibha Parmar, and John Greyson (Routledge: New York, 1993), 250–51.

31. Tony Fisher, "Isaac Julien: Looking for Langston: Montage of a Dream Deferred," *Third Text* 4, no. 12 (1990): 61.

32. Fisher, 60.

33. Kaja Silverman, *Threshold of the Visible World,* 106.

34. José Esteban Muñoz, *Disidentifications: Queers of Color and the Performance of Politics* (Minneapolis: University of Minnesota Press, 1999), 62–63.

35. Fisher, "Isaac Julien," 65.

36. Fisher, 67.

37. Silverman, *Threshold,* 105.

38. Julien, "Mirror," 11.

39. Silverman, *Threshold,* 108.

40. Julien, *Looking for Langston,* DVD.

41. Manthia Diawara, "The Absent One: The Avant-Garde and the Black Imaginary in *Looking for Langston,*" in *Representing Black Men,* ed. Marcellus Blount and George Philbert Cunningham (New York: Routledge, 1996), 206.

42. Essex Hemphill, *Conditions* (Washington, D.C.: Be Bop Books, 1986).

43. Essex Hemphill, "Under Certain Circumstances," in *Ceremonies: Prose and Poetry* (New York: Plume, 1992), 152.

44. Julien, *Looking for Langston,* DVD.

45. Silverman, *Threshold,* 111.

46. Hemphill, "If His Name Were Mandingo," *Ceremonies,* 141.

47. Hemphill, "Does Your Mama Know About Me?," *Ceremonies,* 38.

48. For an account of the "dialectic of gazing positions" in this scene, see Rachel Jane Carroll, "Can You Feel It? Beauty and Queer of Color Politics in *Looking for Langston,*" *Criticism* 60, no. 4 (Fall 2018): 496.

49. Silverman, *Threshold,* 113.

50. Silverman, 28.

51. Fanon, *Black Skin, White Masks,* 84.

52. Silverman, *Threshold,* 29.

53. Fanon, *Black Skin, White Masks,* 85.

54. Hemphill, "Does Your Mama Know About Me?," 39.

55. Julien, *Looking for Langston,* DVD.

56. Donnelly, "Langston Hughes on the DL," 44.

57. For a compelling reading of this poem's ambiguities and the nature of its closing "*Where?*" see Chad Bennett, *Word of Mouth: Gossip and American Poetry* (Baltimore: John Hopkins University Press, 2018), 123–25.

58. Judith Butler, *Bodies That Matter: On the Discursive Limits of "Sex"* (New York: Routledge, 1993), 121.

59. Donnelly, "Langston Hughes on the DL," 36. See C. Riley Snorton, *Nobody Is Supposed to Know: Black Sexuality on the Down Low* (Minneapolis: University of Minnesota Press, 2014).

60. Donnelly, "Langston Hughes on the DL," 51.

61. Laurence Goldstein, *The American Poet at the Movies: A Critical History* (Ann Arbor: University of Michigan Press, 1994), 78.

62. Martin Duberman, "Donald Webster Cory: Father of the Homophile Movement," in *The Martin Duberman Reader: The Essential Historical, Biographical and Autobiographical Writings* (New York: The New Press, 2013), 173.

63. Dorian Webster Cory, *The Homosexual in America: A Subjective Approach* (New York: Greenberg, 1951), 110.

64. Donnelly, "Langston Hughes on the DL," 41.

65. Davidson, *Guys Like Us,* 102.

66. Roy DeCarava and Langston Hughes, *The Sweet Flypaper of Life* (New York: Simon and Schuster, 1955), 58.

67. DeCarava and Hughes.

68. Caroline Blinder, "Looking for Harlem: The Absent Narrator in Roy DeCarava and Langston Hughes's *The Sweet Flypaper of Life* (1955)," *CoSMo* 13 (2018): 194.

69. Sonia Weiner, "Narrating Photography in *The Sweet Flypaper of Life,*" *MELUS* 37, no. 1 (2012): 156.

70. DeCarava and Hughes, *The Sweet Flypaper of Life,* 66.

71. DeCarava and Hughes, 70.

72. Blinder, "Looking for Harlem," 200.

73. DeCarava and Hughes, *The Sweet Flypaper of Life,* 72.

74. DeCarava and Hughes, 77.

75. Donnelly, "Langston Hughes on the DL," 43.

76. Hughes, "Passing," in *The Collected Works of Langston Hughes: The Short Stories,* ed. R. Baxter Miller, 16 vols. (Columbia: University of Missouri Press, 2002), 15: 46–48.

77. DeCarava and Hughes, *The Sweet Flypaper of Life,* 27.

78. DeCarava and Hughes, 28.

79. Langston Hughes, "To Alan Green, July 1 1944," in *Selected Letters of Langston Hughes,* eds. Arnold Rampersad and David Roessel (New York: Alfred A. Knopf, 2015), 259.

80. Terrance Hayes, "Sonnet," in *Hip Logic* (New York: Penguin, 2002), 13.

81. For a reading of this poem's relation to sound and laughter, see Edward Allen, *Modernist Invention: Media Technology and American Poetry* (Cambridge: Cambridge University Press, 2020), 243–44.

4. Frank O'Hara's Moving Pictures

1. This particular evening is described, and the letter quoted, in Brad Gooch, *City Poet: The Life and Times of Frank O'Hara* (New York: Knopf, 1993), 456.

2. For more work on O'Hara and race, see Peter Stoneley, "O'Hara, Blackness, and the Primitive," *Twentieth Century Literature* 58, no. 3 (Fall 2012): 495–514; Aldon Nielsen, *Writing between the Lines: Race and Intertextuality* (Athens: University of Georgia Press, 1994); Michael Magee, "Tribes of New York: Frank O'Hara, Amiri Baraka and the Poetics of the Five Spot," *Contemporary Literature* 42, no. 4 (Winter 2001): 694–726; Nick R. Lawrence, "Frank O'Hara in New York: Race Relations, Poetic Situations, Postcolonial Space," *Comparative American Studies* 4, no. 1 (2006): 85–103; and Mark Goble, "'Our Country's Black and White Past': Film and the Figures of History in Frank O'Hara," *American Literature* 79, no. 4 (2007): 57–92.

3. Barry Reay, *New York Hustlers: Masculinity and Sex in Modern America* (Manchester: Manchester University Press, 2010), 5.

4. Reay, 11.

5. O'Hara's review, "Sorrows of the Youngman: John Rechy's *City of Night,*" was later collected in *Standing Still and Walking in New York,* ed. Donald Allen (Bolinas: Grey Fox Press, 1975), 161–64.

6. John Rechy, *City of Night* (New York: Grove Press, 2013 [1963]), 15.

7. Reay, *New York Hustlers,* 86. The cruising spaces of the Times Square

movie theaters are described vividly in Samuel R. Delany, *Times Square Red, Times Square Blue* (New York: New York University Press, 1999).

8. Sarah Riggs, *Word Sightings: Poetry and Visual Media in Stevens, Bishop and O'Hara* (New York: Routledge, 2002), 81.

9. Stoneley, "O'Hara, Blackness, and the Primitive," 501.

10. Stoneley, 502.

11. Goble, "Our Country's Black and White Past," 82.

12. Stoneley, 501; Goble, 59.

13. Aaron Deveson, "A Time to Dance: Frank O'Hara Reading Edwin Denby," *Concentric* 37, no. 2 (September 2011): 170.

14. Rechy, *City of Night*, 39–40.

15. Wayne Koestenbaum, "Frank O'Hara's Excitement," in *My 1980s & Other Essays*, 78.

16. Koestenbaum, 75.

17. O'Hara to Grace Hartigan, December 20, 1957, Box 1, Folder 8, Allen Collection. This radio recording, entitled "Evergreen Review Presents: Poems to Music and Laughter, 1959," can be found in the Rare Book & Manuscript Library Collection, Columbia University, Barney Rosset Papers, MS#1543, Box 57.

18. John Gruen, *The Party's Over Now: Reminiscences of the Fifties—New York's Artists, Writers, Musicians, and Their Friends* (New York: Viking Press, 1972) 144–45.

19. Koestenbaum, "Frank O'Hara's Excitement," 76.

20. Goble, "Our Country's Black and White Past," 58.

21. Boyd McDonald, *Cruising the Movies: A Sexual Guide to Oldies on TV* (South Pasadena, Calif.: Semiotext(e), 2015), 212.

22. Joe LeSueur, *Digressions on Some Poems by Frank O'Hara* (New York: Farrar, Straus & Giroux, 2003), 78.

23. Laurence Goldstein, *The American Poet at the Movies: A Critical History* (Ann Arbor: University of Michigan Press, 1994), 154. For further insights into the relation between camp and the passé, see Matthew Tinkcom, *Working Like a Homosexual: Camp, Capital, Cinema* (Durham, N.C.: Duke University Press, 2002).

24. Richard Dyer, *Heavenly Bodies: Film Stars and Society* (New York: Routledge, 2003 [1986]), 177.

25. Dyer, 150.

26. LeSueur, *Digressions*, 77.

27. Vito Russo, *The Celluloid Closet: Homosexuality in the Movies* (New York: Harper & Row, 1987 [1981]), 4.

28. Barthes, "Leaving the Movie Theater," *The Rustle of Language*, trans. Richard Howard (Berkeley: University of California Press, 1989), 346.

29. Barthes, 345–46.

30. Frank O'Hara, "A Journal: October-November 1948 & January 1949," in *Early Writing* (Bolinas, Calif.: Grey Fox Press, 1977), 106.

31. David K. Johnson, *The Lavender Scare: The Cold War Persecution of Gays and Lesbians in the Federal Government* (Chicago: University of Chicago Press, 2004), 16.

32. LeSueur, *Digressions,* 54.

33. LeSueur, 55.

34. Frank O'Hara, *Act & Portrait: Al Leslie Film,* in *Amorous Nightmares of Delay: Selected Plays* (Baltimore: John Hopkins University Press, 1997), 165. Hereafter abbreviated *AN*.

35. Susan Sontag, "Notes on 'Camp,'" in *Against Interpretation and Other Essays* (New York: Farrar, Straus & Giroux), 288. For an account of O'Hara's "flippancy," see Prudence Bussey-Chamberlain, *Queer Troublemakers: The Poetics of Flippancy* (London: Bloomsbury, 2019), 69–101.

36. Bussey-Chamberlain.

37. Daniel Kane, *We Saw the Light: Conversations between the New American Cinema and Poetry* (Iowa City: University of Iowa, 2009), 81–82.

38. Kane.

39. Richard Moore, "Transcript of 'Frank O'Hara: Second Edition'" in *Homage to Frank O'Hara,* ed. Bill Berkson and Joe LeSueur (Bolinas, Calif.: Big Sky, 1978), 217.

40. Richard Moore, "'Frank O'Hara: Second Edition': Outtakes from the NET Films Series *USA: Poetry*" (video). The American Poetry Archive, The Poetry Center, San Francisco State University, 1978. Viewed in the Woodberry Poetry Room, Lamont Library, Harvard University; also available on You Tube: https://www.youtube.com/watch?v=344TyqLlSFA.

41. Reay, *New York Hustlers,* 194.

42. Chad Bennett, *Word of Mouth,* 149.

43. Boyd McDonald, "A Hearty Heterosexual Looks at the Picture Biz," in *CUM: True Homosexual Experiences from S.T.H. Writers* (Gay Sunshine Press: San Francisco, Calif., 1983), 21.

44. Richard Moore, "Transcript of 'USA: Poetry: Frank O'Hara,'" in *Homage to Frank O'Hara,* ed. Bill Berkson and Joe LeSueur (Bolinas, Calif.: Big Sky, 1978), 216.

45. Moore, "Transcript of 'Second Edition,'" *Homage,* 219.

46. Moore, 219.

47. Moore, 219.

48. Featured in *Alfred Leslie: Cool Man in A Golden Age: Selected Films* (London: LUX, 2009).

49. Moore, "Transcript of 'Second Edition,'" 219.

50. Kane, *We Saw the Light,* 82–83.

51. Moore, "Transcript of 'USA: Poetry,'" 215.

52. Lytle Shaw, *Frank O'Hara: The Poetics of Coterie* (Iowa City: University of Iowa Press, 2010), 58.

53. Riggs, *Word Sightings*, 81.

54. Mary Douglas, *Purity and Danger: An Analysis of Concepts of Pollution and Taboo* (New York: Praeger, 1966), 40.

55. Barthes, "Leaving the Movie Theater," 345.

56. Leo Bersani, "Is the Rectum a Grave?," 14.

57. Bersani.

58. D. A. Miller, *Jane Austen, or, The Secret of Style* (Princeton, N.J.: Princeton University Press, 2003), 5–6.

59. Leo Bersani, "Sociability and Cruising," 55.

60. Joe Brainard, *I Remember* (New York: Granary Books, 2001), 20.

61. Brian Glavey, *The Wallflower Avant-Garde*, 110–11.

62. Gregory Bredbeck, "B/O—Barthes's Text/O'Hara's Trick," *PMLA* 108, no. 2 (March 1993): 272. See also Bruce Boone, "Gay Language as Political Practice: The Poetry of Frank O'Hara," *Social Text* 1 (Winter 1979): 59–92.

63. Glavey, *The Wallflower Avant-Garde*, 112.

64. Glavey, 118.

65. Arthur Rimbaud, "À Paul Demeny (Charleville, 15 mai 1871)," in *Rimbaud: Complete Works, Selected Letters: A Bilingual Edition*, trans. Wallace Fowlie (Chicago: University of Chicago Press, 2005), 376–77.

66. Rimbaud, 374–75.

5. David Wojnarowicz's Portraits

1. Frank O'Hara, "Sorrows of the Youngman," in *Standing Still and Walking in New York*, 162.

2. O'Hara.

3. See Fiona Anderson, *Cruising the Dead River*, 103–8; Wallace Fowlie, *Rimbaud and Jim Morrison: The Rebel as Poet* (Durham, N.C.: Duke University Press, 1994); Daniel Kane, *Do You Have a Band?: Poetry and Punk Rock in New York City* (New York: Columbia University Press, 2017), 90–104; Carrie Jaurès Noland, "Rimbaud and Patti Smith: Style as Social Deviance," *Critical Inquiry* 21, no. 3 (Spring 1995): 581–610; Jonathan Weinberg, *Pier Groups*, 104–5.

4. David Wojnarowicz, "Reading a little Rimbaud in a Second Avenue coffee shop," n.d., MSS 092, Box 4, Folder 94, David Wojnarowicz Papers, Fales Library and Special Collections, New York University, New York.

5. Wojnarowicz.

6. Anderson, *Cruising the Dead River*, 113.

7. Rimbaud, "Side Show," in *Illuminations and Other Prose Poems,* trans. Louise Varese (New York: New Directions, 1957), 20–23.

8. A *New York Times* obituary from 1975 suggests that Kemeny was a student at Harvard in the graduating class of 1961, so he may well have acquired this New Directions reprint edition at the time of its publication in 1957. Subsequently an editor in New York publishing, Kemeny died after jumping from a subway platform. It is possible, though unclear, that Wojnarowicz somehow acquired this edition secondhand after Kemeny's death. *New York Times,* December 16, 1975, 42.

9. Anderson, *Cruising the Dead River,* 102.

10. *SoHo Weekly News,* June 18, 1980, centerfold, n.p.

11. David Wojnarowicz, "Losing the Form in Darkness," in *Close to the Knives: A Memoir of Disintegration* (New York: Vintage, 1991). References to this edition are given with quotations in the text with the abbreviation *CK.*

12. Cynthia Carr, *Fire in the Belly: The Life and Times of David Wojnarowicz* (New York: Bloomsbury, 2012), 63.

13. Carr. For a survey of Wojnarowicz's poetry, see Hugh Ryan, "Never Not a Poet," Poetry Foundation (2019), https://www.poetryfoundation.org/articles/150527/never-not-a-poet.

14. Carr, *Fire in the Belly,* 63.

15. Carr, "Biographical Dateline," in *History Keeps Me Awake at Night,* ed. David Breslin and David Kiehl (New Haven, Conn.: Yale University Press, 2018), 285.

16. David Breslin, "Chaos Reason and Delight," in *History Keeps Me Awake at Night,* 21.

17. *Arts Magazine,* November 1971, 43–44. The mailed responses to Johnson's project can be viewed in his archive: Box 97: "Rimbaud Box," Ray Johnson Estate, Richard L. Feigen & Co. http://images.rayjohnsonestate.com/www_rayjohnsonestate_com/Box_97_Rimbaud_box.pdf.

18. David Kiehl, "Rimbaud," in *History Keeps Me Awake at Night,* 128.

19. Rimbaud, "À une raison," in *Illuminations,* 38–39.

20. Breslin, "Chaos Reason and Delight," 21.

21. Breslin, 24.

22. Edgar Allan Poe, "The Man of the Crowd," in *Collected Works of Edgar Allen Poe,* ed. Thomas Ollive Mabbott, 3 vols. (Cambridge: Belknap Press, 1978), 2: 507–11.

23. Wojnarowicz, "Reading a Little Rimbaud."

24. *SoHo Weekly News,* June 18, 1980.

25. David Wojnarowicz, "Poetry/Prose-Poems," undated, MSS 092, Box 5, Folder 139, David Wojnarowicz Papers, Fales Library and Special Collections,

New York University, New York. Note that the final 's' in "across" is not struck out, but should be.

26. Jean-Paul Sartre, *Saint Genet: Actor and Martyr,* trans. Bernard Frechtman (New York: New American Library, 1971), 448.

27. Anderson, *Cruising the Dead River,* 103.

28. Wojnarowicz, "Poetry/Prose-Poems."

29. Sontag, *On Photography,* 16.

30. Sontag.

31. "Sylvère Lotringer/David Wojnarowicz," in *David Wojnarowicz: A Definitive History of Five or Six Years on the Lower East Side,* ed. Giancarlo Ambrosino (New York: Semiotext(e), 2006), 182.

32. "Nan Goldin/David Wojnarowicz," in *Definitive History,* 202.

33. "Sylvère Lotringer," in *Definitive History,* 163.

34. David Kiehl, "Peter Hujar Dreaming," in *History Keeps Me Awake at Night,* 174.

35. Sontag, *On Photography,* 16.

36. "Nan Goldin," in *Definitive History,* 203.

37. Wojnarowicz, *Rimbaud in New York 1978–79* (New York: PPP Editions, 2004), n.p.

38. Wojnarowicz.

39. Olivia Laing, *The Lonely City: Adventures in the Art of Being Alone* (Edinburgh: Canongate, 2016), 114.

40. Leo Bersani, "Staring," in *Receptive Bodies* (Chicago: University of Chicago Press, 2018), 108.

41. Bersani, 107.

42. Quoted in Mysoon Rizk, "Constructing Histories: David Wojnarowicz's *Arthur Rimbaud in New York,*" in *The Passionate Camera: Photography and Bodies of Desire,* ed. Deborah Bright (London: Routledge, 1998), 179.

43. Weinberg, *Pier Groups,* 44.

44. Bersani, "Staring," 116.

45. Weinberg, *Pier Groups,* 112.

46. Quoted in Rizk, "Constructing Histories," 179.

47. Rizk, 182.

48. David Wojnarowicz, "Rimbaud in New York—film script," undated, MSS 092, Box 6, Folder 268, David Wojnarowicz Papers, Fales Library and Special Collections, New York University, New York.

49. Anne Friedberg, *Window Shopping: Cinema and the Postmodern* (Berkeley: University of California Press, 1993), 37.

50. Anderson, *Cruising the Dead River,* 116.

51. Sontag, *On Photography,* 30. For a reflection upon the ambivalent gaze

of Arbus's work, see Wayne Koestenbaum, "Diane Arbus and Humiliation," in *My 1980s & Other Essays*, 227–30.

52. Sontag, *On Photography*, 34.

53. *Weight of the Earth: The Tape Journals of David Wojnarowicz*, ed. Lisa Darms and David O'Neill (Los Angeles: Semiotext(e), 2018), 33.

54. David Wojnarowicz, "Doing Time in a Disposable Body," in *Memories that Smell Like Gasoline* (San Francisco: Artspace Books, 1992), 27.

55. Phelan, *Unmarked: The Politics of Performance* (London: Routledge, 1993), 36.

56. Laing, *The Lonely City*, 110.

57. Wojnarowicz, "Doing Time," 28.

58. Wojnarowicz.

59. Anderson, *Cruising the Dead River*, 98.

60. "Nan Goldin/David Wojnarowicz," in *Definitive History*, 202.

61. David Wojnarowicz, "Untitled film script," undated, MSS 092, Box 6, Folder 271, David Wojnarowicz Papers, Fales Library and Special Collections, New York University, New York.

62. Wojnarowicz.

63. Margaret Olin et al., "The Art Seminar," in *Photography Theory*, ed. James Elkins, 162.

64. Sigmund Freud, "Fetishism," in *The Standard Edition of the Complete Psychological Works of Sigmund Freud*, trans. James Strachey, 24 vols. (London: Hogarth and Institute of Psycho-Analysis, 1953–1974), 21: 152.

65. Wojnarowicz, "Untitled film script."

66. Freud, "Fetishism," 21: 152.

67. Kaja Silverman, *The Threshold of the Visible World*, 29.

68. Wojnarowicz, "Poetry/Prose-Poems."

69. David Kiehl, "Room 1423," in *History Keeps Me Awake at Night*, 232–35.

70. Henning Bech, *When Men Meet: Homosexuality and Modernity*, trans. Teresa Mesquit and Tim Davies (Cambridge: Polity, 1997), 206.

71. Quoted in Ben Gove, *Cruising Culture: Promiscuity, Desire and American Gay Literature* (Edinburgh: Edinburgh University Press, 2000), 140.

72. Lee Edelman, *No Future: Queer Theory and the Death Drive* (Durham, N.C.: Duke University Press, 2004), 19.

73. Eve Kosofsky Sedgwick, *Epistemology of the Closet*, 128.

74. Wojnarowicz, "Spiral," in *Memories that Smell Like Gasoline*, 60.

75. Hanya Yanigahara, "The Burning House," in *History Keeps Me Awake at Night*, 69.

76. Wojnarowicz, "Spiral," 59.

77. Wojnarowicz, 58.

78. Laing, *The Lonely City,* 114.

79. José Esteban Muñoz, *Cruising Utopia,* 35.

80. Sarah Ensor, "Queer Fallout: Samuel R. Delany and the Ecology of Cruising," *Environmental Humanities* 9, no. 1 (2017), 152.

81. Anderson, *Cruising the Dead River,* 161.

82. Breslin, "Chaos Reason and Delight," 22.

Coda

1. Eileen Myles, "How I Wrote Certain of My Poems," *Hot Night* (New York: Semiotext(e), 1991), 199. Further references to this edition are given with quotations in the text with the abbreviation *NM.*

2. Davy Knittle, "On Eileen Myles's 'Hot Night': queer / urban / image," *Jacket2* (2017), https://jacket2. org/commentary/eileen-myles's-hot-night -queer-urban-image.

3. Knittle.

4. Sarah Ensor, "Queer Fallout," 150.

5. Eliza Steinbock, *Shimmering Images: Trans Cinema, Embodiment, and the Aesthetics of Change* (Durham, N.C.: Duke University Press, 2019), 9.

6. Maggie Nelson, *Women, the New York School, and Other True Abstractions* (Iowa City: University of Iowa Press, 2007), 197. Indeed, there are numerous comparisons between the aesthetic and compositional principles of Myles's work and those of earlier New York School poets. Compare, for example, Myles's account of the poem "coming on" with Frank O'Hara's recollection of "waiting for the poem to start again" in his "Notes on *Second Avenue,*" *CP,* 496.

7. Nelson, 197.

8. Nelson, 193.

9. Dianne Chisholm, *Queer Constellations,* 132.

10. Knittle, "On Eileen Myles's 'Hot Night.'"

11. Denise Bullock, "Lesbian Cruising," *Journal of Homosexuality* 47, no. 2 (2004): 27.

12. Rita Mae Brown, "Queen for a Day: A Stranger in Paradise," in *Lavender Culture,* ed. *Karla Jay and Allen Young* (New York: Jove Publications, 1979), 69.

13. Brown, 75.

14. Laurie Anderson, *Stories from the Nerve Bible: A Retrospective, 1972–1992* (New York: Harper Perennial, 1994), 146.

15. Anderson, 146–47.

16. Philip Nel, *The Avant-Garde and American Postmodernity: Small Incisive Shocks* (Jackson: University of Mississippi Press, 2002), 154–55.

17. Eileen Myles, "The City of New York," in *Evolution* (New York: Grove Press, 2018), 95.

18. Audre Lorde, *Zami: A New Spelling of My Name* (New York: Crossing Press, 1982), 180.

19. Eileen Myles, "Chelsea Girls," in *Chelsea Girls* (Santa Rosa, Calif.: Black Sparrow Press, 1994), 261. For an account of the city as a repository of queer collective memory in *Chelsea Girls, see Chisholm, Queer Constellations,* 131–37.

20. Myles, "Chelsea Girls."

21. Mulvey, "Afterthoughts on 'Visual Pleasure and Narrative Cinema' inspired by King Vidor's *Duel in the Sun* (1946)," in *Visual and Other Pleasures* (Basingstoke, England: Palgrave Macmillan, 1989), 32.

22. Steinbock, *Shimmering Images,* 4.

23. Myles, "Chelsea Girls," 261.

24. George Chauncey, *Gay New York,* 56.

25. Prudence Bussey-Chamberlain, *Queer Troublemakers,* 114.

26. Eileen Myles, "Poetry in the 80s," https://www.eileenmyles.com/pdf/PoetryInThe80s.pdf, 2–3.

27. Eileen Myles, "The Lesbian Poet," in *School of Fish* (Santa Rosa, Calif.: Black Sparrow Press, 1997), 126.

28. Melvin Dixon, "I'll Be Somewhere Listening for My Name," *Callaloo* 23, no. 1 (Winter 2000), 80.

29. Dixon, 83.

30. Adam Fitzgerald, "Eileen Myles," Interview (2015), https://www.interviewmagazine.com/culture/eileen-myles-1.

31. Myles, "The City," in *Evolution,* 44.

32. Myles, 45.

33. Eileen Myles, "Artist's Statement," Bridget Donahue Gallery, *poems* press release, https://www.bridgetdonahue.nyc/exhibitions/eileen-myles-back-room-poems/.

34. Shaka McGlotten, *Virtual Intimacies: Media, Affect, and Queer Sociality* (Albany: State University of New York Press, 2013), 4.

35. Rem Koolhaas, *Delirious New York: A Retroactive Manifesto for Manhattan* (New York: Monacelli, 1994), 21.

36. McGlotten, *Virtual Intimacies,* 5.

37. Tom Roach, "Becoming Fungible: Queer Intimacies in Social Media," *Qui Parle* 23, no. 2 (Spring/Summer 2015): 55.

38. Garth Greenwell, "How I Fell in Love with the Beautiful Art of Cruising," BuzzFeed (2016), https://www.buzzfeed.com/garthgreenwell/how-i-fell-in-love-with-the-beautiful-art-of-cruising.

39. Roach, "Becoming Fungible," 59.

40. Matthew Numer et al., "Profiling Public Sex: How Grindr Revolutionized the Face of Gay Cruising," in *Radical Sex between Men: Assembling Desiring-Machines* (New York: Routledge, 2018), 199. For an analysis debunking oversimplified critiques of Grindr, see Bryce J. Renninger, "Grindr Killed the Gay Bar, and Other Attempts to Blame Social Technologies for Urban Development: A Democratic Approach to Popular Technologies and Queer Sociality," *Journal of Homosexuality* 66, no. 12 (2019): 1736–55.

41. Roach, "Becoming Fungible," 55.

42. Roach, 56–58.

43. McGlotten, *Virtual Intimacies*, 8.

44. Jonathan Weinberg, *Pier Groups*, 17.

45. For analysis of app profile images, see McGlotten, *Virtual Intimacies*, 127–34.

46. Roach, "Becoming Fungible," 59.

47. Leo Bersani, "Is the Rectum a Grave?," 12.

48. McGlotten, *Virtual Intimacies*, 63.

49. Danez Smith, "gay cancer," in *Homie* (Minneapolis, Minn.: Graywolf Press, 2020), 60.

50. Danez Smith, "Reimagining Ourselves in an Increasingly Queer World," *The New York Times*, June 16, 2019, https://www.nytimes.com/2019/06/16/us/danez-smith-lgbtq-essex-hemphill.html.

51. C. Riley-Snorton, "Afterword: On Crisis and Abolition," in *AIDS and the Distribution of Crises*, ed. Jih-Fei Cheng, Alexandra Juhasz, and Nishant Shahani (Durham, N.C.: Duke University Press, 2020), 316.

52. Smith, "all the good dick lives in Brooklyn Park," *Homie*, 54.

53. Smith.

54. McGlotten, *Virtual Intimacies*, 63.

55. Danez Smith, "a note on the phone app that tells me how far i am from other men's mouths," in *Don't Call Us Dead* (London: Chatto & Windus, 2017), 32.

56. Smith.

57. Roach, "Becoming Fungible," 57.

58. Jericho Brown, "Host," in *The New Testament* (London: Picador, 2018 [2014]), 29.

59. Brown.

60. McGlotten, *Virtual Intimacies*, 74.

61. For an analysis of virtual intimacy's utopian promissory and its relation to Muñoz's "not-yet-here," see McGlotten, *Virtual Intimacies*, 61–77.

62. Smith, "& even the black guys's profile reads *sorry, no black guys*," in *Don't Call Us Dead*, 33.

63. Smith.

Index

sexuality and, 55, 64, 83; soldiers and, 71; space of reading and, 63–64; structure of vision and, 38; succession of, 39; urban desire and, 40; urban multitude and, 63–64
"Whoever You Are Holding Me Now in Hand" (Whitman), 82
Wild One, The, 136
Williams, Dencil, 103
Williams, William Carlos, 87, 123
Wojnarowicz, David, 8, 14, 17, 46, 50, 171, 174, 179, 184, 185; anatomical features of, 173; body parts and, 178; Carr and, 154; cruising and, 173, 178; death/visible and, 181; erotics and, 48, 180, 181; fantasy and, 48, 160–61; gay life and, 12; Genet and, 158; historical moment of, 180; imperfect style of, 183; masturbation and, 158, 162; on memories, 172–73; neck and, 176, 178; peripatetic experience and, 165; photography and, 159–60, 161; poetry of, 22, 151, 152, 153, 155, 159, 164, 166, 167, 168, 169,

177, 181–82, 192; on promiscuity, 160–61; Rimbaud and, 151, 154, 155, 156, 157, 162–63; on Sontag, 159–60; strangers and, 16
Wolff, Janet, 25, 41
Women's Coffee House, 200
"Wound Dresser, The" (Whitman), 68, 69, 70, 73, 74, 77; first appearance of, 71
wounding, 30–31, 50, 74, 175

Yaffa, 189
Yanigahara, Hanya, 183
Yingling, Thomas E., 55
"You Are Gorgeous and I'm Coming" (O'Hara), 150
Your Room Is Awfully Pleasant but I Think I'll Run Along (Acton), 130, 131

Zami: A New Spelling of My Name (Lorde), 196
Zatavksy, Bill, 153–54
Zukofsky, Louis, 87
Zurier, Rebecca, 11

Jack Parlett is junior research fellow in English at University College, Oxford.